C000216446

Elaine Snuggs has provided for us a rich
and spiritual enriching biography. The
has portrayed from careful research and
lived not perfectly but faithfully for Ch
history. How they stood firm in their faith in their moments of trial
will challenge you and will surely prompt the question in any sincere
Christian mind: 'What does Jesus mean to me?'

Mostyn Roberts
Pastor, Welwyn Evangelical Church, and author of biographies of
Francis Schaeffer and Roger Williams

What a lively presentation of some of the women involved in the
English Reformation! Elaine Snuggs has written a most energetic and
revealing account of some of its key figures, albeit not quite on the
front line. Not only does she write the story well, but she captures
something of the spirit of the times. As one reads what took place,
one almost relives it – surely a sign of a most effective writer. As a
student many years ago, my introduction to the English Reformation
came through the biography of the ponderous and repellent figure of
Henry VIII, and later the embittered Mary. Elaine Snuggs makes an
invaluable contribution in providing some much needed 'colour' and
personal testimony.

Peter Barnes
Lecturer in Church History, Christ College, Sydney
Minister of Revesby Presbyterian Church, Revesby, New South Wales,
Australia

A thoroughly enjoyable, informative and uplifting read. Four truly
inspirational women are presented to us clearly and thoughtfully. No-
one could be in any doubt after reading this book, that these women
really knew how to give an answer for the hope that they had in Christ.
Elaine demonstrates how they courageously and wisely articulated this
hope, and faithfully held fast to it until the end.

Jo Coleman
Chair, Grace Baptist Women's Association

Elaine Snuggs' well-researched and informative book about four Reformation ladies is set in the exciting but dangerous times of the Tudor era. Each exhibited outstanding qualities which helped to shape post-Reformation England. All were in some way persecuted for their faith; two of them forfeited their lives. Elaine also gives the reader a very insightful view of the nitty-gritty of life in Tudor times – particularly in the higher strata of society.

Philip Parsons
Author of *A Beginner's Guide to Church History* (Day One, 2019)

Women are too often left out of our history, especially Christian history. This book helps to redress the balance by telling the story of four women from Tudor England who played significant roles in the stirring times in which they lived and maintained a clear evangelical testimony amidst the difficulties that they faced. This very readable and moving account will inform, inspire, edify and challenge men and women.

Robert Strivens
Pastor, Bradford on Avon Baptist Church, Bradford on Avon, Wiltshire

William Tyndale wanted the Bible to be read by the ploughboy and in this highly readable book, Elaine succeeds in demonstrating that Reformation history is not just for the intellectual, but for the ordinary person as well. Four Reformation ladies come to life, as we enter into their many trials and tribulations. Throughout, though severely tested, their faith stood firm and this well researched account is a testimony to the Lord's saving and keeping power. We live in very different times but *The Reluctant Queen and Other Reformation Women* is a challenge and inspiration for believers today.

Pat Mollitt
Retired Pastor's wife

This book provides a fascinating account of the lives of four Tudor women: each of them strong, well educated, witty, articulate, courageous – but above all godly. Our own culture views personal peace, comfort and security as all important, and it is all too easy to slip into that mindset. So it is bracing and convicting to read of the way in which each of these women counted it a privilege to stand and suffer for Christ. The author provides a wealth of detail which effectively conveys the historical context, as well as the personality and faith of each of these remarkable women.

Sharon James
The Christian Institute
Author of several books, including
How Christianity Changed the World

The promise of the Spirit, which is poured out in the new covenant, is for men and women alike. All too often this has been forgotten in the telling of the story of the Church. Women have played significant roles in the advance of the Gospel, and this is especially true during the era of the Reformation. I am therefore thrilled with this new book, especially the inclusion of a chapter on Catharine Willoughby, or the 'Puritan Duchess' as she came to be called. What a remarkable Christian! But so were all of the women highlighted in this new work and there is much that women – and men – can learn from them in our equally challenging day.

Michael A. G. Haykin
Chair & professor of Church History, The Southern Baptist
Theological Seminary, Louisville, Kentucky

THE
RELUCTANT
QUEEN

AND OTHER
REFORMATION WOMEN

ELAINE SNUGGS

CHRISTIAN
FOCUS

All quotations from the Bible are from the Authorised Version.

Cover design by Peter Barnsley

Printed by Bell and Bain, Glasgow.

CONTENTS

To my family

John

Tim and Becca

Elisha and Bethany

Acknowledgements

With gratitude to all those who have helped and encouraged me along the way. Especial thanks to:

Jean Dandy, John and Pat Mollitt, Paul and Christine Crossley, and my daughter-in-law, Becca, for reading through the manuscript, and for their helpful comments and encouragement.

Mostyn Roberts for his Foreword.

Philip Parsons for his enthusiasm, and for his close scrutiny of the text.

Christian Focus Publications for accepting my manuscript and turning it into this book, especially Catherine MacKenzie, Rosanna Burton, and Anne Norrie.

My brother-in-law, Roger, for drawing the maps.

Above all to my husband, John, for his constant support. Also for his practical help in frequently taking over in the kitchen to give me time on my 'project', and in supplying the many computer skills which I lack. I simply could not have managed without him. He even survived living through lockdown with someone whose mind was back in the sixteenth- century for much of the time!

Any errors are mine. Although I have striven for accuracy throughout, it is very possible there may be some mistakes.

FOREWORD

'Why does anyone want to read history?' Sometimes, to my horror, I have heard that asked. I will tell you why everyone should want to read history. Firstly, because it explains where we are today. A tree is not explicable without roots and a trunk; nor a flower without a stem; nor a family without a family tree, even if you only go back a generation or two. We are what we are because of what has gone before us. History gives individuals and a community (whether family, church or nation) their sense of identity. Without it we can survive, perhaps, but we are more lost than we need be, less sure of who we are. Isn't the popularity of programmes like *Who Do You Think You Are?* testimony to our need to be conversant with our past?

Secondly, history helps us to face the future. Without a grasp of our past, we are less able to weather the storms of change within and attacks from without that assail every community as the years go by. History reminds us that the challenges we face are nothing new; old problems recur in fresh guises; circumstances and contexts vary, but not the fundamental forces that drive human beings, whether great or lowly. The mistakes people have made in responding to difficulties help us, if we are wise, to do better this time. Too often, as is frequently lamented, we do not learn from history, but it doesn't have to be that way.

But what if you are a Christian? Even more reason to read history. You need to see how God has exercised His sovereignty in history – what we call His 'providence' in the public sphere as well as in the lives of individuals. You need to see how the Church has survived often turbulent waves on the oceans of succeeding generations; how Christ our Head has governed His body; how Satan has ceaselessly attacked yet never destroyed the Bride of Christ – and of course he never will for Christ has promised He will build His church and the gates of hell shall not prevail against it (Matthew 16:18).

And then there are the lives of countless heroes and heroines of the faith such as we have in this book – worthy successors to those of Hebrews 11, 'of whom the world was not worthy' and with whom we await 'something better' (Hebrews 11:38,40).

These are some of the reasons, whether you are a Christian or not, but especially if you are, why you should read a book like this. Elaine Snuggs has researched widely and deeply to portray for us four remarkable women living through a fascinating period in history, a period with immense consequences for this nation and indeed the world. That period was the Reformation of the sixteenth century as it was ground out in England. The women are both well known (Katharine Parr, sixth and surviving wife of Henry VIII, and Lady Jane Grey, the Nine Days Queen) and not so well known (martyr Anne Askew and Catherine Willoughby, Duchess of Suffolk). In Anne Askew, you will see courage under fire and eventually in death; so too in Lady Jane Grey, executed at sixteen but maintaining remarkable steadfastness of faith in her final days. In Katherine Parr, you will see a woman thrust by God – not Henry VIII ultimately – into a position of prominence and exercising wisdom to survive and quietly exert influence for the gospel, including enabling books to be published and publishing her own spiritual autobiography. As for Catherine Willoughby, the story of her escape and exile with husband and family during Mary's reign, is as exciting as many novels. These were not flawless heroines but in their times of trial showed themselves to be brave, intelligent, educated women, of strong character and radiant spirit, living for the Lord who had saved them and whom they had come to know as the only Saviour and Redeemer by grace alone through faith alone, facing circumstances that, in terms of difficulty and danger, far transcend anything we are likely to have faced.

We need to remember of course that persecution and being in danger of losing one's life is a reality for many of our fellow believers world-wide. We in 'the West' are far from being in danger of our lives, but perhaps that is not the point. What these women show is that the bottom line for a Christian is what a much later martyr, Dietrich Bonhoeffer, once said: when Christ calls a man, He bids him come and die. That is true for us all spiritually; for these four women it was also physically a real threat (for two, actually experienced) and we do well to remember that if we call ourselves Christians, our lives belong to Christ in every way: 'You are not your own, for you were bought with a price' (1 Corinthians 6:19,20).

We may hope that the physical reality of that may not be something we have to face, but it is good to be reminded of what holding fast the faith has meant for many in the past, and does so for many today.

For those in the tradition of the Protestant Reformation, indeed for Christ's disciples of any tradition, these women are our spiritual ancestors. Their DNA is, to some extent, ours. Elaine Snuggs has richly and winsomely given us their stories. To help you understand what you are and to help you face your Christian future, read this book. You will be challenged and inspired to love Christ more, to live for Him better.

Mostyn Roberts

Pastor, Welwyn Evangelical Church

Hertfordshire, UK.

INTRODUCTION

It all began with Lady Jane Grey. Some twenty years ago, I read a Christian novel[1] about her, which stirred and intrigued me. It was a dramatic and moving story, but what particularly caught my interest was her strong Christian faith. I wanted to check that out further, for the trouble with historical fiction is that it is difficult to know where fact ends and imagination takes over. So, like a good ex librarian, I headed to my local library to see if I could find a reliable biography. The book[2] I emerged with was very helpful and challenged much of what I had previously thought I knew about her. She really was not just a quiet, scholarly girl who was plucked from obscurity in the dying days of Edward's reign, but someone of significance who had been brought up with the intent that she would fulfill her parents' ambitions. So what followed was not really too surprising. Though clearly written by someone who had little understanding of Jane's love for God, it did show how important He was in her life. Shortly afterwards, I was lent a book[3] which really opened my eyes. It was written in the nineteenth century and the section telling the story of Jane's life was so sentimental that it was of little interest, but, after it, came real treasure. All of her writings which have survived were reprinted there, and her character, and especially her faith, fairly leapt from the page.

---

1   D. Meroff, *Coronation of Glory: The Story of Lady Jane Grey* (Zondervan, 1979)

2   A. Plowden, *Lady Jane Grey and the House of Suffolk* (London: Sidgewick & Jackson, 1985)

3   N.H. Nicholas, *Literary Remains of Lady Jane Grey* (Harding, Triphook and Lepard, 1825)

I read on, and my quest for the real Jane and all I could find out about her, led me to three other ladies: Anne Askew, Katherine Parr and Catherine Willoughby. I was strongly drawn to them all. What outstanding Christian women, and what lives they had led. They were deeply challenging. I was fascinated by the Reformation and they had each experienced its dramas and dangers and been transformed by its teaching. Yet so much of what I was reading was from secular books and I was surprised that these women were not better covered in Christian literature. The notable exception was Faith Cook's *Lady Jane Grey, Nine Day Queen of England*[4]. Surely their stories were waiting to be told in a way which emphasised the centrality of their faith in their lives. Their lives were linked together so they made a natural quartet, and the seed was sown for a book about all four of them together.

Sometimes, we talk of ordinary people living at extraordinary times, and the times certainly were extraordinary, but there is nothing ordinary about these ladies – quite the opposite – for all were remarkable women. Three lived at the very top of society; two were queens and one a duchess, and even Anne Askew was a gentlewoman (in today's terms, that made her roughly upper middle class). They were well-educated, intelligent and articulate. They had strong characters and personalities, but what is striking above all, is the strength of their love for God, and how He used their lives. They all have left their own witness to that faith in writing. Anne Askew described her examinations in great detail. Lady Jane Grey left several letters and also an account of her debate with John Feckenham. Catherine Willoughby's forty-four letters to William Cecil, Queen Elizabeth's Lord Burghley, have survived, though without his replies to her, and Katherine Parr even wrote a book. She called it *Lamentations of a Sinner,* and in it she lamented her earlier life before her spiritual eyes were opened and she was brought to faith.

The extraordinary times had much to do with the Reformation. The lives of these women were bound up with it, and, among them, they lived through all the most significant Reformation years, from Henry VIII's break with Rome, to the Elizabethan religious settlement

---

4   F. Cook, *Lady Jane Grey, Nine Day Queen of England* (Darlington: Evangelical Press, 2004)

and beyond. The sub-theme of this book, and the thread which runs through it, is the story of the Reformation, a complex story briefly told with broad brush strokes and with a mention of some of its significant people. These were times of instability and upheaval, especially from 1540, when factionalism became entrenched at court in Henry VIII's last years, through the reigns of two of his children, to the achievement of more settled times after the succession of his brilliant second daughter, Elizabeth, in 1558. This period is when much of the action in these ladies' lives occurred. With so much going on around them, and not infrequently impacting on them personally, I have stepped back from their stories at intervals to fill in this information in separate 'background' sections.

I have used the words 'Reformers', 'Evangelicals' and especially 'Protestants' interchangeably throughout to describe the same group of people, despite the fact that the word Protestant was not used in England until the mid 1550s. It seems clearer to use it for the whole period and rather unhelpful not to. I have also, on occasion, mildly modernised some of the sixteenth-century quotations if the meaning seems particularly obscure, or added explanatory words in brackets.

Of course, it is not just language that has changed in the intervening centuries. In Tudor England, people lived, ate, spoke and thought in ways which are strange to us. Living in our age, it is hard to appreciate just how important a part religion played in national life. Everyone was expected to go to church regularly and expected to hold the same beliefs. Before the Reformation, the Church, led by the Pope, declared what these were and, after the break with Rome, the monarch, as Supreme Head of the Church, had a crucial role in deciding its official doctrine. This was upheld by statute and enforced by the power of the state. Thus, the personal religious views of each of the Tudor monarchs was of great importance.

Rather than starting straight in with the life of Anne Askew, we begin with a first chapter which sets the scene, and gives a whistle-stop tour of the events and the people who figured large in the reign of Henry VIII, when the Reformation ushered in times of great change. These were also times when heresy laws meant that deviation from official doctrine was a capital offence and so death was a lurking danger for those who loved their Lord and refused to compromise, as all four women knew only too well. Their lives showed that they had taken to heart the words of the Apostle Paul:

> *For our light affliction, which is but for a moment, worketh for us a far more exceeding and eternal weight of glory; while we look not at the things which are seen : for the things which are seen are temporal; but the things which are not seen are eternal. (2 Corinthians 4:17-18)*

1. Times of Great Change

HENRY VIII AND THE ENGLISH REFORMATION

On 31ˢᵗ October 1517, an Augustinian monk pinned a notice on the door of the Castle Church at Wittenberg in Germany. His name was **Martin Luther** and this public declaration of his **'95 Theses'** was a protest against the way the dubious church practice of indulgences were being sold locally. To his surprise, his actions proved to be a catalyst. Others took his theses, printing them in their thousands, and sending them around Germany. Wherever they went they provoked a strong reaction. This has come to be seen as the **start of the Protestant Reformation**, but what followed was far more than a protest against church corruption. Luther's theology was still developing, but, within a couple of years, his study of the Bible, and most especially of the New Testament book of Romans, would transform his thinking and his relationship with God, and, ultimately, his attitude to the Church. That would be quickly followed by an outpouring of publications, as books flowed from his pen and the new invention of printing took his writings far beyond Wittenberg to other German towns and to other countries. Within a relatively short time, the Reformation would find a foothold across Europe, from Spain to Italy, and from France to Poland, and that in spite of the determined opposition of the Catholic Church and most secular rulers. In time, people from all ranks of society would be impacted, from the aristocracy to peasants.

It was the **Bible** which was at the heart of the movement. The Reformation meant a freeing from the accumulation of much church teaching and tradition, mentally sweeping it away and going back, as it were, to New Testament times to make a fresh start. No wonder it quickly came into conflict with the Church. With the Bible as their guide, people were grappling with deep theological issues and coming to a new understanding of the Scriptures. There would be some differences between them, which could be robustly argued, but, at its core, the Reformation had a real unity in its emphasis on personal faith. Its theology could be summarised in one key doctrine, that of justification by faith, and that was found in its resounding defining statement. **Scripture alone teaches us that salvation is by grace alone, through faith alone, in Christ alone and to the glory of God alone.** For, despite its imperfections, this remarkable time of Reformation saw a wonderful and powerful working of the Spirit of God.

The waters of the North Sea and English Channel divided **Tudor England** from the Continent and the growing religious upheaval, but they could not keep out the flow of ideas. Merchants and travellers brought back news of the new teachings, and some would smuggle in religious literature hidden in bales of cloth. From 1526, the New Testament translated into English by William Tyndale would come in the same way. It was at the ports – London, Bristol, Hull and others – that the work of reform was first felt, and from there it reached other towns, especially those of the south east. These few early English Lutherans were mostly artisans and from the lower classes, but some were intellectuals, with a special work taking place among the theologians and students of Cambridge University. In future days, many of these Cambridge men would become well-known leaders of the Church.

Over one hundred years earlier, England had had her own Evangelical awakener in **John Wycliffe**. He had overseen the translation of the Bible into English, which had been laboriously copied by hand. His followers, **the Lollards**, had taken portions with them as they went out into the byways to preach their simple message, and the Church had looked on with alarm. It had felt threatened and there had been a fierce response from the authorities. Repressive heresy laws came into being, which had been vigorously enforced, and they had dampened down, but not entirely extinguished, the Lollards' work. Now, in the early sixteenth century, these new Reformation beliefs were seen as more dangerous heresy to be rooted out and kept at bay. Religious pamphlets and books and English New Testaments were searched for, seized and burnt, and the King himself, the flamboyant **Henry VIII**, took up his pen and wrote a treatise against Luther, for which the Pope rewarded him with the title 'Defender of the Faith'.

Yet, within a few years, England would break with Rome and found a new national Church. The cause was not theological, but rather came from a decision taken by King Henry in 1527. It was an important decision and yet he could have had no idea just how momentous the consequences would be. Nearly twenty years of marriage to **Catherine of Aragon** had not produced a male heir, only one daughter, the Princess Mary. Catherine was seven years older than Henry and, now in her forties, it was clear her childbearing days were over. Her succession of miscarriages and stillbirths had left her faded, aged and fat. Meanwhile, Henry had fallen in love with the fascinating **Anne Boleyn**, one of Catherine's ladies-in-waiting, and she would accept nothing less than marriage; indeed only marriage could provide heirs to solve the problem of the succession. The King's conscience also played a part. Once he had discovered that the Old Testament book of Leviticus forbade a man to marry his brother's widow, he interpreted his lack of children as a sign of God's displeasure for doing precisely that. So it was that in 1527, he decided to commit himself to Anne and to take the first steps to set Catherine aside and to replace her as Queen.

Because Catherine had been previously married to his older brother, albeit only briefly, Henry had needed a papal dispensation to marry her and now he would look to another Pope to reverse it. He did not anticipate a long or difficult process, but he was very wrong. '**The King's Great Matter**' would take six years of protracted negotiations and frustrating stalemate. Catherine and Anne were both formidable women. Catherine refused to accept any settlement or to go quietly; on the contrary, she vigorously asserted that her first marriage had never been consummated and therefore there were no grounds for denying the validity of her second. Meanwhile, Anne relentlessly urged Henry down the path of annulment and remarriage. The Pope prevaricated and delayed, but his reluctance to act in Henry's favour became increasingly clear. How could he oblige Henry when, from 1527, he was virtually a prisoner of the most powerful man in Europe, the Emperor Charles V, whose troops had sacked Rome in that year? Charles, who was Catherine's nephew, would not countenance any moves against her.

In the summer of 1527, **papal dispensation** to free Henry from his first marriage was applied for, but it was all of another two years before a legatine court convened in England to try the matter, and then it was very quickly adjourned. A young cleric called Stephen Gardiner was beginning to rise rapidly in the Church and in the King's service, and he was involved in the divorce proceedings. He happened to meet someone he had known in his student days at Cambridge University. **Thomas Cranmer** was still at Cambridge, an able but obscure academic. Gardiner updated him on the lack of progress and Cranmer had a suggestion to make. Why not take a very different tack and ask theologians at Continental universities their opinion about the validity of the King's marriage? This was a turning point. It was no quick fix and the situation would rumble on, but Cranmer's own life would never be the same again. He was invited to talk with Henry, the universities were consulted, and Cranmer was lodged with the Boleyn family and taken into royal service to work to find reasons for an annulment.

The legatine court never resumed, for the Pope revoked the case to Rome, which meant that there was now no realistic chance that there would ever be a decision in Henry's favour. More time went by with Henry trying to make progress by putting pressure on the Church, but no nearer to achieving his goal. It was not until 1532 that things finally moved forward. A different way had been found, and a series of Acts of Parliament passed between 1532 and 1534 broke all ties with Rome and took the English Church out of the control of the Pope and into the hands of the King. This other way was centred on the premise, which had gradually been developed, that the monarch was ruler over *all* in his kingdom. So it was the King – and not the Pope – who had authority over the Church, as well as secular affairs. This was not just a cynical ploy to cut through the impossible tangle of the King's Great Matter. Cranmer's extensive research, the replies from some of the European universities, and a book written by William Tyndale, all came together to give a theological and historical basis for this idea which was called the **royal supremacy**. God had appointed Henry to be King of England – and this meant he was head of the Church, as well as head of state.

Theory was all very well, but it had to be turned into reality and Henry had just the man to do it. **Thomas Cromwell** was an experienced lawyer and parliamentarian who was rising in Henry's service and well on his way to becoming his chief minister. He would prove to be extraordinarily able in creating and directing this legislative programme. Cromwell's contribution was complemented by the other key man who also came into position at just the right moment. The elderly Archbishop of Canterbury was doing what he could to resist the King, but he died in 1532, and Henry took the opportunity to appoint Thomas Cranmer as his successor. No one could have been more surprised or dismayed than Cranmer himself. He had been in Germany when the news reached him and he had dawdled, taking as long as possible over the journey home. He was consecrated in March 1533 and, by then, things were moving very quickly indeed, for there was now the most pressing of reasons for urgency. Anne Boleyn was pregnant and her child had to be born indisputably legitimate.

The last act of the King's Great Matter was played out in May in the Priory Church at Dunstable. Cranmer officiated at an ecclesiastical court which pronounced first that Henry's marriage to Catherine was illegal, and then that the secret marriage between Henry and Anne, which had taken place in January, was lawful. Cranmer's judgements had never been in doubt, for Anne was crowned only days later on 1st June. This was the high point of four days of ostentatious celebration, designed to ensure no one could be in any doubt about her new status. For Henry and Anne, though, things would not go completely their way. When their baby was born in September, it was not the much-anticipated prince but a daughter, whom they called Elizabeth.

Henry had certainly not broken with Rome in order to make changes in the Church. He was interested in theology, but his leanings were very conservative, and he would retain his belief in transubstantiation, as well as maintaining hostility to the doctrine of justification by faith all his life. Nevertheless, he had supporters of the Reformed faith around him – his wife, Cranmer and Cromwell – and they did begin to influence him. He appointed Cromwell as his Vicar General, or deputy in religious affairs. The displacement of the Pope had been a fairly popular move, for he was seen as an interfering foreign power, but, for some, this was enough change while others wanted more. Religious division and conflict had now entered the court, the Church, and national life, and it had come to stay.

Anne Boleyn was working for the Reformation even before she became Queen. She was a patron and protector of Evangelicals, encouraging their promotion in the Church, and she tried to protect some who brought illegal English Scriptures into the country. The Bible was important to her. One was placed on a lectern in her private apartments and she possessed a copy of Tyndale's New Testament, even though it was against the law.

The Bible was at the centre of the Reformation. One man who saw the vital importance of translating it into English was a young priest, **William Tyndale**. If he had started his life's work ten years earlier, he could only have used the official Latin Vulgate translation as his source but, when he left Oxford University and was working as a tutor in Gloucestershire, he was poring over a very special New Testament. A Dutchman, Desiderius Erasmus, had, as recently as 1516 , published a New Testament which printed the Greek text alongside his own Latin translation. Suddenly, the New Testament could be studied in its original language, as well as in a Latin text which differed from the Vulgate in the way in which it translated significant texts which had, up to now, supported key doctrines of the Church. As a gifted linguist who knew both Greek and Hebrew, Tyndale felt drawn to undertake an English translation himself. He famously told a Catholic scholar who was denigrating the Bible: 'If God spare my life, 'ere many years I will cause a boy that driveth a plough shall know more of the scriptures than thou dost.'[1]

The authorities, Church and secular, were determined to prevent English translations, which they saw as a threat to the authority of the

---

1   B. Edwards, *Travel with William Tyndale* (Leominster: Day One, 2009), p. 44.

Church, which indeed they were, and were prepared to burn people as well as books. In Coventry in 1519, seven people died at the stake because they had taught their children the Lord's Prayer, the Apostle's Creed, and the Ten Commandments in English. It was too dangerous for Tyndale to undertake his task in England and he would spend the rest of his life in Germany and the Netherlands. Even then, he was not safe, but worked with the threat of arrest hanging over him and, at times, had to move around to keep himself free. He had rare gifts as a translator and in his **New Testament,** he produced a masterpiece which was accurate, memorable and written in English of exceptional quality. It was first published in 1525 and was quickly followed in 1526 by a smaller edition, easier to transport and to hide; and these were speedily smuggled into England and Scotland. So began the Bible burnings, with the authorities on both sides of the Channel seizing as many as they could, but they could not stem the flow.

Tyndale moved on to start translating the Old Testament, but was also prolific in producing other books. In *The Obedience of the Christian Man* published in 1528, he emphasised the foundational principles for Christian living. It was the Bible which was the source of the highest authority within the Church, and the King who was the supreme authority in the state. This book was quickly banned but its influence would be huge especially in the development of the theory of the royal supremacy and in promoting obedience to the King. Tyndale was arrested in Antwerp in 1535 and was executed the following year by being strangled and then burnt. At the stake he cried out, 'Lord open the King of England's eyes.'

As far as the Bible was concerned, there was a speedy answer to this prayer. Two other men were ready to take Tyndale's work forward. In 1535 the first full English Bible, which was translated by Miles Coverdale, had been published, and only months after Tyndale's death, a second complete Bible, the Matthew's Bible, was produced. This was the work of John Rogers, who had rescued and utilised Tyndale's manuscripts and inserted Coverdale's for the significant part of the Old Testament Tyndale had not done. Henry VIII actually allowed both of these Bibles to be published in England. Finally, in April 1539, came the Great Bible, which was Coverdale's achievement and was a revision of the Matthew's Bible. This was ordered to be placed in every parish church. Scripture could now be read by, or to, anyone in their own tongue. Many were eager to do so and the power of the Word of God must have come with peculiar freshness to those who had been deprived of it for so long. Now people could read God's truth directly from the Bible and see for themselves their need of personal repentance, rather than doing penance, and of a heartfelt faith rather than good works and simply obeying the Church. God's Spirit was at work as His Word was set forth in print.

Henry was prepared to take action against some of the visual and traditional aspects of Catholicism, such as pilgrimages, shrines, superstitious relics and images, but by far the greatest upheaval was caused by the **dissolution of the monasteries** which took place between 1536 and 1540. Undoubtedly, there was laxness, corruption and immorality within their walls, but their wealth, especially their vast accumulation of land, made them a particularly tempting target. When their inmates were pensioned off, their lead and roofs were removed and the buildings left uninhabitable, their valuables and land all passed to the King. He sold most of the land on, which meant that, in future, the nobility would be reluctant to undo the Reformation if that threatened their personal estates. The end of the monasteries also removed their significant potential to resist religious change.

Such momentous events did not pass without a backlash. In the autumn of 1536, the sudden flare up of the **Pilgrimage of Grace** brought a desperate crisis. It is reckoned to have been the biggest peacetime revolt, not just of Henry's reign, but in English history. There were complex factors at work behind this rather confusing episode, but the dissolution of the monasteries was a key trigger. The 'pilgrims' marched behind banners emblazoned with the wounds of Christ.

In the meantime, Henry's second marriage was strangely repeating the pattern of his first. Anne had promised Henry a son, but she was not finding it any easier than her predecessor to provide one, and Elizabeth's birth had been followed by a stillbirth. Catherine of Aragon had had to endure Henry's roving eye falling on one of her ladies-in-waiting, Anne herself, and now it was Anne's turn to be put through the same experience, as Henry's interest in her own lady-in-waiting, **Jane Seymour**, became increasingly obvious. Anne's hold on Henry was slipping, not helped by her sharp tongue, while her rival was presenting a demure and gentle contrast to the King. Catherine's death in January 1536 exposed the weakness of Anne's position, for she could now be divorced without affecting the annulment from Catherine. Then, in February, Anne miscarried with a boy. Henry had seen his difficulties with having children with Catherine as a sign of God's displeasure with his marriage, and it was not difficult for him to view his current problems in the same way. He had waited for six long years to marry Anne, but their marriage would last but half that time. Thomas Cromwell began to see Anne as a liability and also as a threat to himself, both to his position and to his policies. He was prepared to free Henry by ruthlessly removing Anne, not through a time-consuming divorce, but quickly and clinically through accusations of adultery. These carried the death penalty for a Queen. Anne was arrested in May 1536 and, though undoubtedly innocent, was tried, found guilty and beheaded in the Tower.

Ten days later, Henry married Jane Seymour and it was Jane alone, of all his wives, who was able to give him what he so desperately wanted: a baby boy. Sadly, all the jubilation at **Prince Edward**'s birth in October 1537 was cut short when his mother died just days afterwards, probably of puerperal fever, a fairly common hazard of Tudor childbirth. Henry had his heir, but now there was no wife to give him a spare. He may well have genuinely grieved for Jane, but there was little delay before the process of looking for a replacement began, this time among suitable European royalty.

Cromwell and Cranmer were using their positions to advance the Reformation and both men acted out of personal conviction. Evangelical men were appointed in the Church, including a small group of bishops, among them Hugh Latimer and Nicholas Shaxton. Cranmer encouraged Henry to consider ecclesiastical changes, although this was met with reluctance. Cromwell personally championed the cause of the English Bible. He encouraged Henry to license the printing of the

Matthew's Bible and used his authority, as well as his own money, to produce the Great Bible, and to bring it within reach of everyone by ordering it to be placed in every church. Even the illiterate could have it read to them. Cromwell saw himself as working for God as well as the King. In March 1538, he wrote to the Protestant Bishop of Salisbury, Nicholas Shaxton. 'I do not cease to give thanks that it hath pleased his goodness to use me as an instrument and to work somewhat by me... My prayer is that God give me no longer life than I shall be glad to use mine office in edification and not in destruction.'[2]

In that year of 1538, it became apparent that Henry's thinking was shifting. He began to indicate that he felt reform had gone far enough, in fact, too far, and needed to be reined in. It was also the year that the rival powers, France and the Empire, stopped their hostilities and concluded peace. The Pope seized his opportunity and called on them both, as well as Scotland, to invade England and depose Henry to restore the Catholic faith. Henry partly deflected the danger by forging a peace treaty with Scotland, but it was these uncertainties which hung over Henry and the Parliament which assembled in April 1539 and which led to the passing of the **Act of Six Articles**. It was a very marked change in direction, a reaffirmation of much traditional Catholic dogma, and was enforced by strict penalties. If anyone denied the real presence of Christ's body in the bread and wine of the mass, he or she was to be burnt at the stake. It was a real setback for the minority of clergy who were Protestant, to say nothing of Cromwell and also Cranmer, who had resisted the Act as far as he had dared.

Even so, just a few months later, in the late summer, Cromwell began to rise again in the King's favour, and Henry endorsed Cromwell's policy of supporting the German Lutheran princes with an alliance to counter-balance the threat from the Emperor Charles V. After seeing an attractive painting of Anne, sister of the Duke of Cleves, Henry agreed to take her as his next wife. Unfortunately, **Anne of Cleves** did not live up to her portrait. She arrived in England late in 1539 and, when Henry first saw her, he was dismayed. Something about Anne repelled him and, if he could have, he would have wriggled out of the

2   A.G. Dickens, *The English Reformation* (London: Collins, 1967) p. 236.

marriage. As it was, with bad grace, he went through with it, but it was unconsummated and he was able to divorce her within months. Anne was no doubt relieved to escape the marriage with her head still on her shoulders and with a generous settlement, and Henry once again had a replacement at the ready in the person of **Catherine Howard**, the pretty teenage niece of the Duke of Norfolk.

Cromwell was not so fortunate. Henry blamed him for the disaster of his fourth marriage and, even though in the first half of 1540 Cromwell seemed to be as secure as ever, Henry had not forgotten. Though the Act of Six Articles had had Henry's support, its prime movers had been the leaders of the Catholic party, the Duke of Norfolk and Stephen Gardiner, who was very influential within the Church as Bishop of Winchester. That same pairing's next move was aimed at Cromwell and when they struck against him, arresting him at a meeting of the Council in June 1540, Henry abandoned him and did nothing to save him, but let his very loyal chief minister be condemned as a traitor. Cromwell was executed on 28th July and the same day, Henry married his fifth wife, Catherine Howard. The Howards and the Catholic faction must have felt their time had come.

Incredibly, Henry's marital saga had yet more drama to come. He doted on his young wife, openly showing his affection for her. What he did not know was that she was not the innocent girl he had thought her to be when they married, and she had been too free with her favours since, despite the terrible risks she ran. In the autumn of 1541, the scandal broke when Cranmer had to pass on information which had been given to him. At first, Henry hoped her misdemeanors were back in the past but, when he realised there was good reason to believe that Catherine had been having an affair as Queen, he hardened his heart and she was doomed. Catherine became the second of his wives to be beheaded in the Tower when she was executed in February 1541. He waited a year before he found his next wife and then, in Katherine Parr, he chose an eminently suitable consort.

Henry did not replace Cromwell with another chief minister. He may have thought he could manage affairs himself without the need of someone wielding the authority of Cromwell, and before him of Cardinal Wolsey, but his last years were marked by increasing factionalism and some measure of decline. He also embarked on a war with France, as well as some expeditions against Scotland, which more than swallowed up all the financial gains from the dissolution of the monasteries, draining the country's resources for very little purpose.

The factions at Henry's court were split along religious lines. He regretted that it was so, but almost inevitably, Reformation changes had led to divisions felt far beyond the Church and that was reflected in the power politics of the day. The **leaders of the Catholic party** accepted the break with Rome and the King's supremacy but wanted minimal change beyond that, and strongly upheld traditional Catholicism. They were led by three members of the Council. Thomas Howard, the powerful Duke of Norfolk, had served the King as a soldier and statesman for most of his reign. Stephen Gardiner, a leading bishop and Cranmer's adversary, had also served Henry for many years and took a more dominant role after Cromwell's fall. Thomas Wriothesley was a prominent administrator, and he would become Henry's last Lord Chancellor.

After Cromwell's death, **Thomas Cranmer took over his role as leader of the other group at court, the Protestants**. He was backed by the King's brother-in-law, Charles Brandon, Duke of Suffolk who, like Norfolk, had had a distinguished career in the King's service and as a soldier. They were supported by two younger men, Suffolk's protegé, John Dudley, Viscount Lisle, and Edward Seymour, Jane Seymour's brother, who was Earl of Hertford. They were both able soldiers and were the up-and-coming men at court. Despite their best efforts, neither side was able to gain a lasting advantage over the other, and the powerful figure of the King, even in his declining years, still dominated the court.

From 1540, as Henry's attitude had hardened against reform, the Catholics had been emboldened, despite Catherine Howard's downfall, when Norfolk had had to sit for the second time in judgement at the trial of a queen and, in each case, the queen had been his own niece. The Act of Six Articles was followed by **further restrictions on religious reform,** especially with the introduction of tight controls on which Bible versions and religious books could be read and by whom. Common people could no longer read the Scriptures. There would be no Catholic triumph though, for **Henry's religious policy** was his own unique middle way. It might look contradictory or random, but there was a guiding principle which steered him through the pressures of foreign threats and of the opposing influences around him, and that was that he would not come down fully on one side or the other. He would shape the Church in his own way and it would contain both Catholic and Protestant elements. Just two days after Cromwell's execution, an unusual and significant event took place at Smithfield. Six men were brought there together for execution, three Catholics and three Protestants. The Catholics were hanged as traitors for denying the royal supremacy and the Protestants were burnt as heretics. It was a deliberately striking visual public statement, a picture of Henry's religious policy. He would not tolerate Catholic resistance to his position as Supreme Head, but neither would he allow Protestants to deviate from the official doctrinal position of the Church, and that had not moved very far at all from pre-Reformation days.

Persecution of Protestant 'heretics' increased, especially in Henry's final year. Since the setback in 1539 of the Act of Six Articles, the key doctrine they fell foul of was that of the real presence. Was Christ present in bodily form in the mass, in the elements which were called the sacrament of the altar? Direct denial of this meant burning at the stake. The question of the mass was an important and contentious issue among Protestants, who individually moved at very different speeds in coming away from the Catholic doctrine of transubstantiation, and towards a replacement theology. Luther had believed that, in some way, the body and blood of Christ were present in the bread and wine of the Eucharist, although these did not change their nature but remained bread and wine. Cranmer and other prominent churchmen for a while also took this view, but many Protestants had moved on in their thinking and had come to believe that the Eucharist was purely a commemorative feast and that Christ's presence was entirely spiritual. For them, the threat of a dreadful death was very real.

This, then, was the situation towards the end of Henry's long reign and it was against this shifting and turbulent background that the first of our four ladies, Anne Askew, came to the attention of the authorities.

2. ANNE ASKEW 1520/1 - 1546

VALIANT FOR THE TRUTH

Whoever smuggled the documents out of Newgate Prison in the summer of 1546 knew exactly what to do with them. Within weeks, Dutch merchants had spirited them across the North Sea and they took them on through the German states until they reached their destination, the Duchy of Cleves and the hands of that most effective propagandist for the Protestant cause, John Bale. As Bale read them, he was struck by the remarkable testimony – the detailed account of the official interrogations, the courage and faith of the writer, and the evidence of the strength of God in her life – especially as it was a woman who faced such suffering. He had been given something special and of rare quality, and he carefully determined how to make the most of the manuscript. He decided that the text would be published in full, and alongside he would write his own extensive comments, comparing her to earlier martyrs of the faith, especially Blandina, who had lived in the second century. *The First Examination of Anne Askew, lately martyred in Smithfield* was printed in October 1546, soon followed in January 1547 by *The Latter Examination of the worthy servant of God, Mistress Anne Askew*. It meant that Anne Askew's story, told in her own words, was quickly and widely circulated, and she would become one of the best known of the martyrs of Henry VIII's reign.

Early life, marriage and conversion

Anne had been born in Lincolnshire some twenty-five years earlier. Her father was Sir William Askew of Stallingborough, a man of some standing. He was a substantial landowner in Lincolnshire and Nottinghamshire, who spent periods of time at court. In 1521, he was appointed High Sherriff of Lincolnshire and, in 1529, he became MP for Grimsby. John Foxe would later comment in his famous compilation of Christian martyrs entitled *Acts and Monuments* that, had it not been for her love of Christ, Anne could have lived a comfortable and prosperous life.

After the death of Anne's mother, Sir William remarried and the family moved to South Kelsey nearer Lincoln. Anne had two sisters, Martha and Jane, two brothers, Francis and Edward and two half-brothers, Christopher and Thomas. Unusually for the time, when learning was more normally seen to be the domain of boys apart from in a few aristocratic households, Anne and her two sisters received a good education, which would have been through tutors at home. This was something which would not have been wasted on the intelligent and articulate Anne. Their parents would have expected their three daughters to make good marriages and her older sister, Martha, was betrothed to Thomas Kyme, the son of another Lincolnshire landowner, but, before the marriage could take place, she fell ill and died. Sir William was unwilling to forego the advantages of the alliance and so Anne was substituted as bride. Anne herself was anything but willing and had to be forced to submit, but in a day when it was the parents who chose who their offspring should marry, she had no alternative but to comply.

After their marriage, Thomas and Anne lived in Friskney, near the coast. Two children were born, but the home was soon disturbed by the differences between the couple. Kyme was a conservative man and a traditional Catholic, whilst Anne came to an understanding of Reformation doctrines, which touched her heart as well as her mind and brought her to a position of evangelical faith. She came to see that her salvation could not come through following the traditions and teachings of the Church, but through repentance and trusting in the sacrificial death of the Lord Jesus Christ. There are no details of when, or exactly how, this happened. Others in her close family seem to have been involved with the Protestant faith and may well have spoken to her about their beliefs. All we know is that her transformation came through regularly reading the Bible over a period of time. What is certain is that Anne could not keep quiet about her new-found faith. To her husband's dismay, she had to talk about it and share it with others.

Word about Anne's enthusiasm spread and, after a while, friends warned her that, if she went to Lincoln, the priests had threatened that she would find herself in great trouble. Anne would have been well aware of the dangers she faced, but far from keeping low and hoping that the priests would forget about her, she made her way to Lincoln Cathedral and installed herself there, sitting calmly and reading the Bible. She remained for six days waiting to see what the priests would have to say to her. It seems that it was the priests who were abashed, nonplussed and unsure of how to handle such boldness. At different times, small groups of them approached her but they all moved on without speaking, and, in the end, only one actually confronted her, though Anne dismissively claimed later that what he said to her was not important enough for her to remember.

The priests had the last word. They urged Kyme to eject Anne from their home and this he did on her return, violently driving her from the house. She had no choice but to go and to leave her children behind. Apart from the upset at being forced from her home and family, Anne was now in a vulnerable position. Not only had she lost the security of having a husband, but her father had died, so she also lacked his protection and support. Where was she to go and what was she to do? Anne made up her mind that she needed to end her marriage and seek a divorce, and she looked to 1 Corinthians chapter 7:12 -15 as her justification. She interpreted this as saying that if a believing wife has an unbelieving husband who will not stay with her, she may leave him. According to Bale, it was Kyme's cruelty in driving her away which made up her mind, and the fact that she could not think him worthy of being her husband when he so spitefully hated God, who was the chief author of marriage.

London 1544

When Anne arrived in London late in 1544, it was to try and obtain a divorce. She was not without friends and family there. Her brother, Edward, had formerly been in the service of Archbishop Cranmer and was now cupbearer to the King, Henry VIII. Her half-brother, Christopher, who had died the previous year, had been a gentleman of the King's Privy Chamber. Her sister, Jane, was married to a known Protestant, George St Paul, who administered the Duke and Duchess of Suffolk's Lincolnshire estates and she most likely shared her husband's faith. Catherine Brandon, Duchess of Suffolk, was a close friend of Queen Katherine Parr.

So it was that through her family connections, Anne had contacts at court. Who exactly she knew, and how well, is simply not known, and even though she shared her evangelical faith with some of the inner circle of the Queen's ladies, there is no evidence that she ever met them, though some have claimed that she did. Anne certainly could have had no inkling that, in the future, those court connections would have terrifying consequences for her.

Anne settled into lodgings near London's legal centre, the Temple. Her cousin, Christopher Brittayne was a lawyer of the Middle Temple, and she would find it helpful to be near the Inns of Court, where she hoped to pursue her divorce. She also came under the spiritual influence of John Lascells, a lawyer of Furnivalls Inn, who had entered royal service. Living in the capital gave Anne neither safety nor anonymity and, within weeks of her arrival, she was being watched. A Catholic spy called Wadlow moved into a nearby house to keep her under observation. In fact, he found nothing incriminating to report, but he did note her piety and how long she spent praying.

First examination 1545
Evidence was being gathered against Anne, including statements she was supposed to have made, and, in March 1545, she was examined at Sadler's Hall by a quest, an official heresy hearing. The quest's spokesman, one Christopher Dare, asked her eight questions. The very first went to the heart of the matter. Did she believe that the sacrament hanging over the altar was really the actual body of Christ? In other words, did she believe that, during the mass, the bread and the wine became the real body of Christ, often called the real presence? The Act of Six Articles of 1539 upheld this traditional Catholic view of the mass, but many Reformers, including Anne, rejected it and found it

abhorrent. Christ had died as a perfect sacrifice for sin and He had risen from the grave. His death and resurrection had taken place in the past, and had fulfilled God's purposes. They were not a sacrifice which could be repeated again and again in the ritual of the mass. The legislation of 1539 meant that investigations for heresy (deviations from officially-accepted doctrine) did not have to look at a range of doctrines but could focus on the litmus test of the mass. If she denied the real presence, she faced a terrible death by burning. What was Anne to do? If she gave a direct negative reply to Dare's question, she would immediately have condemned herself. Anne did not reply. Instead, she asked Dare a question. Why was Saint Stephen stoned to death? When he replied that he could not tell, she retorted that neither would she answer his question. Dare continued with his interrogation, but, if he had stopped to consider, he would have realised the significance of what Anne was asking. Stephen had been killed by the religious authorities of his day for supposed blasphemy but, in reality, it was for following God's Son. He had been the faithful one, not they.

Other difficult questions followed, including about confession, private masses and again about the sacrament of the altar, and Anne answered succinctly, but evasively. It was only the start of her ordeal. The next round of questioning came from the Lord Mayor of London and the Bishop's Chancellor, Dr John Standish. The latter rebuked her for quoting Scripture as St Paul had forbidden women to speak or talk of God's Word. Anne replied that she knew as well as he that Paul's meaning in 1 Corinthians chapter 9, the passage he was referring to, was that women were not to teach in the congregation. 'And then I asked him how many women he had seen go into the pulpit and preach? He said he never saw one. Then I said, he ought not to find fault in poor women unless they had broken the law.'[1]

Anne was imprisoned for the next twelve days in the Counter, the Lord Mayor's prison. Still the questioning continued as she was interrogated by a priest sent by the Bishop of London. The climax came when she was examined by the Bishop of London himself, Edmund

---

1   J. Foxe, *Acts and Monuments* 1563, reprinted in *The Examinations of Anne Askew* ed. E. Beilin, (New York: Oxford University Press, 1996), p. 167 (spelling modernised).

Bonner, and by his Archdeacon, John Wymesley. Bonner spoke first to Anne's cousin, the lawyer Christopher Brittayne, and seemed to be making an effort to put Anne at her ease by encouraging him and others to be present at the interrogation, as well as any learned men of Anne's choice. There seems to have been frustration that Anne had not revealed as much as had been expected and Bonner began in a friendly manner and urged her to speak freely and without fear and to tell whatever troubled her conscience. Anne declared she had nothing to say for she thanked God that her conscience was not burdened with anything.

Anne faced a mixture of questions and of having to respond to statements she was supposed to have made, though she denied some of them. It was all relentlessly directed to the same end, to determine whether she really did hold Reformist views, especially concerning the mass. Anne conducted herself wisely and cannily, sometimes giving a straight answer, mostly being brief and sometimes not answering but asking a question of her own. She stood on Scripture, on what Christ taught and her answers were faithful to God's Word, but she managed to avoid directly incriminating herself. She knew her Bible well and quoted Scripture freely and accurately, but was also careful not to appear to be interpreting it and so placing herself in a position which might be construed as a woman interpreting the Bible before learned men of the Church.

When the quaint language of these exchanges is stripped away there is an astonishing modernity about Anne's speech. We are used to authority being questioned and challenged but Tudor men and women were not. Theirs was a hierarchical society and all, especially women, were expected to know their place and act accordingly with due deference and respect. For women, that meant they were under the authority of their fathers until they married, when they were expected to accept their parents' choice of a husband and then to live under the protection and authority of their husband. Anne's lack of deference is breathtaking. What must her interrogators have made of her? How her words must have jarred. Despite the huge pressure she was under, she was confident and assertive and, by turns, sounded defiant, scornful,

pert and abrasive. Her interrogators should have had the upper hand
but it seems they found her unsettling and difficult to handle. Yet
Anne was not merely challenging the authority of the Church; she was
presenting truth. The Bible was everything to her. What mattered was
what Scripture said, what Christ said. In her great respect for that, she
spoke with scant respect for those she regarded as enemies of true faith.

Bonner accused Anne of saying that the sacrament remaining in
the pyx, or vessel, was only bread. She replied that she had never said
that, though the quest had asked such a question. She had refused to
answer until her interrogator had answered her own question as to
why Stephen was stoned to death. Bonner, like the quest, declined
to go any further with this, but instead charged her with quoting a
certain text of Scripture. Anne answered that she was only referring to
St Paul's words to the Athenians in Acts chapter 17 that God did not
live in a temple made with hands. He asked what she believed in this
matter. 'I answered him I believe as the scripture doth teach me. Then
he inquired of me, what if the scripture do say that it is the body of
Christ? I believe, said I, as the scripture doth teach me. Then asked he
again what if the scripture do say that it is not the body of Christ? My
answer was still, I believe as the scripture informs me. And upon this
argument he tarried a great while to have driven me to make an answer
to his mind. Howbeit I would not, but concluded this with him that
I believe therein and in all other things as Christ and his holy apostles
did leave them.'[2]

Bonner's third charge was that Anne had said 'the mass was
superstitious, wicked, and no better than idolatry'. Anne refuted that
the words were hers, but acknowledged that the quest had asked her
whether private mass relieved departed souls and she had replied, '"O
Lord what idolatry is this? That we should rather believe in private
masses than in the healthsome death of the dear Son of God." Then
said my Lord [Bonner] again what an answer was that? Though it were
but mean (I said) yet it was good enough for the question.'[3]

---

2   ibid., p. 172.

3   ibid., p. 173.

The Bishop said that he had been informed that, when Anne had been asked if she would receive the sacraments at Easter, she had been mocking in her reply. Anne indignantly asked that her accuser should be produced, which Bonner declined. Shortly afterwards, he disappeared and, when he returned, it was with a written confession which was read to her. It was an orthodox confession of traditional Catholic faith. 'I Anne Askew do confess this to be my faith and belief, notwithstanding my reports made before to the contrary…I do believe that after the consecration whether it be received or reserved, to be no less than the very body and blood of Christ, in substance. Finally I do believe in this and in all other sacraments of holy church in all points according to the old catholic faith of the same. In witness whereof I the said Anne have subscribed my name.'[4]

Anne was asked if she agreed with it. 'And I said again I believe so much thereof as the holy scripture doth agree unto, wherefore I desire you, that you will add that thereunto. Then he answered that I should not teach him what he should write.'[5]

The Bishop then read the same confession before a group of churchmen gathered in his great chamber and they encouraged her to sign it. When it was passed to her, Anne wrote, 'I Anne Askew do believe all manner [of] things contained in the faith of the Catholic church.'[6] Anne was using the word 'catholic' in the sense of universal, which was a contentious term to Bonner and other traditionalists. He flew into a rage and swept into his chamber, followed by Anne's cousin, Christopher Brittayne, who had been trying to arrange her release on bail. Now, with some difficulty, he persuaded the Bishop to take his name and that of another lawyer, Francis Spilman, as sureties. Bonner had decided he would take no further action and that he had had enough of this difficult woman, but even so her ordeal was not quite over. She had to endure two more nights in prison and two more appearances, once at the Guildhall and again at St Paul's Church, before 'after much

---

4   ibid., p 174.

5   ibid., p 174.

6   Ibid., p 175.

ado and reasoning to and fro, they took a bond of them of recognisance for my forthcoming. And thus I was at last delivered.'[7]

Release

Anne was not left alone for long though. Just three months later, on 13th of June, she found herself again in the Guildhall arraigned with two others, all accused of speaking against the sacrament of the altar. The only witness proved to be unreliable, and the case was dropped, and Anne was free once more.

John Foxe included Anne's manuscript in his mammoth work *Acts and Monuments of these Latter and Perilous Days Touching Matters of the Church*, a detailed account of the martyrs of the Christian church from the earliest days in New Testament times to the end of the reign of Mary. This was first published early in the reign of Elizabeth l and quickly became universally known as Foxe's *Book of Martyrs*. He records a postscript to these events. Although Anne had not signed the document of confession and recantation presented to her, a year later it was inscribed into the Bishop's register with a note of the witnesses who supposedly had seen her sign it. Foxe pointed out Bonner's duplicity and the falseness of the claim that she had signed anything other than her own brief statement.

Second examination June 1546

Anne's respite was relatively short lived. A year later on 18th June 1546, Thomas and Anne Kyme appeared together before the Privy Council at Greenwich. They had been summoned in connection with their marital dispute, but the issue of their marriage was quickly shelved and Kyme was allowed to return home. Once again, the focus was on Anne and her beliefs. These were dangerous times for Protestant believers. The traditionalist Catholic group around the King had become more active in seeking out 'heretics', especially from within the Church, and at court, and there were a flurry of executions in this the last year of King Henry's reign. This time, Anne was being questioned by some of the greatest in the land, including the Chancellor, Sir Thomas Wriothesley, the Bishop of Winchester, Stephen Gardiner, the Earl of

---

7   ibid., p 178.

Essex, William Parr, and the King's Principal Secretary, Sir William Paget. The Chancellor asked her opinion of the sacrament and Anne replied that she believed that when she was in a Christian congregation and she received the bread in remembrance of Christ's death and with thanksgiving according to His holy institution, she received the fruits of His glorious passion. Gardiner tried to make her answer more directly but with little success, although Anne did tell him she was 'ready to suffer all things at his hands, not only his rebukes, but all that should follow besides, yea and all that gladly'.[8]

About five hours of interrogation ended with Anne back in prison. She was brought before the Council again the following day. The Bishop of Winchester, the Earl of Essex and John Dudley, Lord Lisle, urged her to confess the sacraments to be flesh, blood and bone but Anne steadfastly refused and eventually Gardiner told her bluntly that she would be burnt: 'I answered that I had searched all the scriptures yet I could not find that Christ or his Apostles put any creature to death.'[9] She asked to see the evangelical preacher and former bishop, Hugh Latimer, but this was refused. In fact, he too was under arrest and enduring lengthy interrogations. Feeling very ill, she was now imprisoned in Newgate.

In recording her 'latter examinations', Anne was conscious she was writing for other believers and she concluded this section with the words, 'Thus the lord strengthen you in the truth, pray, pray, pray.'[10] Whereas she had had to be circumspect in responding to her interrogations, now in Newgate she was at pains to set down clearly her doctrine and faith so that her friends and others could have no doubt about what she believed. She included the words, 'The bread being thereof an only sign or sacrament...So that the bread is but a remembrance of his death or a sacrament of thanksgiving for it, whereby we are knit unto him by a communion of Christian love.'[11] As she signed this passage, she gave an indication of how she viewed her predicament. 'Written by me Anne

---

8   ibid., pp. 180-1.

9   ibid., p. 181.

10   ibid., p. 182.

11   ibid., p. 182.

Askew that neither wish death, nor yet fear his might: and as merry as one that is bound towards heaven.'[12]

Ten days later, on 28th June, she was one of four arraigned for heresy at the Guildhall, along with a cleric, Nicholas Shaxton, a merchant, Christopher White and a tailor, John Hadlam. Anne was told plainly that she was a heretic and would be condemned unless she changed her beliefs. The time for any evasion was over. Anne bravely answered that she was not a heretic and did not deserve to die according to God's law, but she would not deny her faith. Again, she was asked if she denied the sacrament to be Christ's body and blood. Yes, she did deny it, 'For the same Son of God, that was born of the Virgin Mary, is now glorious in heaven, and will come again from thence at the latter day like as he went up. Acts chapter 1. And as for that you call your God, it is a piece of bread: for a more proof thereof...Let it lie in the box but three months and it will be mouldy, and so turn to nothing that is good. Whereupon I am persuaded, that it cannot be God.'[13]

All four were condemned by the Lord Chancellor and the Council for their views on the sacrament and Anne was returned to Newgate to await her execution, but not without making an attempt to save her life. She wrote to the King, appealing for his pardon. She was ready to die but she was not seeking martyrdom. She was still compiling her secret writings and she concluded this section with the words, 'I neither wish death, nor yet fear his might, God has the praise thereof with thanks'.[14]

Soon afterwards, attempts were made to persuade her to recant. She was taken to an inn called 'The Crown', where she was visited by Bishop Bonner and Sir Richard Rich, one of the King's Councillors, and afterwards, by Nicholas Shaxton. Shaxton was one of the other three condemned with Anne. As Bishop of Salisbury, in 1539 he had been one of the brave Reformist bishops, along with Hugh Latimer, Bishop of Worcester, who had opposed the introduction of the Six Articles, which had done so much to stop the Reformation in its tracks

---

12   ibid., p. 183.

13   ibid., p. 184.

14   ibid., p. 185.

and indeed to cause it to retreat backwards. As a result, he had had to resign his bishopric and was temporarily imprisoned. Once freed, he had lived in obscurity at Hadleigh in Suffolk, but he was arrested after preaching a sermon in London in which he denied the real presence and he was imprisoned before being brought out to appear at the Guildhall with Anne. After his condemnation, the King had sent Bishops Bonner and Heath to him to persuade him to renounce his beliefs about the sacrament. They achieved their end and Shaxton signed a document of recantation. Now he urged Anne to do likewise but she stood firm, telling him plainly that it would have been better if he had never been born and, in her blunt way, other similar things.

The Tower of London July 1546

As far as Anne was concerned, that should have been that. She had been condemned, had had plenty of opportunity and had resisted the persuasion to recant, and she should have been left alone to contemplate her execution. Nothing could have prepared her for what was about to happen. With no warning, she was taken from Newgate to the Tower of London and into the presence of two Privy Councillors, Sir Richard Rich, and the Lord Chancellor, Sir Thomas Wriothesley.

The summer of 1546 saw the power struggle intensify at court and it was this which had brought them to interview Anne in the chilling surroundings of the Tower. Henry VIII had been failing in health for a while but now it was evident that he was dying. His successor, his son Edward, was only eight years old and there would have to be a long minority. The fearsome, bulky figure of the King had stood between the two rival parties at court, but with the knowledge that he could not keep them in check for too much longer, they were vying to be in the ascendancy, ready to take over the levers of power in the new reign. The two parties had formed on religious grounds, the conservative traditional Catholics, and the Reformers, and Wriothesley and Rich were there on behalf of the Catholics. Anne's condemnation for heresy had been linked to her court connections and was seen as an opportunity which could be exploited to weaken, perhaps even fatally, the Reformist camp. Anne Askew was a small fry who had the potential to bring down much bigger fish. It was a technique which had been used successfully before, to get at important prey through convicting their underlings. If links could be made between Anne, a condemned heretic, and some of the leading Protestant ladies at court, it could lead to their investigation and downfall taking their husbands with them. It might even be possible to implicate the Queen herself, Katherine Parr.

They began by asking Anne to name others who believed as she did and she replied that she did not know anybody. Names were then given to her: the Duchess of Suffolk, the Countess of Sussex, the Countess of Hertford, Lady Denny and Lady Fitzwilliams. These were prominent Protestant ladies, all close to the Queen. Anne Seymour, the Countess of Hertford was married to the King's brother-in-law, Edward Seymour, one of the most influential of those around the King. Catherine Brandon, Duchess of Suffolk, was a very good friend of the Queen. But Anne denied that she had any proof against any of them. She would only acknowledge that she had been told that a man claiming to be from the Countess of Hertford and another claiming to be from Lady Denny gave money to her maid for Anne's support, but added that she had no means of knowing if that was true. She strongly denied that any had provided for her from the King's Privy Council. Pressed again and again to name names, Anne insisted she had none to give. When it was obvious that they were not going to get anywhere with her, the two men resorted to desperate measures. They turned to torture. Anne was strapped to the rack and the two great men turned the terrible device themselves. Incredibly, Anne lay still and did not cry out. In their frustration they kept going until the Lieutenant of the Tower insisted that she was unbound and then she fainted. When she came round, she was on the floor and there she sat for two hours talking to the Lord Chancellor who used flattery and persuasion but without result.

These proceedings were illegal and without precedent. Women were never subjected to torture whatever their background but particularly not a gentlewoman like Anne. In fact, the Lieutenant was so horrified that he hastily took himself off to give an account to the King and to disassociate himself from what was going on. Anne's account is so matter of fact and written so sparely, that it is almost possible not to take in fully the enormity of what happened to her, and the incredible fact that she did not incriminate anybody else. Did Anne have names to give? Was she tempted to cry out anybody's name just to get the agony to stop? Her silence protected others and, though she could not have known it then, that was of crucial importance in the advance of the Reformation. She knew where her strength had come from: 'But my lord God (I thank his everlasting goodness) gave me grace to persevere and will do (I hope) to the very end.'[15]

Anne describes how she was put to bed in a house where she lay in great pain and was once more given the opportunity to recant. The Lord Chancellor was responsible for offering her the stark choice of being looked after or being returned to Newgate to await execution. Once again she stood firm, saying she would rather die than deny her faith. 'Thus the Lord open the eyes of their blind hearts, that the truth may take place. Farewell dear friend, and pray, pray, pray.'[16]

Last days July 1546

When she was back in Newgate, despite her torment, Anne finished her secret account with another declaration of faith, especially her understanding of the sacrament. She had heard that it was said she had recanted when examined by Bishop Bonner the previous year and she was at pains to scotch any such talk and to present the clearest outline of her beliefs. She concluded, 'And Lord I heartily desire of thee, that thou wilt of thy most merciful goodness forgive them that violence which they do and have done unto me. Open also thou their blind hearts, that they may hereafter do that thing in thy sight, which is only acceptable before thee. And to set forth thy truth aright, without the vain fantasies of sinful men. So be it Lord so be it.'[17]

Anne's friend, John Lascells, was also awaiting execution and she wrote to him, assuring him of her steadfastness and telling him that the Council were displeased that it had not been possible to hush up the news of her torture and that it had been spread abroad. 'Well their

15   ibid., p. 187.

16   ibid., p. 188.

17   ibid., p. 191.

cruelty God forgive them.'[18] The last thing to be smuggled out was a prayer to encourage others in the faith.

The end came soon after on 16th July. She was brought to Smithfield with three men, John Helmley, a priest, John Hadlam, a tailor, and her friend, John Lascells, a gentleman of King Henry's court and household. Anne was carried in a chair because she could no longer walk. Each were tied to a stake but, because Anne could not stand up, she was secured with a chain around her waist to keep her upright. Smithfield, the usual place for public burnings in London, was a large open space, but beyond the area roped off around the stakes and pulpit, it was crammed with people. Executions normally attracted large crowds, and the fact that Anne's torture in the Tower had leaked out, no doubt caused extra curiousity on the London streets. Temporary scaffolding in front of the church of St Bartholomew the Great had been erected for the dignitaries, who included Chancellor Wriothesley, the Duke of Norfolk, and the Lord Mayor. The proceedings began when the preacher occupied the pulpit. It was the sad figure of Nicholas Shaxton chosen to preach the customary sermon as part of his public humiliation. Even then, Anne could not keep quiet. As Shaxton spoke she kept up something of a running commentary, commending those things she agreed with, but also disagreeing loudly and calling out where he was not following the Bible. All the while, bundles of wood were being piled around the stakes. When Shaxton had finally finished they were allowed to pray and then the King's letter of pardon was brought offering their lives in return for recantation. All refused to even look at it and Anne declared, 'I came not hither to deny my lord and master.' As the fires were lit, they called out encouraging each other, until they were all consumed.

ANNE'S LEGACY

Anne's most tangible legacy were her writings and the unique insight that they give. She wrote them to encourage other believers in London but sending them to John Bale meant they were saved for posterity, as well as printed and distributed at home and abroad. Bale published

---

18   ibid., p. 188.

them in October 1546 and January 1547. At that time, his works were banned in England but as the situation changed after Henry VIII died on 28th January 1547; there was only a relatively short delay before they could be sold openly. They were printed four times in England before Mary ascended the throne in 1553. John Bale was a friend and help to John Foxe. Both men were collecting evidence about the persecution of Protestants and, in Anne's case, were able to flesh out her account with a few biographical details. Foxe's great work, *Acts and Monuments,* was first published in English in 1563, in only the fifth year of Elizabeth's reign. Anne's extraordinary story lived on in this and in all succeeding versions. The second edition of 1570 was placed in every cathedral and in many parish churches. This ensured that the burnings under Henry VIII and especially his daughter Mary, were deeply embedded in the nation's memory.

Bale's main theme was that Anne was a weak woman made strong by God's strength. Foxe emphasised her unflinching faithfulness, saying that Anne left 'behind her a singular example of Christian constancy for all men to follow'.[19]

Despite repeated opportunities to recant, Anne indeed did not waver in her steadfastness, and her writings show how she depended on God and sought Him in prayer. The urgent repetition of 'pray, pray, pray' stands out in her text. Her love for God was rooted in her knowledge of the Bible. She had clearly read and studied it extensively, and that enabled her, under the pressure of her interrogations, to quote from it so widely and accurately, as she earnestly contended for the faith. There were no half measures with Anne. Bold, feisty and confrontational, she stood up to her interrogators even under intense pressure, displaying both wise prevarication and mental agility in taking her stand. Despite having such facility with words, almost her greatest gift to others was her silence, that incredible silence under torture. Surely it was God-given, as she herself thought. She protected, and may well have saved, lives at court: the Queen's ladies, their husbands, and even the Queen herself, almost certainly owed her a great debt. She had a crucial role to

---

19   ibid., p. 192.

play in keeping the leading Protestants at liberty and so enabling them to be in charge of the country at Henry VIII's death.

Anne's example at her death led to conversions. John Bale received some eyewitness accounts of Anne's execution and he reported that many had come to faith as a result of what they had seen. When he described Anne as a weak woman, he was somewhat wide of the mark. Anne was undoubtedly a very strong woman, but made stronger by her faith and dependence on God, and she was used quite remarkably for His purposes.

3. KATHERINE PARR 1512 – 1548

QUEEN FOR SUCH A TIME AS THIS

In the Spring of 1543, Henry VIII's thoughts were turning to marriage for the sixth and last time. One year earlier his fifth wife, nineteen-year-old Catherine Howard, had been found guilty of adultery and executed. Henry had doted on his pretty young wife and called her his rose without a thorn, but her betrayal had etched deep wounds into his feelings and his pride. Now, though, his eye had fallen on the newly widowed Katherine, Lady Latimer, and the more he saw of the attractive thirty year old, the more convinced he became that she had qualities he wanted in a wife and that he was ready to embark on yet another marriage.

When Katherine realised how seriously the King was interested in her, she was shocked and dismayed. Any lady of sense, and Katherine certainly was one, would hesitate to marry someone with such a marital record as Henry's. Of his five wives, only Jane Seymour had managed to remain his wife, and she had died following child birth. Catherine of Aragon had been divorced, Anne Boleyn divorced and beheaded, Anne of Cleves divorced, and Catherine Howard beheaded. It was not even as though it was just his wives who had suffered. There was a long list, including chief ministers, such as Thomas Cromwell and Thomas More, as well as noblemen, courtiers and kinsmen who had been executed when they fell from favour, disputed the King's supremacy over the Church, or were felt to be a threat. Beneath the glitter and extravagance of court life there was undoubtedly an undercurrent of fear.

Katherine was under no illusion that, if she became his wife, she would have to cope with Henry at his least attractive and most difficult stage of life. The handsome, athletic, charismatic youth who had ascended the throne at the age of seventeen, and had immediately taken as his wife the Spanish Princess, Catherine of Aragon all those years ago in 1509 was now an ageing fifty-two-year-old who bore little resemblance to his former self. He was huge. No longer just tall, but according to the author of the Spanish Chronicles, 'So fat that such a man had never been seen. Three of the biggest men that could be found could get inside his doublet.'[1] His face was puffy and his red hair and beard were streaked with grey. Prematurely aged, problems with his legs were reducing his mobility and causing pain which made his temper, uncertain at the best of times, more unpredictable than ever.

Of course, once Henry had made up his mind, Katherine had very little choice in the matter. How could one consider refusing such a King? A marriage proposal from Henry was really more of a command than a request. Neither was it a totally negative prospect and many would envy whoever became Queen. Acceptance would bring not just Katherine's worldly advancement, but would elevate her family too, especially her brother and sister. She might not have been too influenced by the thought of her own advancement, but she was fond of both her siblings and wanted them to prosper.

As Katherine considered her situation she was all too aware that there was the most personal of reasons for her hesitation. After two marriages which had been chosen for her, she was being courted by the King's brother-in-law, Thomas Seymour. A friend of her brother, Seymour really was tall, dark and handsome and just a few years older than Katherine. His attentions were welcome, Katherine was falling for him and she had been getting ready to consider marrying again, this time for love. Soon after Henry's death she would write candidly to Seymour, 'Truly as God is God, my mind was fully bent, the other time I was at liberty, to marry you before any man I know.'[2]

---

1   A. Weir, *The Six Wives of Henry VIII* (London:Pimlico, 1997), p. 494.

2   Letter from Katherine Parr to Thomas Seymour 1547 in B. Withrow, *Katherine Parr. A Guided Tour of the Life and Thought of a Reformation Queen* (Phillipsburg: P&R Publishing, 2009), p. 161.

Katherine was torn, but this same letter goes on to reveal that there was an even greater influence in her life. Compelling as the King's advances were, it was her love for God and desire to be in His will which cemented her acceptance. 'Howbeit, God withstood my will therein most vehemently for a time, and through his grace and goodness made that possible which seemeth to me most impossible; that was, made me to renounce utterly mine own will, and to follow his will most willingly.'[3] Whatever the struggle, whatever the cost, both Katherine and others who shared her faith came to believe that, like Queen Esther in the Old Testament, she had been chosen to be Queen for 'such a time as this'.

CHILDHOOD

It is a curious fact that Henry VIII's last wife was almost certainly named after his first. At the time of her birth, both of her parents were in royal service and they were regularly at court during Katherine's early childhood. Her mother was lady-in-waiting to Queen Catherine of Aragon and may even have asked her to be godmother to her first child. Her father, Thomas Parr, who was a wealthy man with plenty of charm, was knighted at Henry VIII's coronation. Service at court often ran in certain families and so it was with the Parrs. In 1508, when he was thirty, Thomas Parr had married sixteen-year-old Maud Green, an heiress from Northamptonshire. Thomas had grown up in the same county, but his family came from Westmorland where they still owned estates, including the dilapidated castle at Kendal. Through marriage, they were related to most of the noble families of the north of England. Thomas was on the way up, seeing the gradual rise of his family from the ranks of minor aristocracy through the means of royal connections and advantageous marriages, as indeed were many others around him.

Katherine was born in 1512 and she was followed a year later by a brother, William, and then, in about 1515, by a sister, Anne. Their family life was ruptured when Katherine was five by the sudden death of her father after a very short illness. He probably died of a new and frightening disease called the sweating sickness. His twenty-five-year-

---

3   ibid., p. 161.

old widow was left with three very young children to bring up. What she did next, or rather what she did not do, was surprising. At a time when it was most unusual to be single, Maud, who was a strong-minded, capable woman, did not re-marry. Instead she devoted herself to the care of her children, whilst retaining her position as lady-in-waiting.

The family were based at Rye House near Hoddesdon in Hertfordshire and, despite the loss of their father, the children had a secure and loving childhood. Their father's brother, Sir William Parr, was a close and supportive uncle, who would try to fill the place of their father for the rest of his life, and Maud herself, intelligent and resourceful, noted for her common sense, did her best to care for them and prepare them for their future lives. Education was a priority and all three children received an excellent one. Katherine learnt French, Latin and Italian as well as mathematics, and through her studies developed a love of learning which would stay with her throughout her life. She was also taught practical social skills, such as the art of good conversation, music and dancing.

FIRST MARRIAGE 1529–1533

Katherine's future security depended on her marriage and her mother set about this very early, entering into marriage negotiations for her daughter before Katherine was even eleven. Eventually they fell through and it was not until 1529, when Katherine was sixteen, that she married Sir Edward Borough, son and heir to Thomas, Lord Borough of Gainsborough in Lincolnshire. Her husband was a little older than her, in his early twenties, and she joined him at his father's house, Gainsborough Old Hall. It was a very different world to the one she had grown up in. At that time, Lincolnshire was sparsely populated and an isolated part of the country and it would have seemed flat, bleak and unfamiliar after her southern childhood. She must have felt cut off from her friends and family and needed to adapt to her new life. This would not have been helped by her father-in-law, who was a difficult man and dominated his household.

Very significantly, the family were involved with the Protestant faith, employing a chaplain with Reformist views. Lord Borough would go on to become Anne Boleyn's chamberlain and be an enthusiastic supporter of the changes brought about by the Reformation. Possibly, her time in Lincolnshire was Katherine's first contact with evangelical faith. She had been brought up, as had all around her, in the traditional Catholic Church. Her mother was religious and had encouraged her children to reverently love God. Katherine would come to reject the church of her youth and to see the emptiness of its ceremonies and rituals. She began to realise that she was a sinner and that she deserved God's punishment, but also that her sins could not be removed by the Church's sacraments, such as confession and penance. Only God's Son, the sinless Jesus Christ, could meet God's demands and take her punishment for her. That was why He had died on the cross – to save her and all who put their trust in Him, and in Him alone. This, the doctrine of justification by faith, after all, lay at the heart of Luther's teachings, and of the Reformation itself. Luther had first seen this teaching in Romans but there were many other New Testament passages with a similar message such as Ephesians 2:8-9: 'For by grace are ye saved through faith; and that not of yourselves: it is the gift of God: Not of works, lest any man should boast.' These things became real to Katherine and gave her a deep love for her Saviour. Much later, she would clearly testify to her faith in her book, *Lamentations of a Sinner*. Tantalisingly, she gives no clues as to when her conversion happened. Did she respond quickly when she first heard Lutheran teaching at Gainsborough or was it gradually over a period of time, perhaps many years later?

Only two years into her marriage, death cast its shadow over Katherine again. In December 1531 her mother, Maud, died. Katherine must have felt her loss keenly, for they were a close family and Maud's strong personality would have left a large void. She had lost both her parents before she was twenty and there was more to come. Edward Borough died in the Spring of 1533, leaving Katherine a very young widow. Coping with a double bereavement, her life changed abruptly. Although there was no family home for her to move back to, Katherine left Lincolnshire. Her movements for the next year or so are uncertain, though she may have stayed with relatives in Westmorland. If so, she was even further away from her siblings, who were both prospering at court. Maud had launched them on their future paths. She had secured a very advantageous match for William. He had been married even before Katherine, to Lady Anne Bourchier, the daughter and heiress of the Earl of Essex. The marriage offered much in the way of land and wealth and the expectation of future titles, but it was a disaster as, from the start, Anne sustained a strong dislike for her husband, despite his easy charm. Katherine's sister, also Anne, was one of the Queen's ladies and would serve as lady-in-waiting to Jane Seymour and to each of Henry's succeeding wives.

SECOND MARRIAGE 1534–1543

For Katherine's future path, marriage was the only realistic option and, in the summer of 1534, she married her father's cousin, Sir John Neville, Lord Latimer. At forty, he was nearly twenty years older than Katherine. He had been widowed twice and was left with two children from his first marriage. The Nevilles were one of the foremost families in the north of England and Katherine was now mistress of a large household. Latimer's primary residence was Snape Castle in Richmondshire, part of the North Riding of Yorkshire, near Bedale, in part of what we now call the Yorkshire Dales. Lord Latimer also had a town house at the Charterhouse in London. Katherine had moved up in the world, as well as further north and further away from her family roots in the south, except for the occasional visit to the capital.

Katherine had to quickly grow into her new responsibilities. Her husband needed to be away from home quite frequently. As a member of the House of Lords, he had to attend parliamentary sessions as well as fulfil his responsibilities as a member of the Council of the North. This was the body charged with representing the authority of the King in the northern portion of his kingdom, both defending it against incursions from Scotland, and being ready to deal with threats from over-mighty northern magnates, who, so far from the seat of government in London, were prone to assert their independence, sometimes even to the point of rebellion. Katherine's new husband was a man of experience, a former soldier and an important player in the politics of the north. His young wife had to run his home in his absence as well as acting as a mother to his children. Katherine was her mother's daughter; and she would have almost certainly brought to her new role not only resilience, energy and capability, but also an attractive cheerfulness.

Katherine's stepchildren

She would need all of those qualities in handling her stepson. At the time of her marriage John Neville was fourteen, only seven years younger than she was herself and he was a very difficult boy who must have caused her much concern throughout her marriage. He would grow into an unstable man, violent even, but Katherine did not distance herself from the family tie and his wife, Lucy, would become a lady-in-waiting when she was Queen. Fortunately for Katherine, John's younger sister, nine-year-old Margaret, was a very different proposition. Margaret had been too young to really know a mother's love before, and Katherine supplied not only that but also, in supervising her education, encouraged her to love both learning and godliness. They forged a close relationship. Ten years or so later, when Margaret wrote her will, she said she was 'never able to render to her Grace [Katherine] sufficient thanks for the godly education and tender love and bountiful goodness which I have evermore found in her Highness'.[4] In the same document she also expressed her faith, 'I bequeath, yield up and commit to the hands of my most merciful [heavenly] father my soul, yet all my whole substance, as well spiritual as well as corporeal, most steadfastly trusting unto his mercy that he through the mercies of my saviour and only mediator Jesus Christ will now perform his promise unto me that death may have no power over me but that through his grace I may boldly say, "O death where is thy victory? O hell where is thy sting?", being above all other things most certain that trust in him shall not be confounded.'[5]

For Katherine, her faith must have been a difficult issue during this marriage. If she had not already come to personal faith at its beginning, she would do so before its end, and she would have had to be very careful and circumspect about her beliefs. Latimer was typical of the

---

4   L. Porter, *Katherine the Queen: The Remarkable Life of Katherine Parr* (Pan, 2010), p. 60.

5   ibid, pp. 228-9.

northern lords, a staunch upholder of the traditional Catholic faith, and while she was his wife, Katherine gave no outward indication of divergence of opinion. Latimer did, however, have a Protestant friend, a neighbour, Sir Francis Bigod. The two families were closely connected and so again we have a known link between Katherine and Reformed faith.

Reformation changes

During the early years of their marriage, Lord Latimer was in London more than usual, in attendance at the 'Reformation Parliament'. It was not what he would have personally wanted, but he sat through the proceedings which took the English Church out of the Catholic Church and the control of the Pope, and into an uncertain future with Henry VIII as its Supreme Head. This great change was swiftly compounded by another one – the dissolution of the monasteries. In 1535, royal commissioners visited monasteries across the land, assessing their spiritual condition and their wealth. Direct action against them began in March 1536 when Parliament passed an Act to close all the smaller houses, which was followed ominously by the setting up of another commission. There was much hostility to these moves, particularly in Lincolnshire and the northern counties, which, on the whole, were firmly rooted in traditional Catholicism. In October 1536, this hostility spilled over into what was known as the Pilgrimage of Grace. Both Katherine and her husband were to be closer – far, far closer – to the action than they cared to be.

The Pilgrimage of Grace 1536–1537

The rebellion began on 1st October at Louth in Lincolnshire. Rumours and resentment abounded and, within days, it had become a major uprising. However, it lacked leaders and coherence and, by the time the Duke of Suffolk arrived in Lincoln a couple of weeks later, at the head of a hastily assembled army, the rebels had faded away and the Lincolnshire insurrection was over. But the danger had not yet passed. The action now moved to Yorkshire where a lawyer, Robert Aske, assumed the leadership of another sudden and swiftly-moving uprising. He proved to be an effective leader of men who were motivated by a complex range of issues. Religious conservatism, concern for the fate of the monasteries, and of the rise of the new religion, were prominent, but there were also many economic and social factors. Aske merged the rebels into an effective force which was frighteningly large. He used the name 'pilgrimage' to emphasise that this was no conventional rebellion, but a movement completely loyal to the King, meant to appeal directly to him and to remove him from the influence of those they saw as his evil advisers, who were the real target. There were other significant leaders, major landowners, men of the northern nobility, most with sympathy for the religious aims of the movement, but some forced into active support because they were threatened and they feared for their lives. Lord Latimer was one of them.

In the middle of October, Snape Castle was invaded during the night by a mob, including some of his own tenants, threatening violence and demanding that Lord Latimer join them. He was forced to swear the rebel's oath and to lead them off to link with the main rebel force, which would swell to over thirty thousand strong. This was an extremely dangerous moment for the crown. There was no standing army in Tudor times, and the sheer speed of events and size of the rebel contingent meant that Henry did not have the military capacity to take them on. To make matters worse, this was no ill-disciplined rabble but well led, with many trained soldiers used to fighting the Scots. The Duke of Norfolk, with as many troops as he could muster on the government's side, including Katherine's brother William, advanced to Doncaster with a woefully inadequate force. Lord Latimer was a member of the rebel delegation sent to meet him. Norfolk stalled and caused delays, promising that the King would seriously consider the rebel's demands and that all would have a full and free pardon if they dispersed. Despite some misgivings, his terms were eventually accepted in early December, and the most serious crisis of Henry's reign seemed to be over as the pilgrims returned home.

Katherine must have been very relieved to see her husband again. Her anxious wait, presumably with little news, would not have been eased if she had known that his life would have been worth nothing if the rebels had any thought that he was shamming and not truly on their side. Whilst he was with them, Latimer had appeared to be enthusiastic for their cause, which may have been genuine, but it could equally have been forced. For now, some fragile stability was restored, and Aske was even invited to court for the Christmas festivities, but Katherine's husband and the other northern lords knew that they were not out of the woods yet. Latimer had escaped the clutches of the rebels, but how would the King view his role, and would the plea of acting under duress cut any muster against likely charges of treason? Both sides viewed him with deep suspicion and both could yet prove dangerous. He was between the proverbial rock and a hard place.

Early in January, Latimer left for London to put his case in person, but he never reached the capital. He was at Buntingford when he received orders from the Council of the North to return at once in case of further unrest. He headed back and then at Stamford he was greeted by frightening news: 'I learn that the commons [common people] of Richmondshire, grieved at my coming up [to London], have entered my house at Snape and will destroy it if I come not home shortly. If I do not please them I know not what they will do with my body and goods, my wife and children.'[6] For Katherine, it would have been a terrifying ordeal, to be at the mercy of suspicious and unpredictable men who had taken over her house, and who were holding her and the children hostage to ensure Latimer remained committed to their cause. Fortunately, when Latimer returned he was able to pacify and eject the mob. The rising was flaring up again in Yorkshire and also west of the Pennines but this time the Crown's forces were ready and able to suppress it completely, with the excuse of this further insurrection to break their word and execute the ringleaders.

The aftermath of the Pilgrimage of Grace

The Latimers spent the first half of 1537 in anxious suspense waiting to see what Sir John's fate would be. If he were found guilty of treason, not only would he be executed, but all his estates and property would be forfeited to the crown. He appealed to anyone who might help and the Duke of Norfolk spoke for him and in midsummer sent him to London to defend himself in person. He was immediately arrested

6   ibid., p. 104.

and sent to the Tower but was released not long after, saved partly by the years of useful service and strong loyalty of his wife's family. They had unquestionably been on the right side in the recent troubles. Not only had Katherine's brother been in Norfolk's army but her uncle, Sir William Parr, had helped the Duke of Suffolk restore order in Lincolnshire.

One result of these traumatic times was to loosen the Latimers' ties with the north. They moved first to Worcestershire and then to Stowe Manor in Northamptonshire. Here, Katherine was near her Uncle William and various other relatives. After years mainly in the east and north she could enjoy close family connections again and also be nearer her brother and sister in London. Her uncle and both her siblings were supporters of the new faith.

In the autumn of 1542, the Latimers settled into their London home to spend the winter in the capital. Lord Latimer was ailing. He made his will in October and his health deteriorated over the next months. He died in February 1543. The main estates were left to his son John, but Katherine was left comfortably off and with the responsibility of looking after her stepdaughter, Margaret. She had very little time either to grieve or to adjust to her new circumstances. Thomas Seymour must have had his eye on her whilst her husband was fading and very quickly made his intentions known, and then she came to realise that she had not one but two suitors for her hand. Henry was not one to brook a rival and cleared the field by sending Seymour abroad as ambassador to the Spanish Netherlands. He also followed a familiar pattern of advancing the family of the woman he intended to marry. Her brother, William, had the honour of becoming a Knight of the Garter, and also Lord Warden and Keeper of the Western March (the Scottish borders). Before the end of the year, his mother's ambition for him would finally be fulfilled when he became the Earl of Essex. His marriage to Anne Bourchier was over as she had left him, but even so, he had been gifted her father's title. Katherine's sister Anne was not forgotten either as her husband, William Herbert, was knighted and given lands in Wales.

KATHERINE THE QUEEN 1543–1547

Katherine must have accepted Henry's proposal in June. They were married on 12th July in the Queen's Privy Chamber at Hampton Court. It was a quiet wedding in the presence of a few family and friends and Katherine was proclaimed Queen later that day.

Katherine became Queen to general approval. After Katherine Howard's disgrace, the fact that she was older, a respectable widow with a mature outlook, was seen as an advantage. Henry was a shrewd judge of character and others recognised that he had made a good choice. A poised, capable lady, intelligent, cultured, and caring with a pleasant manner and a warmth which drew people to her. She brought a much needed calm and dignity to the role of Queen. Thomas Wriothesley wrote to the Duke of Norfolk, describing her as 'a woman in my judgement, for certain virtue, wisdom and gentleness, most meet for his Highness. And sure I am that his Majesty had never a wife more agreeable to his heart than she is. The Lord grant them long life and much joy together.'[7]

In the past, Katherine has often been depicted as a woman past her prime, dull, intellectual, staid and a good nurse. This portrayal sits oddly with her real character. She was indeed intellectual and also caring, ready to cheer and distract her husband when his leg was particularly painful, but she was energetic, vibrant, lively and attractive. Of course she had faults too. She could be outspoken and over-confident, and she had a fiery temper.

Her previous marriages had provided useful experience for her. She had twice before had to adapt to significant changes in her way of life, she had been married to an older man and had been a stepmother, but she had also spent little time at court and nothing could have prepared her for the speed with which she became Queen. Yet remarkably, she took to her new role with aplomb.

Katherine as Queen

Katherine energetically took on the mantle of royalty. The Queen was expected to look the part. It was important that she wore expensive, ostentatious clothes and jewellery, and Katherine entered fully into

7   Weir, *Six Wives*, p. 498.

that as into every other aspect of her role. She also used her position to promote the arts, becoming the patron of several artists, as well as musicians, poets and scholars.

A rather attractive eyewitness picture of the diplomatic dimension of court life was given in the winter of 1544 by the secretary of the Duke of Najera, a nobleman who served the Emperor Charles V at his court in Brussels. He was granted an audience with both Henry and his new Queen, separately, as was the norm. Katherine, supported by her brother and various of her ladies, as well as the Lady Mary, entertained her visitor with music and dancing. The Duke was delighted with his reception and recorded his impression of Katherine as having 'a lively and pleasing appearance and is praised as a virtuous woman'.[8] Katherine forged a good personal relationship with the Emperor's ambassador, Chapuys, so backing up the formal diplomacy of her husband.

Katherine as wife and Queen Regent

Henry may not have been her choice of a husband, but Katherine entered into her marriage with the same mixture of duty and enthusiasm that she brought to her position as Queen. She was fully committed and cheerfully so, despite her affections having once been engaged elsewhere. Katherine was an intelligent companion and they shared many interests. Unexpectedly, they had had the opportunity to spend the first six months of their marriage away from court and in each other's company. The usual summer progress, when the King visited a particular area of his kingdom to see and to be seen by his subjects, was extended because plague had broken out in London. Much of the autumn was spent away from the capital at Ampthill in Bedfordshire and then Christmas was celebrated at the great palace at Hampton Court, before they were fully settled back in London in the new year.

Just over six months later, Henry embarked on one last foreign adventure and this brought Katherine the most demanding of her responsibilities as Queen. Henry led an expedition to France and, when he departed in July 1544, he left Katherine in his place as regent. It was an important position, and a great honour for Katherine, which showed how much her husband trusted and respected her. He clearly

---

8   Porter, p. 160.

thought she was up to the challenge. Henry had a last fling at a military campaign, even though his ailing body was long past the physical rigours of soldiery and he had to be carried in a litter or awkwardly hoisted on to his horse. While he was leading his troops, and capturing the port of Boulogne, Katherine successfully kept things going at home. Though she had a regency council to help her, for the three months Henry was away she ruled the country in his stead. Efficient and practical, she was more than competent at handling the detailed workings of government, and making the decisions that were needed. When she heard of the fall of Boulogne she was quick to thank God for the victory and immediately wrote to the Council of the North to share the good news in the troubled Scottish borders and ordering that they 'shall cause thanks to be given to God, by devout and general processions in all the towns and villages of the North, and also signify to the Wardens of the Marches this great benefit which God has heaped on us'.[9]

While he was away, Katherine kept up a steady flow of letters to Henry keeping him informed of state affairs as well as more personal family news. These reveal the affectionate state of their union, and that they had drawn close together in that first year of marriage. Her letters assured him that she was missing him and of her love for him. In an early letter she declared, 'Although the distance of time and account of days neither is long nor many of your Majesty's absence, yet the want of your presence, so much desired and beloved by me, maketh me that I cannot quietly pleasure in anything until I hear from your Majesty...I mind nothing less, but a plain, simple relation of the love and zeal I bear your Majesty, proceeding from the abundance of the heart.' She referred to her husband as 'a noble Prince, at whose hands I have found and received so much love and goodness, that with words I cannot express it'.[10]

Katherine's wifely support would be increasingly needed as Henry's condition worsened over time and, as the pain rose, so did his temper. Always unpredictable and with a suspicious nature, he became more

9   ibid., p. 220.
10   Letter from Katherine Parr to King Henry VIII July 1544. Withrow, pp. 136-7.

volatile and his mood swings more alarming. He found Katherine's calm presence soothing, and she would sometimes sit with his bad leg, which was smelly, resting in her lap.

Katherine as stepmother

It was not just Henry who appreciated Katherine but all three of his children were drawn to her. From the first, she sought to get to know them and bring them together as a family. The court was no place for young children quite apart from the danger of disease, and the royal children were brought up in their own separate households. Both Elizabeth and Edward had lost their mothers when they were very young, Elizabeth at two and Edward as a newborn baby, and Katherine was the first of their stepmothers to be a real mother to them.

On that first summer progress of 1543, just weeks after their marriage, Henry and Katherine visited the royal household at Ashridge in the Chiltern Hills to see both Edward and Elizabeth. Katherine took great interest in them both, in their progress and their education. In turn, their tutors would encourage the royal siblings to write to their new stepmother and they became regular correspondents. The following summer when Henry was in France and Katherine absorbed in her role as regent, she gathered the three to her at Hampton Court, where for a while they could be together as a family. As she maintained contact with her husband through her letters she regularly reported that his children were in good health. It was not often possible to bring the royal family together physically, though Katherine did what she could to encourage that, but she did draw them closer together as a family unit. She provided a loving centre to it, giving her stepchildren much needed emotional stability.

At the time Katherine married their father, Mary was twenty-seven, just four years younger than Katherine; Elizabeth was almost ten and Edward was five. All three were in awe of their father and, despite their privileged upbringing, suffered emotionally from the loss of real family life. Mary was the only one to have ever known it but, when Henry separated from her mother in 1527, he ripped his wife and daughter apart too, for they were not allowed to see each other again. Later, Mary was put under enormous pressure to accept that her parents had not been legally married and that she was illegitimate, even to the point that she was warned that her life might be in danger if she held out any more in defiance. Eventually, she had had to give in, but her relationship with her father had never been fully restored. In more recent times she had begun to spend more time at court, and she and Katherine, so close in age, became good friends, perhaps more like sisters than stepmother and stepdaughter. Chapuys, who was the Emperor Charles V's ambassador, had for years looked out for the Lady Mary's interests on behalf of his royal master, who was Mary's cousin. He was delighted to see Katherine's encouragement of Mary and reported back favourably on the new Queen and the fact that 'She favours the Princess [Mary] all she can'.[11]

Elizabeth, too, had once been the heir to the throne. Even though she had been so young, she could remember when the splendour and deference of her childhood had suddenly been withdrawn at a stroke. She became the Lady Elizabeth, no longer Princess, the bastard of a disgraced and executed mother. She was a precocious and intelligent child, largely overlooked by her father and it was left to her governess to bring her up and care for her. No wonder Elizabeth responded to Katherine's kindly interest and genuine affection.

Edward might have been the lawful heir and the pride of his father, but he too lived in his own establishment, though sometimes he was joined by Elizabeth. He was also precocious and intelligent and, like Elizabeth, would prove to be a gifted scholar. He was perhaps a cooler character than Elizabeth, but he too responded well to Katherine, as was displayed in his letters to her. He regularly addressed her as 'My dearest mother' and he told her that she held 'the chief place in my heart'.[12] Shortly after his father's death he would write to Katherine, 'Wherefore since you love my father, I cannot but much commend you, since you love me, I cannot but love you again: and since you love God's word I will love and admire you from my heart'.[13]

11 A. Fraser, *The Six Wives of Henry VIII* (London: Arrow Books, 1998), p. 372.

12 ibid., p. 385.

13 S. James, *Kateryn Parr: The Making of a Queen* (Aldershot: Ashgate, 1999), p. 138.

There was one significant way in which Katherine tried to help her stepdaughters. Before Henry left for France in 1544, he left his affairs in order in one important respect: he established the line of succession to the throne. While Edward was his direct heir, both of his daughters had been declared illegitimate and had been explicitly excluded from the succession. In February 1544, Parliament passed the Act of Succession which reinstated Mary followed by Elizabeth if Edward died without heirs of his own. Henry did not relent enough to change their designation as bastards, but at least their position in the succession had been restored, important both for the country and for his daughters' status and security. Katherine had encouraged him to do this and no doubt she would have been delighted with the outcome.

Katherine's intellectual pursuits

Of all Henry's wives, Katherine was the most intellectual. She had had a good education herself and she took a particular interest in Edward and Elizabeth's academic studies. They were excellent scholars; indeed, by the standards of today quite exceptional. Katherine also encouraged the ladies of her inner circle to provide the best education for their children, girls as well as boys. In the thinking of the day there was a strong link between religion and education and Katherine herself combined the two in her intellectual pursuits. Her love of reading turned to attempts at writing which in turn led her to producing books for publication. She was one of the very few ladies to do so in Tudor England, certainly the first and only Queen.

As early as April 1544, *Psalms or Prayers Taken Out of Holy Scripture* was published in English. The original had been published in Latin in 1525, the work of John Fisher, Bishop of Rochester, who would later be executed for denying Henry's supremacy over the Church in England. In translating this, Katherine gave the original Catholic text a new Protestant emphasis. She did the same the following year with *Prayers Stirring the Mind unto Heavenly Meditations* published in June 1545. It was more commonly known as *Prayers and Meditations* and was based on Thomas à Kempis's classic work *Imitation of Christ* but shortened, and in English, and with a new emphasis on the grace of God. It was deliberately produced inexpensively to bring a religious work to a wide audience. This was so successful that it ran to five editions before 1548.

Again in 1545, Katherine organised and financed the translation of Erasmus' *Paraphrases of the Gospels*. It was the work of a team of translators and the Lady Mary was persuaded to undertake the book of John. It would be published in 1548. The editor of the work, Nicholas Udall, praised Katherine's skill in organising so large a project. The common thread throughout her literary ventures was the use of the vernacular, the English language as opposed to Latin, which excluded all but the elite. Latin was the language of scholarship and also of the Church. She wanted to bring religious literature and the Bible itself to as many people as possible and in their mother tongue.

When Katherine became Queen she took as her motto the phrase 'To be useful in all I do'. She fulfilled that well, pouring energy and enthusiasm into her role as Queen, wife and mother, but she would have also wanted to be useful in God's service. It is clear that her faith and her love for her Saviour undergirded every area of her life, including writing her books. Her faith brought her along a very dangerous path for she had married Henry at a particularly significant moment. We now need to step back and look at the bigger picture.

BACKGROUND. HENRY'S LAST YEARS. THE GROWING STRUGGLE BETWEEN CATHOLICS AND PROTESTANTS

The period 1539 to 1540 had been quite a turning point in the Reformation story. Protestant advances had been abruptly reversed in 1539 by the Act of Six Articles which upheld some key traditional Catholic doctrines. More calamity for the Reformers was to come the following summer when Thomas Cromwell, Henry's brilliant chief minister, was arrested and swiftly executed. His enemies, the leaders of the religious conservatives, had engineered his downfall and Henry had not intervened to save him, although he probably lived to regret it as there was no one else approaching his calibre to replace him.

Henry had had to accept that, for some time, those of influence in his court were divided on the grounds of their religion. What mattered most to him was that they were all united in their loyalty to the crown. It was not what he would have chosen but he was far too powerful and too wily a politician to be ruled by them, and the fact that they were his faithful servants, even if they did have their own agendas, meant he could manage the situation. For three years from 1540, the traditionalists held the initiative and, in 1543, they seemed to be threatening complete ascendancy. In May, Parliament passed the Act for the Advancement of True Religion, which seriously restricted access to the Bible and other religious books. There was a short list of what was acceptable and other Bible translations and books were banned. Only females from the upper classes, and noblemen, clerics and the gentry were allowed to read the Bible, and that only privately. At almost the same time, the changes to church doctrine and practice published in *The King's Book* were all reversions to more traditional forms.

Religious persecution of Protestants was hotting up too, even against some of the King's household. This mounting pressure on the Reformers culminated with a sustained attack on Thomas Cranmer. There were two specific attempts, one in the summer, and again in November of 1543, to bring him down. This time Henry did not step aside as he had with Cromwell. Instead he gave Cranmer his personal protection and he survived, for Henry had a special relationship with Cranmer. Cromwell had once told him, 'You were born in a happy hour, for do or say what you will, the king will always well take it at your hand.'[14] When Henry had selected him for his archbishop, Cranmer had been a curious choice. He was no church or court politician, unlike his opponent, Stephen Gardiner, who was his complete opposite. Cranmer was a scholar, whose theology gradually and thoughtfully developed over a period of time. He was mild, timid and very gifted at developing liturgy; a thinker rather than a doer, he avoided factionalism. It was his honesty and integrity and avoidance of politics which drew Henry to him, that and his reliable loyalty to the King, for he believed that Henry's royal authority came from God and therefore he was to be obeyed. Cranmer would be God's man in a key position for twenty years and his unique relationship with Henry kept him safe.

---

14   Dickens, p. 234.

That summer of 1543, the summer when Henry and Katherine were married and Cranmer's fate hung in the balance, would turn out to be the high point for the Catholics. Things began to even up noticeably after that, but even so, the last years of Henry's reign were dangerous times to be an evangelical. There were increasing arrests of Protestants leading to more burnings, which all reached a peak in 1546. As the King's health was clearly giving way, the traditionalists became increasingly desperate to remove Protestants from positions of power before he died, as both Anne Askew and Katherine Parr found out to their cost.

KATHERINE THE QUEEN CONTINUED

Katherine the Reformist Queen

Katherine would not have been well known at court when she became Queen. The conservative faction may have wondered if she was one of them, as, after all, she had been married for nine years to a Catholic lord, and they would have been waiting and watching for indications as to where her religious sympathies really lay. Katherine was wise and cautious – but not overawed or intimidated. She felt that it was God's purpose for her to be where she was. Queen Esther in the Old Testament was told by her uncle, Mordecai, 'Who knoweth whether thou art come to the kingdom for such a time as this'[15] – she went on to protect her people, the Jews, from destruction. Queen Katherine felt that she, too, had become Queen 'for such a time as this' so that she could use her position to do whatever she could to serve God and advance His kingdom. Within the limits of what it was possible for her to do, that is just what she did.

Choice of tutors for Edward and Elizabeth

The unusually long period Katherine was able to spend with her new husband at the very beginning of their marriage, away from the demands of life at court, not only gave them a chance to get to know each other better and to draw closer together, but also provided Katherine with the opportunity to begin to influence Henry. Very important decisions

---

15   Esther 4:14.

were being made about Prince Edward. He turned six that October and that was the time chosen for him to begin his formal education. Male tutors were appointed. They were led by Richard Cox, a fellow of King's College, Cambridge and former headmaster of Eton College. He was joined the following summer by John Cheke, Professor of Greek at St John's College, Cambridge and the outstanding classical scholar of his day. These two men, as well as others close to the young prince, were Protestants. At the very least, Katherine would have approved of their appointment, but she almost certainly had some influence in their choice, especially of Cheke, who had been a pupil and protégé of her almoner. John Cheke developed a good relationship with Edward. He was always with him and became one of the very few people to win his affection. This small group of gifted men were to have a great influence on Edward's life. Not only did they give him a first-class education but they also taught him the Reformation doctrines which they believed and which he came to accept and believe for himself.

Also, in 1544, Katherine was to have a hand in the choosing of Elizabeth's new tutor. William Grindal was from the same group of Cambridge academics as Edward's tutors, and as well as being an outstanding Greek scholar, he shared their commitment to the Protestant faith. Like Edward, Elizabeth would be brought up under the influence of evangelical teaching.

Ladies of Katherine's household

When Katherine became Queen, she gathered about her members of her own family. Margaret Neville, her stepdaughter, moved to court with her. Her sister, Anne Herbert, was a lady-in-waiting and became Chief Gentlewoman of the Queen's Chamber. Katherine appointed her uncle and father figure, Lord Parr of Horton, as Lord Chamberlain of her household, though he was not well enough to be at court very often. Her cousin, Lady Maud Lane, her aunt, Lady Mary Parr, and others gave her friendship and companionship, and also shared the Queen's religious commitment. So did some of the noble ladies around her, especially Catherine Brandon, Duchess of Suffolk, her close friend. One of Katherine's chaplains, Francis Goldsmith, has left a brief description of life in her household. She had 'made every day

like Sunday, a thing hitherto unheard of, especially in a royal palace...
God has so formed her mind for pious studies, that she considers
everything of small value compared to Christ...Her piety cherishes the
religion long since introduced not without great labour to the palace'.[16]
Katherine and the like-minded ladies around her spent time studying
the Bible together, discussing religious books, including, no doubt,
some which were banned, and hearing Protestant preachers such as
Hugh Latimer and Nicholas Ridley.

Literature
Katherine also tried to advance the cause of the gospel outside of her
immediate circle. She acted as a patron to a significant group of scholars
and clerics and, at the same time, encouraged publishers of Reformed
religious literature. Her own writings, and her strong emphasis
on replacing Latin with the English language to bring learning and
especially the Bible within reach of all who could read, were part of
the same pattern. Katherine was using every means at her disposal to
further the advance of evangelical faith.

So far, her own publications had been mainly adaptations of the
work of others but, sometime towards the latter part of her time as
Queen, she began to write an entirely original book centred on the
gospel of Christ and her own experience of faith. It would later be
published under the title *Lamentations of a Sinner*, but for the moment
it was kept secret and away from prying eyes. The contents would not
have been at all acceptable to her husband; indeed, they would have
been distinctly dangerous.

Katherine under attack
Not that Katherine was immune from danger anyway. A little over a year
into her marriage, from the autumn of 1544, an event occured which
meant her religious sympathies would have been public knowledge.
Stephen Cobbe, a schoolmaster, was accused of heresy and of printing
radical religious books. When he was tried in October 1544 before the

---

16   Porter, p. 168.

Court of the Aldermen in London, Katherine sent a member of her household to plead for him and he was released. Increasingly, there was too much evidence of Katherine's true religious motivations for her enemies among the religious conservatives to have any doubts about her and the obstacle that she was to their influence with the King. They were indeed her enemies for they began to work against her and to relentlessly seek to remove her. Katherine herself, great conciliator that she was with her gift of drawing people together, had tried to maintain pleasant relationships with both sides and seems to have been unaware of her danger until it was almost too late.

During the winter of 1545 to 1546, Henry's health deteriorated. He was weary and weakening as he found it ever harder to drag his great bulk around and the pain in his legs was often severe. His affection for Katherine and the fact that she made him such an excellent wife had meant he had turned a blind eye to the goings on in her household but he had always had the capacity to turn suddenly on those close to him. With his intense pain, he was not just unpredictable but could not bear to be crossed. The solid ground Katherine had felt she was standing on was beginning to move beneath her.

Events of 1546

In February 1546, Katherine received a letter from Cambridge University asking her to intervene with Henry on their behalf. They feared that the endowment of their colleges was under threat. She replied very confidently that their fears were misplaced, and that they had Henry's full support; indeed, he was likely to found new colleges. She also chided them that they had written to her in Latin rather than English. Maybe Henry felt the correspondence was rather a wakeup call, that Katherine was getting too confident of herself and getting involved in too many things which in his eyes were not really her concern. Almost immediately, there were rumours that she was losing the King's favour. Worse still, there were even reports that there was to be a new queen. They reached Katherine herself and, not unnaturally, she was very angry. The rumours would die away again but they had perhaps exposed a weakness in Katherine's position, which not all her sterling qualities as Henry's wife could completely remove. To the end of his life, Henry hoped for a second son. The Act of Succession of 1544 made provision for the children Katherine Parr might bear him, but, after two and a half years of marriage, there had been no signs that Katherine could produce another royal baby.

From that spring, Gardiner and the Catholics were on the offensive. There was a new surge in prosecutions of Protestants and even arrests at court. Those men close to power with evangelical leanings needed to be removed, while there was still the opportunity before the King died. A most effective way would be to find incriminating evidence that their wives, who were part of Katherine's inner circle, had been reading forbidden books or believed 'heretical' doctrine. At the end of June, the desperate attempt was made to force Anne Askew to implicate those ladies or even the Queen herself. It failed and produced nothing whatsoever which could serve their purpose. But around that very time, another attempt was made to remove Katherine and this one was much more deadly. This time, the person who provided the opportunity her enemies were looking for was Katherine herself.

Henry was leaving his apartments at Whitehall Palace less and less frequently, as he was finding it so difficult to move around. As he had stopped visiting his wife, increasingly she would go to visit him instead. Often they would discuss religion. It was a subject that interested them both, but Katherine was becoming too forward. She was making the mistake of contradicting her husband and even, as he saw it, of lecturing him. It seems that quite probably, out of concern for his soul and in her eagerness to share God's Word, she got carried away and simply forgot herself. One evening, Henry had had enough. To her surprise, he abruptly changed the subject, though he appeared calm and affectionate until she had retired to her own quarters. As soon as she had gone, he gave voice to his annoyance and frustration. 'A good hearing it is when women become such clerks, and a thing much to my comfort, to come in mine old days to be taught by my wife.'[17]

The person who Henry was letting off steam to was the last one to let such an opportunity go to waste. It was Stephen Gardiner, Bishop of

---

17   J.H.M. D' Aubigne, *The Reformation in England,* Vol 2. (Reprinted Edinburgh: Banner of Truth Trust, 1985), p. 475.

Winchester, and he played up the incident for all he was worth. He told the King how unfortunate it was that the Queen should argue with her husband. He praised Henry for his learned understanding of theology. How unseemly it was for any of Henry's subjects to 'reason and argue with him so malapertly' and he hated to hear it. He cleverly insinuated that Katherine was not only nurturing heretical beliefs but behind them lay the possibility of treason. He would reveal all if Henry gave him his protection and authorised him to act. Henry gave him the assurances he needed and Gardiner emerged triumphantly and, together with Thomas Wriothesley, set to work to engineer Katherine's downfall. It was too big a step to go directly after the Queen, but they would first attack her closest ladies. Her sister, Anne Herbert, her cousin Lady Lane, and Lady Tyrrwhit were all to be arrested and examined and their rooms rigorously searched to find incriminating evidence, especially in the form of prohibited books. The Queen herself would then be arrested and conveyed to the Tower under the cover of darkness.

Up to this point it looked as if nothing could save Katherine from sharing the same fate as Anne Boleyn and Katherine Howard. They had both been suddenly whisked to the Tower, where they were executed after facing charges which were concocted in Anne's case, but almost certainly true in Katherine's. Then Henry let someone else in on the plot, one of his physicians, Dr Wendy. One evening when Katherine had just left him, completely oblivious to what was afoot and unaware of any change in his affections for her, Henry told Dr Wendy what was about to happen but swore him to secrecy.

Soon afterwards, a lady of the court found a document which had been dropped in the palace, picked it up and took it straight to the Queen. When Katherine saw it she was struck with terror. It was the actual indictment against her, signed by Henry and ready for use. She was in an agony of fear and shock, crying out loud and hysterical. No wonder. She had not seen it coming and she knew that the danger was all too real. Was she going to be destroyed in the same way as her predecessors? She must have been appalled that the affectionate relationship she had with the King and with all his children appeared to count for nothing! How could it be happening?

Word reached Henry that his wife was in great distress and some of his physicians, including Dr Wendy, came to see her. Dr Wendy realised something of what was going on and sent the others away. He was able to confirm to Katherine the danger she was in. He advised her to be humble and submissive to her husband and she would regain his favour. Then Henry, hearing she was still very unwell, had himself carried to her. Katherine gathered herself together and explained that she feared that she had displeased the King and he had completely forsaken her. Henry comforted and reassured her until she gradually calmed down. His visit had encouraged her, but Katherine knew that she was still far from safe.

The next evening, accompanied by her sister and Lady Lane, she made her way to the King's bedchamber. Henry was sitting there with several of his gentlemen. He greeted his wife courteously and soon began to talk about religion and sought her opinion. Katherine demurred. God had given men superiority in wisdom; how could she as a weak woman give her opinion, so she must refer her judgement on this and everything else to Henry's 'wisdom, as my only anchor, Supreme Head and Governor here on earth, next under God'. 'Not so', said the King; 'you are become a doctor, Kate, to instruct us, as we take it, and not to be instructed or directed by us.' Katherine replied that Henry had misunderstood her, for she thought it very unseemly for a woman to teach her husband, when it should be the other way round and she should learn from him. She had mainly disputed with Henry to distract him from the pain in his leg and also that she might profit from his learned replies. With apparent relief the King responded, 'And is it even so, sweet heart, and tended your arguments to no worse end? Then perfect friends we are now again, as ever at any time heretofore. It does me more good at this time to hear the words of your mouth, than if I had heard present news that a hundred thousand pounds in money had fallen unto me.'[18] Henry showed his delight by embracing and kissing her, and they stayed talking together, perfect harmony restored. Katherine had been tested and had come through with flying colours. She had had to humble herself and to emphasise her humility, but her

18   ibid., pp. 480-1.

conscience may well have been touched and in her heart she might well have felt that she was correcting the too forceful stance she had previously taken. She believed that the Bible taught that it was the man who was head over his wife and how much more should that be the case when the husband was the King.

The next afternoon, Henry, who was in the best of moods, and Katherine were enjoying a walk in the park with some of their attendants, when forty armed men were seen marching towards them with Wriothesley at their head. They had come to arrest the Queen. Henry took his Chancellor to one side and berated him. 'Fool, beast, arrant knave.' Shocked and dismayed, Wriothesley and his soldiers were forced to scuttle away. Henry rejoined his wife and Katherine, who had not heard what was said, tried to excuse Wriothesley, and asked Henry to assume that whatever offence he had committed had been done in error. 'Ah, poor soul!' said the King, 'thou little knowest how evil he deserveth this grace at thy hands. On my word, sweet heart, he hath been to thee a very knave'.[19]

Henry, wily operator that he was, had allowed the plot to develop for his own purposes. Katherine had learnt her lesson and would not overstep the mark again. By going along with them, Henry had also flushed out the antagonism of Wriothesley, and especially Gardiner, towards his wife and exposed just how far they would go. For many years he had used Gardiner's skills for his own purposes, but he disliked his crafty cleverness and would never trust him again for daring to strike at his wife. What exactly was in Henry's mind? The only things that are certain are that Katherine gave him the reassurance he wanted and was immediately restored in his affections and favour, and that Henry, through both Dr Wendy and the 'mislaying' of the warrant, gave her every chance to find out about the conspiracy in time. The Catholics had overplayed their hand and their hold on power was slipping away. What had looked as if it would be their moment of triumph turned out to be disastrous for them.

---

19   ibid., pp. 481-2.

Henry's last months

The King and Queen were together from July until the beginning of December and then Henry chose to set himself apart. He was ill and did not want Katherine or the Lady Mary or any of his family to see his decline. It must have been hard for Katherine to be kept away at Henry's time of need, but she had no choice in the matter. She spent a strange Christmas with the court at Greenwich whilst Henry was in London, the first time they had been apart at Christmas, and then she joined Henry at Westminster but was still unable to see him.

Henry was slowly dying. He was not too ill though to settle affairs for the future. He had never liked or trusted the Duke of Norfolk, but it was Norfolk's son, the earl of Surrey, who provided Henry with the opportunity to remove them both. Surrey, an arrogant and foolish young man, not only began to throw his weight around but recklessly displayed the arms of Edward the Confessor, so emphasising the ancient royal lineage of his family. Henry would not brook a whiff of disloyalty or any possible rival to his son, and both Surrey and his father were arrested in December. Surrey was executed on 19th January and his father, who had been condemned for concealing his son's offences, was due to die on 28th January.

On 26th December Henry named a Council of Regency to rule for his nine-year-old son. Its sixteen members were strongly dominated by Protestants. There was one striking omission and Sir Anthony Browne was close enough to the King to cautiously query with him whether he had accidentally forgotten to include the name of Stephen Gardiner. 'Hold your peace', growled the King, 'I remembered him well enough, and of good purpose have left him out...I could myself use him, and rule him to all manner of purposes, as seemed good unto me, but so you will never do'.[20]

Henry had done everything he could to ensure his son's reign began with political stability and, in doing so, that Evangelicals would hold the levers of power. In God's providence, the plots of the previous summer to remove Katherine and the leading Protestants at court had

---

20   Dickens, p. 271.

failed, and now, in Henry's last days, he himself took steps to remove key Catholics and to assure Protestant domination in the new reign.

On the freezing cold night of January 27th 1547, Henry was near to death and asked for Cranmer. The King could no longer speak, but, when Cranmer asked him to give a sign that he was trusting in God's mercy, he gripped the archbishop's hand. Shortly afterwards, he died and the towering presence who for nearly thirty-eight years had dominated national life, as well as his sixth wife's life, was no more.

QUEEN DOWAGER 1547–1548

Katherine would grieve for a husband she had grown fond of and who most of the time had shown her kindness and affection. When Henry was buried at St George's Chapel, Windsor on 16th February, she looked down on the scene from the Queen's closet above the choir. He was laid to rest with his third wife, Jane Seymour, the Queen who had managed to give him a son and heir.

Katherine had been well provided for in Henry's will. She would be a very wealthy woman, as well as possessing several properties, including at Hanworth and Chelsea. Henry had stated that he was rewarding her for her 'great love, obedience, chastity of life and wisdom'.[21] Katherine would also still be the first lady in the land. Until nine-year-old Edward married, the Queen Dowager had precedence over all, including Henry VIII's two daughters.

Coronation of King Edward VI

Edward VI's coronation followed closely after his father's funeral on 20th February. There is no record of whether Katherine was there. The ancient ceremony had been shortened from the normal eleven or twelve hours to about seven on account of Edward's young age. The new King had insisted that, in addition to the three swords carried in the procession before him, which were emblems of his three kingdoms, the Bible, which is the sword of the Spirit, should also be carried. Cranmer, in his sermon, charged his new monarch to see that God was truly worshipped within his realm and idolatry destroyed. He was to

---

21   Fraser, p. 396.

act as a second Josiah, the Old Testament King who also became King as a young boy. He had been eight years old at the time of his accession. Josiah faithfully followed the Lord and restored worship as God had commanded and had removed and destroyed all the signs of idolatrous worship which had flourished in the previous reigns. Cranmer quoted 2 Kings chapter 23 verse 25, 'Now before him there was no king like him, who turned to the Lord with all his heart, with all his soul, and with all his might, according to all the law of Moses; nor after him did any arise like him.' Cranmer told Edward that, as king, he had been chosen by God and given the gift of His Spirit to better rule and guide His people. There would be many other sermons in the following weeks comparing Edward to Old Testament kings such as David and the young Solomon, and especially Josiah.

Edward Seymour, Duke of Somerset and Lord Protector

The previous day when Edward had processed in great magnificence from the Tower to Westminster, his uncle, Edward Seymour, had ridden close by his side. Seymour, now elevated to the rank of duke, the Duke of Somerset, had also taken over the vacant role of head of state. Henry VIII had left power in the hands of the sixteen members of the Council of Regency, but clearly they could not all rule together. Someone had to be in over all charge and Seymour had acted swiftly and decisively to make sure he was that person. The Regency Council had accepted him as Protector, regent in all but name. Somerset was a committed Protestant. With him in charge of the realm, Cranmer as Archbishop of Canterbury and Edward the figurehead monarch, the stage was set for them to work together and establish an unmistakably Protestant Church. The steps would have to be slow at first but they would gradually gather pace.

Almost immediately after Henry's death, there was a feeling of relaxation. The Duke of Norfolk, expecting to be executed the next day, found himself unexpectedly reprieved. He would remain a prisoner in the Tower, but his life was no longer forfeit. It was a sign of less threatening times. The new regime was not looking to put people to death, especially not for their faith. The dangers of the last reign had gone, for the Act of the Six Articles along with the earlier heresy legislation, which had provided the legal basis for the burnings, would all be repealed.

Chelsea

In early March, Katherine left the court. For the first time in her life, she was fully independent and could decide for herself what she would do. She moved to the Old Manor House at Chelsea, which was a large red brick house, built only ten years earlier. It overlooked the Thames and was surrounded by five acres of beautiful gardens. Her stepdaughter, thirteen-year-old Elizabeth, moved with her, although by now she had lost one of her other stepdaughters. Margaret Neville had lived with her for more than a decade and had died in 1545 at the age of twenty. It had been a real loss for Katherine as she and Margaret had been very fond of each other. Elizabeth brought her own small household with her, including her tutor, William Grindal. As Katherine and Elizabeth adjusted to their change in circumstances and dealt with their grief, they welcomed a newcomer into their home. Nine-year-old Lady Jane Grey was Elizabeth's cousin. She was the granddaughter of Henry VIII's sister, Mary, and, like Elizabeth, she was very well educated and an outstanding scholar. It was the common practice among the aristocracy to send their children to receive the advantage of education and of learning social graces in a different establishment to their own home. Katherine was a most suitable person to have charge of her at this time and she settled well into her new surroundings. Jane and Elizabeth do not appear to have become close but Jane and Katherine were drawn to each other. Here was another young girl who needed mothering and loving and Katherine was very good at doing both. Jane had left a family home where both her parents were alive, but which lacked the warmth and concern for her welfare which she found at Chelsea, and she would probably grow to love Katherine more than her own coldly ambitious mother. Jane was also drawn to Katherine's godliness. Jane had been brought up as a Protestant and she knew the Bible and its gospel teachings. Now that all restraint was removed, Katherine could worship freely with her household and listen to sermons from her chaplains and from Miles Coverdale when he became her almoner. She could read and study what she chose. It was an atmosphere Jane would have loved and she would flourish under Katherine's care.

Courtship and marriage

Once before Katherine had been widowed, and almost immediately she had been courted by Thomas Seymour, the new King's younger uncle. Now, history was to repeat itself. Thomas had not married and, after Henry had died, he was ready to resume his long interrupted courtship. Katherine was just as ready to respond to it. Four years before, she had put duty and following God's will first, even though she had been getting ready to accept Thomas as her husband. Now, there was no reason why they could not marry and Katherine was very quickly falling back in love with him.

Some have questioned whether Seymour truly loved Katherine or whether he was just marrying her to advance his ambitions, and think that, if he could, he would have chosen Elizabeth in preference, but there is no reason to think it was not a love match on both sides. She had not been the exalted wealthy person she now was when he had first pursued her. Marriage to the widowed Lady Latimer would not have brought him much in the way of either wealth or status. Even marriage to the Queen Dowager had a downside. Katherine was 34, almost middle aged by Tudor standards, and, after three childless marriages, it would be doubtful that she could provide him with an heir.

As for Katherine, Thomas Seymour was an attractive proposition. As the King's uncle he was close to the royal family. Still in his late thirties, he was tall and good looking, loud and merry, with a splendid voice. He had had a good career in Henry VIII's service as a diplomat and in the military and he was a dashing, adventurous sort of man. According to a fellow courtier he was 'hardy, wise and liberal….fierce in courage, courtly in fashion, in personage stately, in voice magnificent, but somewhat empty of manner'.[22]

At first, Katherine was insistent that they would have to wait to get married and mentioned a delay of two years. There needed to be a suitable period of mourning, and because she was Henry VIIII's widow,

---

22   A. Weir, *Children of England: The Heirs of Henry VIII* (London: Pimlico, 1997), p. 36.

they would also need permission from the Council or the new King. She must have been aware that there would inevitably be talk that after being married to the King, she would be marrying beneath her. The sensible Katherine knew it was wisest to take their time, and let things settle down, before embarking on another marriage, but Seymour was having none of it and urged a period of two months instead. Katherine was someone with strong emotions, and in the end her feelings overcame her common sense, and they were secretly married, probably in May. Then, they had to face the consequences.

Only their very closest family knew of their union and Thomas had to visit his wife secretly. How to get permission for something which had already taken place and how to limit any backlash? If they were not to admit that they were already married, it was impossible without an element of deceit. The first casualty was Katherine's previously close relationship with the Lady Mary. When Mary was appealed to for support, she was upset that Katherine could already be contemplating marriage so soon after her father's death and her frosty reply was an indication that their friendship would not be what it was. It was not easy for either Thomas or Katherine to actually see the King to ask his permission in person, but after some letters from Katherine, he wrote on the 25th June to express his pleasure at their marriage, so giving the official sanction which they needed. His stepmother had a special place in his affections and at this stage he was probably still fond of his lively younger uncle. When the news came out, some were shocked and others openly dismayed and none more so than Thomas's brother Edward, the Lord Protector, and his wife Anne, who were simply furious.

Tensions within the Seymour family

Katherine's fourth marriage had brought her headlong into a family divided within itself. Both brothers were intensely ambitious and resentful of the other. Katherine's well-known gifts as a conciliator were no use here, for she very quickly began to quarrel with the Protector and his wife on her own account, though in her case it was none of her making and justice was on her side. Somerset wrongly kept jewellery which should have been hers by claiming they were property of the state, and was even granting leases on her dower lands without her knowledge or consent. His Duchess refused to accept that Katherine had precedence over her. She claimed that, as the Protector's wife, she was the first lady of the land and would not give place to the wife of her husband's younger brother. It was intolerable behaviour for Katherine to accept and made her very angry. On one occasion she wrote to her husband, 'This shall be to advertise you, that my lord, your brother, hath this afternoon made me warm. It was fortunate we were so much distant, for I suppose else I should have bitten him. What cause have they to fear having such a wife.'[23]

Thomas's antagonism towards his brother had its roots in disappointed expectations. At the very beginning of the reign, there had been a sharing out of honours and roles amongst the top courtiers and Thomas had anticipated doing better than he had. Why did his older brother take so much as Protector, guardian of the King's person and Duke of Somerset whilst Thomas had so little? This despite the fact that Thomas had been made a baron and Lord Seymour of Sudeley, and had become a Knight of the Garter and Lord Admiral of England. This resentment would fester and only grow over time.

It was not an edifying start. Katherine and the Seymours had been on the same 'side' in the old reign. Although she had not been close to her, Anne Seymour had been one of her ladies and had participated in the Bible studies and heard the sermons in the Queen's apartments. Now, with religious pressures removed and important work to be done, petty quarrelling was an unsightly distraction. Anne was well known for her immense pride and Thomas had no intention of subsiding quietly. Despite the happiness it brought her, there was a very sad element to Katherine's marriage. Her husband did not share her faith and he was also simply unworthy of her. Though he was known as a Protestant and there was no doubting his outward allegiance to the new religion, it is clear that, unlike Katherine, he had no experience of living faith. All too soon, Thomas began to excuse himself from family devotions and it was obvious he had no real interest in the spiritual things which Katherine held dear.

---

23   Letter from Katherine Parr to Thomas Seymour 1548. Withrow, pp. 167-8.

After their shaky beginning, Thomas and Katherine could settle into married life together at the pleasant manor of Chelsea. The hitherto mainly feminine household was now enlivened by the rather boisterous presence of Seymour. It was a happy and fulfilling time for Katherine. Married to the man she loved and with two young girls to mother and supervise, Katherine could now see two earlier literary projects of hers come to fruition. The *Paraphrases* of Erasmus, the gospel translation project she had been so closely associated with, was finally published and orders were given for it to be placed in every church. After they were removed in the next reign, they would be reinstated when Elizabeth was Queen. Providing the *Paraphrases* in churches meant that Katherine's desire of bringing them before a humble readership was achieved.

Lamentations of a Sinner

In November 1547, her *Lamentations of a Sinner* was finally published. It was now safe to do so and this book, into which she had poured so much effort, could be brought into the public domain. It was written from the heart and was the product of much study of various Reformed writers, influenced by Calvinism as well as Lutheranism, and sprang from her deep knowledge of the Bible. Although the dense sixteenth-century prose is hard reading today, she presents her theme in a straightforward way and uses vivid and down-to-earth illustrations. She herself was the sinner saved by grace. She did not hesitate to describe her ignorant and complacent rejection of the truth of the gospel, which turned to joy at the salvation she received through the death of the Lord Jesus Christ. She could do nothing. Christ had done everything. She wants 'to confess and declare to the world, how ingrate, negligent, unkind and stubborn, I have been to God my Creator: and how beneficial, merciful and gentle, he hath been always to me his creature, being such a miserable and wretched sinner'.[24]

'I had a blind guide called Ignorance, who dimmed so mine eyes, that I could never perfectly get any sight of the fair, goodly, straight, and right ways of his doctrine; but continually traveled uncomfortably in foul, wicked crooked, and perverse ways. Yea, and because they were

---

24   Katherine Parr, *Lamentations of a Sinner* 1547, reprinted in Withrow. Quotations are from pp. 90, 91-2, 96, 97, 99-100, 112-13, 122.

so much haunted of many, I could not think but I walked in the perfect and right way, having more regard to the number of the walkers, than to the order of the walking...I forsook the spiritual honouring of the true living God and worshiped visible idols and images made of men's hands, believing by them to have gotten heaven, yea to say the truth I made a great idol of myself, for I loved myself better than God. And certainly look how many things are loved or preferred in our hearts before God, so many are taken and esteemed for idols and false gods.'

'If I should look upon my sins, and not upon thy mercy I should despair: for in myself I find nothing to save me, but a dunghill of wickedness to condemn me. If I should hope by mine own strength and power to come out of this maze of iniquity and wickedness, wherein I have walked so long, I should be deceived. For I am so ignorant, blind, weak and feeble that I cannot bring myself out of this entangled and wayward maze: but the more I seek means and ways to wind myself out, the more I am wrapped and tangled therein...It is the hand of the Lord that can and will bring me out of this endless maze of death.'

'For I am most certain and sure, that no creature in heaven nor earth is of power, or can by any mean help me, but God, who is omnipotent, almighty, beneficial, and merciful, wellwilling and loving to all those that call and put their whole confidence and trust in him [Acts 4:12]. And therefore, I will seek no other means, nor advocate, and mediator between God and man, to help and relieve me.' 'But when God of his mere goodness had thus opened mine eyes, and made me see and behold Christ, the Wisdom of God, the Light of the world, with a supernatural sight of faith [1Cor 2:14] all pleasures, vanities, honour, riches, wealth, and aids of the world began to wax bitter unto me...then began I to perceive that Christ was my only Saviour and Redeemer, and the same doctrine to be all divine, holy, and heavenly, infused by grace into the hearts of the faithful, which never can be attained by human doctrine, wit, nor reason, although they should travail and labour for the same to the end of the world.'

Her exhortations on how to live the Christian life included encouragement for women to be obedient, godly wives and to learn from their husbands at home. She described her husband (at the time of writing) in Old Testament terms as Moses. 'But our Moses, and most godly, wise governor and king, hath delivered us out of the captivity and bondage of Pharaoh. And I mean by this Moses, king Henry the eighth, my most sovereign favourable lord and husband...And I mean by this Pharaoh the bishop of Rome, who hath been and is a greater persecutor of all true Christians, than ever was Pharaoh of the children of Israel. For he is a persecutor of the gospel and grace, a setter forth of all superstition and counterfeit holiness.'

She repudiated the argument of Catholics that Bible reading was harmful. 'It is a lamentable thing to hear how there are many in the world that do not well digest the reading of scripture, and do commend and praise ignorance, and say that much knowledge of God's word is the original of all dissension, schisms, and contention, and makes men haughty, proud, and presumptuous by reading of the same. This manner of saying is no less than a plain blasphemy against the Holy Ghost. For the Spirit of God is the author of his word, and so the Holy Ghost is made the author of evil.' By contrast, Katherine's love for the Bible permeates her whole book.

Pregnancy and Elizabeth's departure

In the winter of 1547/8, most unexpectedly and joyously, Katherine found that she was expecting a baby. It must have been something she thought would never happen. Sadly, delight in her pregnancy had to give way to increasing concerns about Elizabeth, or, to be precise, concerns about Elizabeth and Thomas. Thomas had been indulging in teasing and horseplay with Elizabeth. To begin with, Katherine sometimes joined in, but, after time, both she and Kat Ashley, Elizabeth's devoted governess, became worried that things were going too far. Thomas might protest that the fourteen-year-old Elizabeth was like a daughter to him and it was innocent fun, but he was not to be trusted. His behaviour was totally inappropriate and flirtatious and included early morning romps in Elizabeth's bedroom, involving much laughter and horseplay and though others may have been around, it was not a seemly way to carry on. The day came when Katherine found Elizabeth in his arms and she acted swiftly and decisively to protect them all. Elizabeth was immediately sent away to stay with Kat Ashley's sister, Lady Denny, and Katherine was left to deal with her hurt and sense of betrayal. She had lectured Elizabeth before her departure, but they had parted on good terms, and Elizabeth would soon write to express her sorrow, so their relationship, though rocked, was not greatly damaged. The pain her husband had caused them both would not have been so easy to handle.

Sudeley

In June 1548, Katherine left Chelsea for Hanworth because of fears of the plague. Soon after, the family travelled west to Thomas's estate at Sudeley for Katherine to give birth in the peace of the country. Sudeley Castle stands just outside the ancient town of Winchcombe, in the beautiful area we now call the Cotswolds. Seymour had been having rooms prepared at great expense to turn the castle, which had seen better days, into a luxurious dwelling fit for the Queen Dowager. Lady Jane was with her, along with members of her household such as Miles Coverdale, the Bible translator, who was her almoner, and John Parkhurst, her chaplain. It was a relaxing sociable summer with a succession of friends and relatives coming to visit. Katherine did not always feel well and was tired, but she must have looked forward to the arrival of her long-awaited baby, although in those times she would have been considered old for a first-time mother.

Katherine gave birth to a healthy baby girl on 30th August. She was named Mary. As with her sister-in-law and predecessor as Queen, Jane Seymour, joy at the birth was cut short by the dreaded signs of puerperal fever. As the fever advanced, Katherine was taken over by delirium and accused those about her of laughing at her grief. It was mostly directed at Thomas, an outworking no doubt of some of her hurt. Her distress eased as the fever left her and, once more in her right mind, she dictated her will. She left everything to Thomas, and, displaying her love for him, wished that she could leave him far more. She died on 5th September. It was all so sudden. Thomas was stunned and, to begin with, overwhelmed by his grief, and others would have felt Katherine's death keenly – her stepchildren and Lady Jane.

Katherine was buried in the castle's chapel three days later. Custom dictated that her husband was not present. The chapel had been hung with black cloth embroidered with the Queen's escutcheons and the surroundings and funeral procession were appropriate for the internment of a Queen of England. Miles Coverdale led the service and preached. Lady Jane Grey was the chief mourner, at ten years old a tiny figure dressed in black. The service was short, in English, and distinctly Protestant. Psalms were sung in English, three lessons from the Bible read and offerings placed in the almsbox. Miles Coverdale was at pains to explain that the giving of alms was for the benefit of the poor, not to pay for masses for the soul in purgatory as in the past. Also, that the tapers carried in the procession and placed around the coffin were to honour the person and not for any other purpose. He then preached his sermon and concluded the service with prayer. So ended the first Protestant funeral service for an English Queen.

As for Katherine, she had known where she expected to go when she died. She had chosen to close *Lamentations of a Sinner* with these words. 'I beseech God we may...be found such faithful servants, and loving children, that we may hear the happy, comfortable, and most joyful sentence ordained for the children of God, which is: "Come hither, ye blessed of my Father, and receive the kingdom of heaven prepared for you before the beginning of the world."'[25]

KATHERINE'S LEGACY

Katherine's most obvious claim to fame is that she was the one who survived. The well-known couplet about Henry's wives goes:

Divorced, beheaded, died;

Divorced, beheaded, survived.

She was the only one of Henry VIII's wives who was both alive and still married to him at the time of his death. Anne of Cleves outlived them both, but of course, she had been divorced. Even so, if Katherine had not married her King, she would still have made her mark. Her body of literary work was probably unique in Tudor England and *Lamentations of a Sinner* was one of only a very few books of prose by a woman to be published in sixteenth-century England. Of course, the fact that they were written by a Queen encouraged people to read

---

25   ibid., p. 130.

them. Her books were intended to be spiritually useful and to be as accessible to as many as possible, especially *Lamentations of a Sinner*. Here, she could write freely of those things which were most important to her. She also championed the use of English for the same reason – to bring religious literature and especially the Bible to the many – and not just to the elite.

Interest in education and learning was a key theme of her life. In encouraging the choice of gifted Reformist tutors for both Prince Edward and the Lady Elizabeth, she helped to shape not just their intellect, but the faith of two Tudor monarchs and so to advance the Protestant Reformation. It is very hard to overstate how important that was. There was never any proper doubt that either of them would be anything other than Protestant monarchs. Edward had to be content to let others wield real power and rule on his behalf while he was a child, but what he wanted made a difference. Knowing that he was expected to leave his minority and rule for himself must have helped to shape the direction of policy under the Duke of Northumberland, his second 'regent'. Northumberland was preparing for power to transfer to Edward on his sixteenth birthday in October 1553, when he would reign fully as King.

Influence can be hard to quantify and define exactly, but Katherine was clearly someone who greatly influenced those around her – and she influenced for good. She lived as a godly woman and was a godly example. Margaret Neville, Edward, Elizabeth, Lady Jane Grey and others saw her strong sense of duty, as well as her love for her Lord, at close quarters. The anomaly in her life was her fourth marriage. How could someone like Katherine Parr come to marry someone like Thomas Seymour? It was a marriage of a believer with an unbeliever. It was a marriage where the wife had married someone greatly beneath her, not in rank, but in character. Seymour's handsome and attractive exterior masked huge ambition and a selfish, shallow and ill-disciplined interior, and he cast a shadow over her last eighteen months. They say love is blind. When Katherine was able to choose a husband for herself, despite her common sense and intelligence, she was ruled by her heart and not her head and fell hopelessly in love with him.

Historians have picked one precise moment when Katherine was Queen, when they believe her example had very significant consequences. In the summer of 1544, Katherine was Regent and the ten-year-old Lady Elizabeth was living with her. She was a witness of the capable way Katherine dealt with state affairs. Elizabeth saw how calm and competent she was and that, as a woman, for a short time, Katherine was able to not just survive but effectively flourish in a man's world as she governed the country. It is said Elizabeth never forgot the experience and it gave her the confidence to know a woman could be in charge. She could make a go of ruling a country without a husband at hand, even in sixteenth-century England.

Katherine became Queen in the summer of 1543 at a critical moment for the Reformation. Catholic traditionalists were in the ascendancy and it was beginning to look as if they might be unstoppable. Henry's personal preferences were very much for the old religion with certain elements removed; which had already been effected. Gardiner and Norfolk were riding high and Thomas Cranmer was in a dangerous place. It looked as if he was about to be removed like Thomas Cromwell. Yet in that summer, not only did Henry protect Cranmer, but something shifted and Protestant opinions began to be more influential at court. Then, Edward's tutors were chosen. Once more, slowly, and little by little, the cause of Reform grew stronger. What changed things? Some historians have highlighted that the turning point came when Katherine married Henry and think it may well have been her influence which started to move things. Dr David Starkey has pointed out that, although it could not be entirely due to Katherine, the only circumstance that changed that summer was that she became Queen. She, unusually, had Henry largely to herself during the first six months of their marriage because of their extended summer progress and, as someone with a strong sense of mission, she seized her opportunity and used it well.[26]

She may have had little choice in taking on the role, but Katherine had proved a success as Queen, and as a wife and stepmother. At the

---

26   David Starkey, *Six Wives: The Queens of Henry VIII* (London: Chatto & Windus, 2003), p. 729.

same time, from the very beginning, she had used her royal position and had worked consistently to do whatever she could to advance the Reformation and make biblical truth known, and had not been held back by fear of the consequences.

It is noticeable how much respect and admiration Katherine has aroused, not just in her own day but in ours too. Modern biographers, even those who appear to have little interest in her faith, write of her with praise and admiration. There is a fragrance about Katherine's life and a warmth about her which still draws people. It is the warmth of grace and graciousness, and it was a response to the grace which God had shown to her, a sinner who had lamented over her sins and had been saved by grace.

4. Lady Jane Grey 1537 - 1554

Faithful to the End

When the news reached London about eight o'clock in the morning on Friday 12th October 1537, the whole city erupted and rejoiced. Church bells pealed, Te Deums were sung and two thousand rounds from the Tower of London's guns thundered through the air. There was a sense of release amidst the elation for it had been a long wait. Queen Jane Seymour's delivery had taken all of three days and two nights, but it had ended triumphantly in the birth of a healthy baby boy. Henry VIII had a male heir. Rarely can the response of monarch and people have been so closely aligned – spontaneous joy and relief. As Henry held his baby son in his arms, he wept. He had been waiting for this moment for over twenty-five years, ever since his first wife, Catherine of Aragon had also born a son, but cruelly, he had died just a couple of months later. Since then, his three marriages had only brought two girls and a succession of miscarriages and stillbirths. In the joy of the moment all of that could be forgotten for now.

The church bells continued to peal all through the day and on into the evening. Shops and workshops were shut and people flooded the streets. Bonfires were lit. There were impromptu banquets and other gatherings of people eating and drinking together. Banners and garlands festooned the streets and free wine flowed from the conduits and from hogsheads. In the evening, the Lord Mayor rode through the city and personally thanked the people for their response. The celebrations continued well into the next day.

Messengers took the news throughout the country and everywhere there were the same scenes of joy and excitement. When Bishop Hugh

Latimer heard in his Worcester diocese, he put pen to paper and wrote to the King's chief minister, Thomas Cromwell. 'Here is no less rejoicing in these parts from the birth of our prince, whom we hungered for so long, than there was, I trow, at the birth of St John the Baptist...God give us grace to be thankful.'[1]

The hope of a secure male succession to the throne had been born along with the tiny baby, who was named Edward by his joyful parents. In Tudor times, society was ordered and hierarchical, and power, influence and authority was invested in men. That was the norm in everyday life, but how much more did that apply to the governing of the country. How could it be right for a nation to be ruled by a woman? It seemed to be something quite unnatural. A female ruler was virtually unknown in England. The only example that history could give was the reign of Matilda, way back in the twelfth century and that had hardly been encouraging. Her father, Henry I, had made his barons swear allegiance to Matilda whilst Henry was still alive, but that had not stopped most of them supporting the rival claims of her cousin Stephen when Henry had died, and civil war had followed. That was a long time ago, but civil war was not a distant prospect in Tudor England, and nobody wanted to return to the grim seesaw of the power struggles and bloody battles of the Wars of the Roses of the previous century. That had only been brought to an end when Henry VIII's father, Henry Tudor, for the Lancastrians, had won his famous victory over the Yorkist King Richard III at Bosworth, and Richard's crown, lying on the battlefield, had been retrieved and placed on his head.

Henry's right to the crown was slender to say the least, but by marrying Elizabeth of York, whose claim was superior to his own, he had united the rival factions of Lancaster and York, the houses of the red and the white roses, and had founded the Tudor dynasty. After that, it was a matter of holding on to power and leaving a stable succession. A stable succession meant having a male heir, or preferably a male heir and a male spare. Henry Tudor, who reigned as Henry VII, had needed his spare when his oldest son, Arthur, had died in his mid teens, and his younger son, Henry, had become his heir, but Henry VIII himself

---

1   A. Plowden, *The House of Tudor* (Stroud: The History Press, 2010), p. 139.

would not have that advantage. Almost immediately after his baby Edward had been christened, Jane Seymour began to be unwell with the first signs of the dread of Tudor childbirth, puerperal fever, and shortly afterwards Henry's joy at the birth of his tiny son gave way to grief and shock at the loss of his wife.

There was a very practical element to such thinking about the succession. Did women have the capacity to rule? That was entirely untried and unknown in England. One of Henry VIII's daughters would go on to be one of England's most famous and successful monarchs, Elizabeth I, but that was in the future. There were three good reasons to fear a female succession. 1. If the Queen was married to foreign royalty, her husband would try to influence English policy for the advantage of his own country. 2. If the Queen was married to an Englishman there would be the danger of internal rivalry and factionalism. 3. In both cases of a married Queen, it might be her husband who wielded the real power in the land and there was the possibility she might be side-lined as little more than a figurehead. The only way to avoid these outcomes with certainty was for the Queen to remain unmarried – but then she could not have children to succeed her. These possibilities were not just theoretical and they would all be displayed in some measure in the reigns of Edward VI's three female successors.

So a boy mattered very much and the country gave thanks. Meanwhile, in that same month, another Tudor royal baby was born. Hardly with the same fanfare, for there is no record of the date or place of birth, but the King's niece, Frances Grey, Marchioness of Dorset, gave birth to a baby girl. She was called Jane, almost certainly in honour of the Queen. What no one could have foreseen was that these two cousins, born so close together, would live lives which bore remarkable and strong parallels with each other. More than that, both of their lives would be influenced, and ultimately dominated, by the two great issues of the day – the Reformation and the succession to the throne.

CHILDHOOD

Lady Jane Grey's family home was at Bradgate Park in Leicestershire. Today, its ruins lie at the heart of a country park on the outskirts of Leicester. When Jane was born the house was newly built. It was constructed of brick, which was fashionable and expensive, and had white stone facings. Bradgate had been built for comfort and ostentation, and not for defence. It was the first unfortified great house in the county. Just two storeys high, with towers and an impressive gatehouse, it was a grand building. The house was surrounded by formal gardens, a tiltyard, and a park six miles in circumference. Outside of the park was rolling woodland, part of the forest of Chartley, and excellent hunting territory. The interior was magnificent, lit by large windows and hung with expensive tapestries.

Jane's family

Bradgate had been largely built by about 1520 by Jane's grandfather, Thomas Grey, Marquess of Dorset, although Jane's father finally finished improving it soon after her birth. Thomas Grey came from an old Leicestershire family and had had a career both at court and as a soldier. He could claim royal connections as his father was Edward IV's stepson. When Thomas Grey died in 1530, his heir was his thirteen-year-old son, Henry, who acquired not only Bradgate but several other estates in Leicestershire, as well as the title Marquess of Dorset. Thomas had been a wealthy man and his son was left amply provided for. He was, however, a minor and he became a ward of the King. In 1533, Charles Brandon, Duke of Suffolk, and an old friend of Henry's father, bought his wardship and almost immediately arranged a marriage between Henry and his own eldest daughter, Frances. They were married in May of that same year at Suffolk Place, the Brandon's imposing London house, Henry aged sixteen and his bride, fifteen.

Henry Grey was proud of his own links to the monarchy, but in marrying Frances he had married into the royal family. His mother-in-law, who died soon after the wedding, was Mary Tudor, younger and favourite sister of King Henry VIII. As a lively and beautiful eighteen-year-old she had married the French King Louis XII, who was in his fifties. Before she had agreed to the marriage, Mary had extracted a promise from her brother that, when the King died, she could choose her next husband and they had both known who she had in mind – Henry's close friend, Charles Brandon. As it happened Mary was released from her marriage almost as soon as it began. Louis died just three months later on 1ˢᵗ January 1515. King Henry curiously chose Charles Brandon to be his emissary back to France to wind up Mary's affairs, retrieve as much as he could of her dowry and then to escort her back to England. Henry was cautious enough to make Brandon promise to not get entangled in any way with Mary whilst in France. What neither man reckoned with was Mary herself. Weeks of seclusion as a widow, and very real fears that, once again, she would be pressurised into a political marriage, made her desperate and extremely emotional, and Brandon found himself unable to withstand her insistence that, if they were to be married at all, it had to be at once. They were married at Cluny very quietly in February 1515. It was utterly reckless. Henry was close to both of them and Mary did have his promise that she could choose her next husband, but no one that near to the throne could marry without the King's express consent, and anyone who knew Henry knew that it was very dangerous to take liberties with him. In the end, the storm blew over, but the King had been very angry and the couple had had an unnerving wait before they heard that they would have to pay heavily for their actions, repaying all the costs of Mary's first marriage, a huge amount which hung over them for the rest of their lives. They returned to England in May and to an elaborate second wedding at Greenwich. So Mary achieved what few other royal princesses of the time could hope for, to marry the man of her choice for love – although to her dying day she would still be known as 'The French Queen'.

All of this made her eldest daughter not just the niece of the King, and the granddaughter of a king, Henry VII, but also the daughter of a queen. These were things Frances was in no danger of forgetting, for she was acutely aware of her royal heritage.

Early in 1538, Henry Grey was twenty-one and so reached his majority. He now had control of his estates and he made Bradgate his main home. As he moved in, he forced his mother to move out, treating her unkindly and even preventing her from taking many of her personal possessions with her. Henry and Frances, along with their infant daughter, established themselves at Bradgate, improving their magnificent house and living a luxurious lifestyle. When the Greys dined in public in their great hall, up to two hundred guests ate with them. Sumptuous food was provided and served with great ceremony. Each course was carried in to a fanfare of trumpets. They had at least three hundred servants. In fact, they were living beyond their means, always in debt and in need of money, which was not helped by their love of gambling.

When Lady Jane was born, her parents had already had two children, a boy and a girl, but they had both died in infancy. They would go on to have two others, Katherine, who was born in 1540 and Mary in 1545. Katherine would be the beauty of the family, but Mary was humpbacked and would later be described as ugly. All three girls were particularly small, but Mary was unusually so. In many families, she would have been kept at home and neglected, but Mary went about with the rest of the family and received the same education as her sisters.

Education

There would have been a regular pattern to life in Jane's early years. The day began with prayers, followed by breakfast, and once Jane reached four or five, there would be formal lessons either side of dinner. After supper she learnt to dance, so necessary for future life at court, or worked at her needlework. She would have first learnt to read when she was three or four, probably taught by her nurse, Mrs Ellen, who would be her close companion all her life. The chaplain, Dr Harding, started Jane's formal education and was later replaced by John Aylmer. Aylmer was a gifted young man in his early twenties, who was a protégé of Henry Grey. When he finished his studies at Cambridge University about 1541, he came to Bradgate as a chaplain and as Jane's tutor. He believed in teaching through kindness and they developed a real bond. In Jane he had a very apt pupil. She was a natural academic and through his teaching he encouraged her growing love of learning.

The core of Jane's education were the classics, Latin and Greek, as well as religious instruction. Over time, she would also learn French and other modern languages, as well as history and music. Jane and her sisters received an excellent education as befitted their rank and their parents' expectations, who wanted them to be educated to the highest standards comparable with their cousins, Prince Edward and the Lady Elizabeth. They would also have been taught good manners from an early age and to obey their parents unquestioningly.

Privilege and Jane's parents

Although Henry and Frances had been brought up as Catholics, they were both now committed to the Protestant cause. So, from an early age, the Grey sisters not only lived very privileged lives at the top of society, but were also very favoured to be taught the Bible and its doctrines, especially by Dr Harding and John Aylmer. But, despite their privileges and advantages, they were unfortunate in their parents. Henry Grey behaved badly to his mother and both he and Frances displayed the same selfishness and lack of affection to their daughters. Frances was the dominant one of the two – greedy, ambitious, arrogant and domineering. Although Henry was also ambitious, he was weak and lazy, lacking any obvious sense of drive and purpose. Like other parents of the time, they tightly ruled their children, but especially with Jane, they would show little genuine concern for her welfare and a consistent harshness in their dealing with her.

Katherine Parr

As Jane approached her ninth birthday, change was in the air. The nobility had a well-established custom of 'placing out' their children. They were sent to a family, usually one of higher standing than their own, to learn social graces and especially to improve their marriage prospects. For Jane there was only one possible household for her to join – that of the Queen, Katherine Parr, but the strange autumn and winter of 1546, as King Henry's life was drawing to a close, was not the right time. So she came to the household of the Queen Dowager, as she had become by then, at her manor in Chelsea in the spring or early summer of 1547. When she arrived, Katherine would have welcomed an unusually small girl for her age, slender and graceful, with auburn hair and freckles. The Lady Elizabeth was already there but the four-year age gap between them was probably too great at that age for them to become real friends and it is also possible that Elizabeth was aloof with Jane. She had something of a reputation for haughtiness. Katherine

Parr's new husband, Thomas Seymour, joined them that summer and would have livened things up with his boisterous good humour.

The atmosphere at Chelsea was very different to what Jane was used to at home. She was praised and treated with warmth and kindness by the motherly Katherine, who grew increasingly fond of her, and, unsurprisingly, Jane responded well to such treatment. Academically it was stimulating, as each of the girls studied with their own tutors, but were encouraged by Katherine's keen interest. Both girls were highly intelligent and very advanced in their education for their ages. Tudor children were expected to grow up quickly, to pass through childhood as speedily as possible, and to be able to take on adult responsibilities, especially marriage, at an early age – which we would shrink from today. Part of that process for these royal cousins was to develop their minds in something of an academic hothouse.

Jane also flourished under the religious teaching in the house. Katherine's chaplains and her almoner, Miles Coverdale, led regular devotions and Katherine was now free to read the Bible and any religious literature without any concerns about the consequences. Her house would have been somewhere where the Reformed faith was preached, discussed and promoted. Jane had been taught from the Bible from her earliest days, and knew the need to trust not in her own good works or anything she could do, but in what Christ had done for her. In dying on the cross, He had died for her and for all who would put their trust in Him. At some stage, as like her cousin Edward, she would move beyond a mere mental acceptance of these things to a personal faith and trust in Christ for herself. It was a faith which shaped who she was and would come to dominate her life. Her time with Katherine Parr and the circle around her would have encouraged and helped her in these things, as would Katherine's book *Lamentations of a Sinner*, published when she had been at Chelsea about six months.

Jane's place in the succession

Living with the Seymours was not the only big change in Jane's life at this time. Henry VIII's will had quite dramatically altered her status. The Act of Succession of 1544 had reinstated Mary and Elizabeth after Edward in the succession, but had also given Henry the right to further name the order of succession in his will. In his will, he had confirmed the order of his three children, though once again without taking the label of illegitimacy away from his daughters, but he had then laid down the succession should all three die without heirs. He ignored the line of his older sister, Margaret, who had married the King of Scotland, and instead turned to the line of his younger sister, Mary. After the Lady Elizabeth the crown would pass 'to the heirs of the body of the Lady Frances, our niece'. In other words, not to Frances herself, but to her children and first to her oldest child, Lady Jane. In the new reign, Jane was third in line to the throne. Of course, in time, all three of her cousins would hope to marry, and even Mary was still young enough to bear children, but just at this moment, Jane stood immediately behind them in the succession.

Jane's parents would have been well aware of Jane's significance. Both of the Greys were very ambitious, but although they were prominent in the ceremonial life of the court, Henry Grey lacked the aptitude to take on a more significant role. Both Henry VIII and the Duke of Somerset, Protector of the new King, failed to use him in any meaningful way in government and they evidently made the same judgement that he was unsuited. This made Henry and Frances look to their children to fulfill their own ambitions, and as they had not been able to produce a son, then it was to Jane that their attention fell. The fact that she was now so much more important only highlighted this and especially in relation to her marriage. She might only be nine years old but they would be looking to arrange the very best marriage for her, the one best suited to her rank and position, and to their ambitions.

Ward of Thomas Seymour

There was someone else who was not slow to grasp the possibilities of Jane's situation and that was Katherine Parr's new husband, Thomas Seymour. Seymour's festering sense of grievance over what he saw as the unfair inequality between his position and that of Edward VI's other uncle, his own brother, Edward, developed into a campaign to undermine the Protector and to advance his own influence in whatever way he could. He saw Lady Jane as a useful asset and he was not slow to do something about it. He persuaded Jane's parents to let her become his ward. He dangled the prospect before them of the best marriage alliance of all – that Jane should marry the King. As the King's uncle, he would use his influence to bring about a match between them. At first, Jane's parents were cautious; they would be handing over control of their daughter and they were hesitant to put too much credence on Seymour's confident words. They were all too aware that the influence that mattered in the King's life was that of the Protector and were not at all sure that Seymour's undertaking was anything more than fine words. What did sway them was his proposal to pay £2,000 for Jane's wardship and to arrange her marriage. Some money passed hands and the rest would follow over time. The Greys were always in need of money and, in effect, they sold their daughter's future to Seymour.

With Jane already ensconsed in the Seymour's household, this arrangement brought no obvious change for her. Katherine moved between her properties at Hanworth and Chelsea and her apartments at Whitehall. Jane saw the King on some of her visits to court during her childhood and, like the Lady Elizabeth, she treated him with exaggerated respect. The honour due to the sovereign had to be reflected in the strict etiquette they observed in his presence, such as curtsies, kneeling when spoken to and walking backwards when withdrawing from him, even though Edward was still a child and Elizabeth was his own sister.

Death of Katherine Parr

The even tenor of life with the Queen Dowager continued for about a year. Jane almost certainly had no idea why Elizabeth left suddenly in the early summer of 1548, and shortly afterwards she accompanied the Seymours to their castle at Sudeley. Here, Jane spent a pleasant summer with many visitors, spending time with Katherine and had the joy of seeing the new baby. Then she would have picked up the sense of fear of the adults around her as fever set in, followed by the shock of Katherine's death. She almost certainly loved her more than her own mother, and would have felt the loss deeply of someone who had brought love and kindness into her life without demanding anything in return. When Katherine died, probably the happiest period of Jane's life came to an end. She had a special role as chief mourner at Katherine's funeral, and then it was time to return home.

Return to Thomas Seymour

At first Thomas Seymour was overwhelmed at his loss. In a daze he began to disband his wife's household, but then as he grew calmer he began to think more clearly. He did not want to let go of Jane and he wrote to her parents to say that he was ready to take her back. He was retaining the ladies of Katherine's household and his mother was coming to take charge, so all was suitable for Jane to return. The Greys were not inclined to agree. They were disappointed that no progress had been made on Jane's marriage to the King and they were disturbed by the changes they had noticed in her since her homecoming. She had grown independent during her time away and they detected signs that she had been spoilt. She needed her mother to take her in hand. They would take Seymour's advice in the question of her marriage and still looked for the fulfilment of his promise of a match with Edward, but Jane would remain at Bradgate.

Thomas Seymour was not easily put off. Letters went back and forth and then he visited the Greys and forcibly and persuasively worked on them until they gave in. He promised that, once he had freed the King from the influence of the Protector, he would make sure he married Jane. He also paid over five hundred pounds, out of the two thousand he had agreed with them for he knew well that they were influenced by money.

Jane was probably content to return to Seymour either to Hanworth or to his grand London house, Seymour Place. She had written to him whilst at Bradgate and her letter reads as if she had grown fond of him. She called him a loving and kind father. Thomas had plenty of charm and when he wanted was full of good humour and Jane may have only ever seen the best side of him.

Fall of Thomas Seymour

In fact, Seymour was living on the edge and there were plenty of warning signs for Jane's parents to pick up on and safely remove their daughter from his care, but they did not. Marriage to Katherine had curbed Seymour's wilder side but now there was nothing to rein him in and he very quickly began to run out of control. For a start, now he was a free man again, his thoughts turned to the Lady Elizabeth and he began sending her messages and to show an all too obvious interest in her. His friends warned him of the considerable danger he was running. The Council would never give permission for their marriage and would be highly alarmed and suspicious at the very thought of it. Elizabeth wisely steered clear and gave him no encouragement.

As for Elizabeth's brother, the King, Seymour had tried to cultivate his relationship with him ever since Edward had succeeded to the throne. He had bribed one of Edward's servants very early on which meant he could communicate with him through that servant. As the Protector kept Edward very short of money, and was also distant and austere with him, and kept him away from any meaningful involvement in government, Thomas saw his opportunity. He regularly sent the boy money and fostered his image with Edward as the friendly and amusing uncle, so much more affable than his older brother. To begin with Edward had responded, but although he was glad of the money, in time he developed an aversion to both uncles and saw through the way Thomas was trying to use him for his own ends.

In the autumn of 1548, the incessant plots and plans buzzing around in Seymour's head of how to wrest power away from his brother, and to take control of the young King, now spilled over into dangerous talk and action. Ineptly, and also with insufficient secrecy, Seymour began to plot a coup, looking to his closest friends and associates for support. They included Henry Grey and Katherine Parr's brother, William, now Marquess of Northampton, who bluntly told him he was likely to fail. Seymour was increasingly losing touch with reality and, as his preparations advanced, others warned him of their futility. Finally Seymour, apparently frustrated at his lack of support, decided to kidnap the King. He broke into Edward's bedchamber on the night of 16th January 1549. Edward's dog started barking and Seymour shot it dead, so alerting the household. Although Seymour fled, he was arrested the next day at Seymour Place.

It was not hard for the Privy Council to gather evidence against him. Finally, Lady Jane's parents took action and whisked their daughter away from his home and back to Bradgate, and then they did all they could to distance themselves from the schemer. Henry gave the Council all the evidence he had, exonerating himself in the process. It must have been a huge relief that no further action was taken against him. Others were also forthcoming with information and, as Seymour had hardly been discreet, his treason was all too obvious. He was convicted by an Act of Attainder, which meant that there was no need for a trial. Thomas Seymour was beheaded on Tower Hill on 20th March 1549.

Return to Bradgate

As Jane settled back into life with her family again, she must have been suffering from a mixture of grief and shock. Her pain at the loss of her surrogate mother had not had long to heal, and was followed within months by her abrupt and unanticipated departure from London which was not cushioned for her by any warning beforehand. Then, the shocking and gruesome death of a man she was fond of, a substitute father figure for her.

Little had changed at Bradgate in the nearly two years she had been away. It was Jane herself who had changed, as she and her family would gradually find out. She had returned without the glittering marriage her parents had been looking for but, as far as that was concerned, they were were quick to retrieve the situation. For the moment, marriage with the King looked like a very distant prospect and so instead they agreed to an alliance with the eldest son of the most powerful man in the land, the Lord Protector, Edward Seymour, Duke of Somerset. He was another Edward, the Earl of Hertford, a little younger than Jane and an intelligent and attractive lad. However, it was not long before the arrangement would prove to be not so advantageous as it had first appeared.

BACKGROUND. ENGLAND UNDER THE DUKE OF SOMERSET 1547–1549

Religious changes

The new reign brought together evangelicals in power who could move the Reformation forward. The head of the Church, Archbishop Thomas Cranmer, the head of state, Edward Seymour, Lord Protector, and the titular head of state, King Edward VI, by personal conviction were all wanting to build on Thomas Cromwell's foundations and take things on from where they had stalled in 1539. Even so, they faced significant problems and could only proceed very cautiously and cannily. The majority of the bishops were Catholics, as were most of the nobility and landed gentry. That caused difficulties within the Church, but especially within Parliament, where it was problematic to get legislation through the House of Lords. There was also resistance to further religious change throughout the country. Whilst there were those with strongly held views for either traditional Catholicism or the new evangelicalism, there were many in the middle, the mostly silent majority, and some were confused and most were feeling that they had seen enough religious changes and wanted no more threats to the old, familiar, established order of things.

The first Parliament of the reign met in the autumn of 1547 and repealed the Act of Six Articles of 1539 as well as all the other treason and heresy legislation from previous reigns, so bringing in freedom from the dreadful burnings of the past. In the first two years of Somerset's regime, all restrictions on printing, reading and teaching from the Bible were lifted, the removal of all images remaining in any church or chapel was ordered, and the clergy were allowed to marry.

Now that England was free from persecution, it became a haven for Continental Reformers. Men of the calibre of Martin Bucer, Peter Martyr and John à Lasco arrived to settle, along with many others. They began to influence theological thought, especially that of Cranmer. Most were doctrinally aligned with the Swiss Reformer, Ulrich Zwingli. Cranmer's own theology was gradually changing. Naturally a moderate man, and wanting to hold the Church together, his prayer book of

1549 was revolutionary in that it was in English, but otherwise it was a compromise. It was a move in the direction of Protestantism but with the intention that Catholics would be helped to accept it too. In fact, some passages could be interpreted in very different ways by those holding opposite doctrines. The Bishop of Winchester, Stephen Gardiner, was by now imprisoned in the Tower for resisting change in the Church, and he provocatively announced that he was ready to use it – certainly not a commendation that Cranmer had wanted. The new Book of Common Prayer was the only form of service allowed. Non-compliance was dealt with by fines or imprisonment for clergy, but no longer by execution.

Rebellion

Despite its weaknesses, the Prayer Book caused problems. There was an uprising in Devon and Cornwall in the summer of 1549 demanding its withdrawal and a return to the old faith. There were other regional disturbances but the most dangerous was Kett's rebellion in Norfolk. This was a Protestant movement caused by local issues, especially enclosures of common land. At one, time the rebels numbered sixteen thousand, but John Dudley, Earl of Warwick, very effectively and bloodily put down the revolt. By the autumn, the country was calm again.

Somerset's faith in action

In some ways, the Duke of Somerset was a man before his time. He was ruled by his evangelical convictions and he had good, even noble, ideals. He was genuinely concerned for the welfare of the lower classes and he became popular amongst them. They called him the 'Good Duke'. He was strongly opposed to religious persecution and there was less of it while he was in power than in any other part of the Tudor period. Calvin wrote to him to encourage him to advance the cause of Christ. 'I implore you, in the name of God, to apply your principal care and vigilance to this point; that the doctrine of God be preached with an efficacy and power which may produce fruit, and never to rest, under all circumstances, until you have accomplished a full and entire

Reformation of the Church.'[2] One practical example of the outworking of Somerset's faith was during his military campaign against Scotland in 1547, when, as well as fighting, he also distributed Bibles through the Lowlands.

Somerset's weaknesses

Somerset was someone with great strengths but also obvious weaknesses. Sadly, he let himself down by his pride and self-aggrandisement, especially in connection with the grand residence, Somerset House, he was building in London. It did not help that his wife was a woman notorious for her sense of pride, and she clearly influenced him. Several ecclesiastical buildings were removed, including the cloister of St Paul's Cathedral, to provide the site and building materials for this house. John Knox claimed that Somerset became cold towards God's Word and preferred to supervise the building work than to listen to sermons. It was altogether a poor witness to his faith and Somerset's house was seen as a symbol of the greed of the Protestant nobility.

The Protector was labouring under great difficulties which were probably beyond his capabilities to resolve. When Henry VIII died, the nation was in debt (the huge windfall from the dissolution of the monasteries had been blown on the French war) and the religious divide was threatening instability, as was widespread unrest over enclosures in the countryside. Inflation and the plague were also both taking a toll. Somerset's position was weakened by the fact that he was only a nobleman and did not have the authority of a monarch. Worst of all, he gradually lost all the support he had started with. The King turned against him relatively quickly, for he treated Edward as a child, keeping him at arm's length from what was going on. He was high-handed, and frustrated and infuriated the other Privy Councillors. His popularity with the lower orders made them trust him even less and his brother's treason undermined him further, tainting his image with the

---

2   Letter from Calvin to Somerset from Geneva 22nd October 1548 in George Gorham, *Gleanings of a Few Scattered Ears During the Period of Reformation in England of the Times Immediately Succeeding AD 1533 to AD 1588* (London: Bell & Daldy, 1857), p. 61.

cold-blooded execution of his own brother. Thomas's crazy schemes did more than he could have realised to bring down his brother with him.

John Dudley

Someone was watching, quietly waiting for the two brothers to destroy each other, and biding his time to make his move. John Dudley, Earl of Warwick, ambitious and very capable, was a natural plotter and when he had defeated Kett's rebellion, he judged his moment had come. He garnered sufficient support on the Council, and used the kudos he had acquired from his recent exploits, as well as the troops he still had at his disposal, to make his strike. In October 1549, Somerset was arrested and sent to the Tower, but was released in February. He even returned to the Council, but his authority had gone and it was Dudley who was now in control. He became President of the Council, but let the title of Protector drop. He rewarded his supporters with titles and tightened his grasp on power.

John Dudley was certainly not driven by high ideals. He was a highly ambitious and ruthless individual who had steadily risen in influence and authority during the reign of Henry VIII. Handsome, in his forties, and with a strong personality, he was an affectionate family man with five sons, who had already displayed his capabilities as a military commander, administrator and diplomat. Early in his life, he had learnt a hard lesson about the untrustworthiness of princes. His father, Edmund Dudley, a lawyer, had served Henry VII as a financial adviser. He had been very effective, probably too effective for his own good. When his royal master died the new King, Henry VIII, had taken the popular, though unwarranted step, of having him and another hated administrator, Richard Empson, arrested. In an early display of the King's ruthlessness, which would be evident throughout Henry's reign, Dudley was executed when his son, John, was only nine. That had not affected Dudley's loyalty to the crown over the intervening years and he now established a good relationship with his twelve-year-old King. He knew what interested young boys and, crucially, he treated Edward with the respect due to one who was getting old enough to have some involvement in his own government.

JANE THE 'TEENAGER' 1549 -1553

Roger Ascham's visit

In the summer of 1550, Roger Ascham, a Yorkshireman then in his thirties, approached the house at Bradgate Park. He was one of the group of Cambridge scholars who had provided tutors for Prince Edward and the Lady Elizabeth and he was a friend of both Jane's tutor, John Aylmer and Bradgate's chaplain, James Haddon. He was also acquainted with the family. He had known Lady Jane at Chelsea when he had become tutor to Elizabeth while she was living with Katherine Parr. He had also seen Jane several times at court and he thought a lot of her.

As it happened, the Greys were out hunting and Ascham was shown in to the hall where the only member of the family available to see him was sitting. Ascham was so struck by their ensuing conversation that he must have written it down soon afterwards, for he incorporated it into his book, *The Schoolmaster* which was published twenty years later. Jane was absorbed in her book and Ascham was fascinated to see it was Plato's *Phaedo* and her evident enjoyment of it. He asked her why she was not hunting with the rest of her family. She smiled and replied that their sport was only a shadow of the pleasure she found in Plato. 'Alas! Good folk, they never felt what pleasure means.' Ascham asked. 'And how attained you, Madam, to this true knowledge of pleasure? And what did chiefly allure you to it, seeing that few women and not many men have arrived at it?'

Jane responded, 'I will tell you and tell you a truth which perchance you will marvel at. One of the greatest benefits that ever God gave me is that He sent me, with sharp, severe parents, so gentle a schoolmaster. When I am in [the] presence of either father or mother, whether I speak, keep silence, sit, stand or go, eat, drink, be merry or sad, be sewing, playing, dancing or doing anything else, I must do it, as it were, in such weight, measure and number, even as perfectly as God made the world – or else I am so sharply taunted, so cruelly threatened, yea, presented sometimes with pinches, nips, and bobs [blows] and other ways – which I will not name for the honour I bear them – so without measure misordered, that I think myself in hell – till the time comes when I must go to Mr Aylmer, who teacheth me so gently, so pleasantly, with such fair allurements to learning, that I think all the time nothing whiles I am with him. And when I am called from him I fall on weeping, because whatever I do else but learning is full of great trouble, and whole misliking unto me. And thus my book hath been so much my pleasure, and bringeth daily to me more pleasure – and more – that in respect of it, all other pleasures, in very deed, be but trifles and troubles to me.'[3]

In his book, Ascham used this conversation to make the point that learning should be pleasant and that harsh punishments, which were then commonplace, should be avoided. Instead, what stands out now is how an interested enquiry from a friendly person caused Jane to pour out her unhappy tale. If her parents had thought Katherine Parr had been too soft with her, they had certainly made up for lost time since. Parents' standards in those days were very different to ours; they expected total obedience and physical chastisement was normal, but even so, Jane's accusation that nothing she did was ever good enough for them rings concerningly true. The incident laid bare an unhappy state of friction between Jane and her parents.

There is no evidence that Jane was deliberately wilful or rebellious. That would have been against her upbringing and the teaching of the Bible, but as she was growing up she must have been beginning to show her independence of thinking and strength of character, and was probably becoming more outspoken. Just what her parents did not want to see or hear in a daughter. They expected passivity and a docile nature, and were no doubt frustrated that Jane did not fit their mould, and as a result it seems they made her life a misery.

There was most likely a very particular cause of annoyance, which would have inflamed things. Jane's parents loved gambling and members of their household gambled too. Over time their chaplain, James Haddon, persuaded the Greys to forbid their employees to indulge but he could not prevent them from continuing to gamble themselves and so the situation rumbled on. John Aylmer supported

---

3   H. Chapman, *Lady Jane Grey* (London: Jonathan Cape, 1962), p. 47.

Haddon in his stand and almost certainly so did Jane, which would not have gone down well with her parents.

Correspondence with Reformers

Roger Ascham had visited Bradgate on his way to the Continent. He was taking up a post as a diplomat in Germany. It was partly through Ascham but even more through a poor Swiss student, John Ulmer, who had looked for and gained Henry Grey's patronage, that a correspondence began between Jane and some of the leading European Reformers. These included Martin Bucer and also Henry Bullinger, Zwingli's successor as pastor of the church at Zurich. After first addressing themselves to Henry Grey, it was normally Jane who was the one to reply. Her letters to Bullinger spanned a period of over two years. She was deeply conscious of the honour being done her that such a busy and respected Protestant leader should be writing to her personally, advising her and exhorting her 'to embrace a genuine and sincere faith in Christ her Saviour'.[4] She felt free to ask him many questions, including the best way to study Hebrew. Even at such a distance, a friendship began to develop and gifts were exchanged. Jane thanked him for his book, *Decades*: 'From that little volume of pure and unsophisticated religion, which you lately sent to my father and myself, I gather daily, as out of a most beautiful garden, the sweetest flowers'.[5]

Haddon and Aylmer were sending their own letters and took the opportunity to ask Bullinger to write to Jane about some issues which were concerning them, for they felt that some matters were becoming too prominent in her life. Aylmer feared that Jane was becoming too interested in her appearance and was spending too much time practising her music. Would Bullinger tell Jane what was appropriate for a young person professing godliness?

Jane was acquiring quite a reputation for her scholarship. Roger Ascham considered that academically she outshone even his outstanding

---

4   A. Plowden, *Lady Jane Grey: Nine Days Queen* (Stroud: Sutton Publishing, 2003), p. 65.

5   N. Tallis, *Crown of Blood: The Deadly Inheritance of Lady Jane Grey* (London: Michael O'Mara Books Limited, 2017), p .112.

pupil, the Lady Elizabeth, and others felt that she was more gifted than the King. Several of the letters Jane was receiving from abroad were highly complimentary to her, extolling her virtues and gifts in an almost excessive way. Aylmer and Haddon on their part and the other Reformers on theirs, were no doubt truly glad to praise her for her erudition and for evidence of her spiritual life, but there was almost certainly another factor at play. The Continental evangelicals had been struck by the same thought as Thomas Seymour, and indeed by Jane's parents. What an excellent and most suitable bride Jane would make for King Edward. The two young cousins shared the same faith and their union would give England a godly couple to rule the country. Jane's correspondents seemed to think it was a very likely prospect. It appeared to be a common hope in their circles, but in fact, Edward's journals reveal that it was never a possibility. He was expecting to marry a foreign princess as kings normally did, to further the strategic interests of the country, and not to please himself, and he would become betrothed to Elizabeth of France.

For Jane, these letters seem to have been a source of real pleasure, but she must have found it difficult to reconcile the lofty praises of herself that she read in some of them with the continuous criticism from her parents. She had to accept and cope with the two extremes and it is a sign of her growing maturity that she appeared to do so. The difficulties and challenges of her childhood were surely a good preparation for the stern trials that lay ahead. Similarly, her regular reading of the Bible and of Christian books, and the gradual growth of her faith, were laying a solid foundation for the time when she would be called on to react to extraordinary circumstances and to severe testing.

Henry Grey's rewards

In November 1549, with Somerset in the Tower and John Dudley strengthening his hold on power, Henry Grey received his reward for supporting Dudley's coup. He was given a place on the Privy Council. At last he had a position of influence, but he does not seem to have valued it too much as his attendance declined with time.

A more significant elevation came about two years later. In the summer of 1551, the Grey family were shocked to hear of the sudden deaths of Frances's two half-brothers from the sweating sickness. For Jane, it was another reminder of the sometimes swift and unexpected nature of death. The title of the Duke of Suffolk died with the boys, but it was recreated for Frances's husband and, in October, Henry Grey was made Duke of Suffolk in the same ceremony as John Dudley became Duke of Northumberland. Dukes were at the very top of the peerage and there were very few of them. They were only outranked by the royal family themselves. Northumberland was enhancing his power and prestige and Henry Grey was seeing the fruits of his support for him. The Grey family were now spending more time in London and at court, and less at Bradgate.

Royal visit

In November 1551 Jane, now aged fourteen, took her place at a formal court occasion for the first time, when she was present at the visit of Mary of Guise, Regent of Scotland and mother of the young Mary Queen of Scots. Jane, along with her parents, attended a grand dinner and reception at Westminster given in honour of Mary. Neither the Lady Mary nor the Lady Elizabeth were there, and both were very infrequently at court. The Greys seemed to have had little contact with Elizabeth, but had much more to do with Mary, who was a similar age to Frances, and the two were friends.

Incidents with Mary

Mary loved to give gifts and on one occasion she sent a beautiful and elaborate dress as a present to Jane. It was 'of tinsel cloth of gold and velvet, laid on with parchment lace of gold'. As Jane gazed at it thoughtfully, she said, 'What shall I do with it?' 'Marry, wear it to be sure' replied Mrs Ellen, her old nurse. Jane objected, 'Nay, that were a shame to follow my Lady Mary against God's word, and leave my Lady Elizabeth which followeth God's word.'[6] Elizabeth had some time ago adopted a plain, unadorned style of dress. This had won her approval from some Reformers, including John Aylmer. Jane was clearly drawn to the idea of copying Elizabeth, but this was hardly something her parents would have countenanced. Dress was a very important part

6   Chapman, p. 67.

of displaying rank and status, and Jane would be required to look as showy as anybody else at court.

Another incident provides a snapshot of Jane's character and thinking, and it involved the Lady Mary again. Jane's family were staying with Mary at one of her houses at Newhall in Essex. Despite the fact that it was illegal, the mass was still celebrated daily. Jane may well have been struggling to contain her disapproval. At any rate, when the opportunity presented itself, she made her feelings known. One day she was walking through the chapel with one of Mary's ladies, Lady Anne Wharton. The host (the bread) was on the altar and Lady Wharton curtsied to it. Jane asked her what she was doing, 'Why do you do so? Is the Lady Mary in the chapel?' Lady Wharton answered, 'No, Madam. I make my curtsy to Him that made us all.' To which Jane replied, 'Why, how can He be there that made us all, and the baker made Him.'[7] Lady Wharton reported the conversation to her mistress and it is said that Mary never felt the same about Jane again.

In time, Mary would come to play a very significant part in Jane's life. There were others around her who would also make decisions which would decide her future – her cousin the King, her parents, and also a man who Jane both disliked and feared – John Dudley, Duke of Northumberland.

BACKGROUND. ENGLAND UNDER THE DUKE OF NORTHUMBERLAND 1549-1553

Religious changes

The pace of religious change quickened once Northumberland came to power. Some Catholic bishops were imprisoned and deprived of their office for their opposition to reform, including Edmund Bonner, Bishop of London. They were replaced by strong Protestants such as Nicholas Ridley as Bishop of London, and John Hooper, as Bishop of Gloucester and Worcester, which made it easier to make progress. Cranmer found himself pushed to move quicker and further, both by strong Protestant voices from within the Church, such as Hooper and John Knox, and by leading Continental Reformers, especially Martin

7   ibid., p. 72.

Bucer. Northumberland himself pressured Cranmer and pressed for a more strongly Protestant settlement. Some of the changes meant that church property, both land and possessions, could be sold to refill the nation's empty coffers and some sales profited Northumberland and his allies personally. Northumberland knew too that further reform was what the King wanted.

The centrepiece of the Edwardian Reformation was the Prayer Book of 1552. That of 1549, like so many compromises, had ended up being criticised from all sides. Cranmer built on the beauty of his earlier liturgy, and while avoiding the extremes of evangelical doctrines, he made changes which meant that the Anglican Church was now unequivocally Protestant. The mass was finally abolished. The real presence was gone. Instead, there was a communion service, a service of remembrance. 'Take and eat this in remembrance that Christ died for thee, and feed on him in thine heart by faith with thanksgiving.'

The following year, Cranmer's Forty-Two Articles provided a statement of faith for the Church, taking elements from Lutheranism, Calvinism and Zwingliism. With some alterations, they would form the basis of the Church of England's enduring Thirty-Nine Articles, which would be published in Elizabeth's reign.

The changes had brought the Church a long way in five years. They were visible in parish churches and cathedrals. Statues had gone and wall paintings had been covered up, in some places replaced with Bible verses. Stone altars for the sacrifice of the mass were knocked down and, in their stead, communion tables were placed in the body of the church, in the chancel or nave, nearer the people, who were no longer spectators but partook of both the bread and the wine. These were physical reminders that the visual, ritualistic religion of the past, with its emphasis on spiritual magic and mystery, had been replaced by the dominance of the Word, and an entirely new emphasis on the importance of preaching and teaching.

There are glimpses of the impact of Bible exposition on ordinary people. Bishop Hooper wrote to William Cecil, secretary first to Somerset and then to Northumberland: 'You and I, if we should kneel all the days of our life, could not give condign thanks to God for that he hath mercifully inclined the hearts of the people to wish and hunger for the word of God as they do. Doubtless it is a great flock that Christ will save in England.'[8] Scottish preachers met with a good response in northern England, where people were eager for their teaching despite the fact that Catholicism was particularly strong in the north and the Scots were viewed as the enemy. A.G. Dickens, in his classic work on the Reformation, saw this as showing strongly how there was a yearning for religious instruction in a society which had previously been denied sermons.[9] The Emperor Charles V regularly received negative reports from his ambassador about the way the Reformation was influencing the common people and that Protestant preaching was turning them against the Catholic faith.[10]

Catholics were treated mildly throughout the reign but two Anabaptists were put to death. The fact that only two people suffered for their faith, by far the lowest figure for the whole Tudor period, is noteworthy. The term Anabaptist covered a wide range of doctrinal positions, and they were feared at the time partly because of some of their more extreme beliefs, and partly because of concern that they would cause social unrest.

Difficult times

The Duke of Northumberland had to contend with the same difficulties as his predecessor. The country was in desperate financial straits. Inflation and land enclosures were causing real hardship, and the threat of plague was eclipsed by the prevalence of the frightening sweating sickness, which could bring death within hours of the first symptoms. Northumberland was better equipped to tackle these issues. An unpleasant man and a greedy one, he nevertheless had considerable abilities, and he took effective action to bring in financial and administrative reforms.

---

8   Dickens, pp. 334-5.

9   ibid., p. 324.

10   D. MacCulloch, *The Boy King: Edward VI and the Protestant Reformation.* (Los Angeles: University of California Press, 2002), p.108.

The death of Somerset

Northumberland had unfinished business with the Duke of Somerset. He laid his plans carefully over a period of time so that he could remove his rival entirely. Somerset was, after all, the King's uncle and his widespread popularity among the common people made it potentially dangerous to move against him. It was not until October 1551 that Northumberland felt able to arrest him again. Somerset was accused of treason, of plotting to murder the Council and reinstate himself in power. Some witnesses were bribed to give false evidence. The outcome was not in doubt and Somerset was beheaded in January 1552. He died with dignity, affirming his loyalty to Edward and his faith in Christ. There were scenes of near riots as the mob expressed their displeasure at his death.

Northumberland and Mary

Northumberland's other main opponent was the Lady Mary. As an ardent Catholic, Mary fell foul of the changes in the Church early in the reign. She demanded that religion should be left as it was at the time of the death of her father, until Edward should reach his majority and was able to take charge of his kingdom himself. This became a common Catholic stance. She had refused to stop having mass celebrated in her house and the Duke of Somerset had reluctantly given her permission to continue. Northumberland took a much harder line and quickly clashed with her. She was told Somerset's promise was for her and her alone, not for anybody else in her household and was only a temporary arrangement. By 1551, Edward was involved in the ongoing conflict and was writing to her to demand that his laws were obeyed. Mary had hoped that Edward himself might be more lenient with her than his Council, but this communication, followed by a meeting between them in March, shattered that illusion, for the two siblings were on a collision course over religion. It mattered particularly because, although Mary was living quietly, she was Edward's heir and a popular figure with many. Her high profile disobedience could not be countenanced. Northumberland increased the pressure on her and by the end of 1551 Mary had had to give way. Her household were denied the mass and Mary herself could only celebrate illegally, alone and in utmost secrecy.

Edward

Both of Edward's sisters mainly avoided the court, though Elizabeth, as a Protestant had no barriers in her relationship with her brother. Edward was growing up displaying many of the gifts and abilities of his father. He did not have his physical presence or the same athletic prowess, but he was fond of archery and other sports, as well as having an outstanding academic brain. He had a keen interest in the practicalities of government, and a strong desire to take up his destiny as King. Northumberland greatly encouraged him. He spent much time informing Edward about affairs of state in private, treating him with respect but at the same time moulding him to his own viewpoint. He arranged for Edward to attend Council meetings, which he did regularly from 1551. Edward was gradually growing into the role of King, and expected to attain his majority on his sixteenth birthday in October 1553, but before then, it was still Northumberland who wielded all the power.

In the spring of 1552, Edward caught measles. He had always been a healthy boy and had led an active life enjoying plenty of outdoor exercise, but although he appeared to make a good recovery, it was this illness which triggered a fatal decline in his health. There was a susceptibility in the Tudor family to tuberculosis and the teenage boys in the family seemed particularly vulnerable. Edward's half-brother, the illegitimate Duke of Richmond, his uncle, Henry VIII's older brother Arthur, and his cousin, Henry Brandon all succumbed to fatal illness in their teens.

Edward seemed to be back to normal by the end of June when he started his summer progress through Sussex, Hampshire, Wiltshire and Berkshire. It was a strenuous itinerary which took him away for nearly three months, and, coming on top of the measles, it seems to have completely undermined his health. He looked noticeably unwell on his return and as the autumn and winter progressed so did his cough and other symptoms. It was becoming clear that he was seriously ill. Northumberland and the government carried on as usual as if nothing was wrong, but it was obvious to all at court that the King was declining rather than getting any better.

THE SUCCESSION

At the beginning of February, Mary came to London to see her brother. She had to wait three days before he felt well enough to admit her and then he was in bed for her visit. They spoke together in a friendly way but Mary was shocked to find him so ill. The Duke of Northumberland and some of the Council treated her with a new respect, much as if she was the Queen already. The clear inference was that they were accepting that it would not be too long before she succeeded Edward and would be their new monarch.

Edward improved a little in March and opened Parliament, although the Lords and MPs had to go to him, but it was only a temporary respite and his doctors knew that he did not have long to live. Northumberland kept both of his sisters away from court and sent them falsely optimistic accounts of his health. The Imperial ambassador believed that Northumberland's reports showed that he was trying to build bridges with Mary and restore himself in her favour.

For a man of action, Northumberland was moving curiously slowly as Edward's illness developed, almost as if he could not bear to believe it was happening. He had built a strong position for himself. Edward trusted him and was amenable to most of his suggestions. If Northumberland was in control of the King for now, he was also pretty much in total control of the country. This was resented by the Council. There were many, both in and outside of government, who feared as well as disliked and distrusted him, but Northumberland had the upper hand. Clever and devious, with a magnetic personality, he managed and manipulated those around him.

Edward's impending death was a huge blow to Northumberland's prospects. Everything he had built was dependent on Edward continuing as King. He was under no illusions as to what would happen when the crown passed to Mary. He would immediately be removed from power, but more than that, he would almost certainly lose his life. There had been no love lost between him and Mary up to now and she would see to it that he followed earlier fallen leaders, such as Thomas Cromwell and the Duke of Somerset, to the executioner's block.

For the King, the thought of his oldest sister succeeding him was equally appalling. At some stage, he came to realise that he was not going to recover from his illness. For a fifteen-year-old, who had been full of life and promise and with the high calling of fulfilling his role as King of England before him, it must have been very hard to come to terms with. On top of that, knowing that Mary would undo all the work of Reformation so far achieved, would have been devastating. So both Edward and Northumberland had the same desire; to block Mary from becoming Queen. One of them came up with a plan to achieve this, and what one suggested the other accepted and they both worked together to bring it about.

Henry VIII had left a glimmer of a legal loophole. Both his daughters were still officially classed as illegitimate. Normally illegitimacy was a barrier to inheritance, but not necessarily an insuperable one. On the other hand, Henry, in both the Act of Succession of 1544 and in his will, had unequivocably declared Mary, and then Elizabeth, to be his heirs after Edward. The legislation and will combined were legally binding, leaving no possibility that someone could subsequently change anything without further legislation. Henry had been allowed, in what were unique circumstances, to declare his line of succession and no one else, neither his underage son nor the acting head of state, were able to tamper with it.

In the middle of April, Edward left Westminster and moved to Greenwich. He was growing weaker and he was confined inside, still coughing, with a continuous fever and with ulcers starting to break out. According to the Imperial ambassador, what he was coughing up was greenish-yellow and black and sometimes pink, like the colour of blood.

Jane's marriage

At the end of April, Jane's parents told her that she would shortly be married. A betrothal had been arranged between her and Lord Guildford Dudley. Lord Guildford was the youngest son of the Duke of Northumberland and the only one not yet married. Jane was horrified and immediately refused to comply, something which was unheard of in her day. Girls knew they had to obey their parents in accepting whomever they had chosen to be their husband. She clung to the fact that she was still contracted to Edward Seymour, Earl of Hertford, the former Protector's son, and so she was not free to marry elsewhere. Hertford was an attractive young man and was on good terms with the family. He would visit the Greys in London and Frances even called him 'son'. It is very possible Jane had grown fond of him. It is also possible that she was clutching at straws, anything which would prevent her from having to marry Guildford. Jane was highly intelligent and she well knew that her parents would never let her marry Hertford, not once his father had been executed and the family were disgraced, with his mother imprisoned and their property confiscated. Jane probably did not know Guildford very well. He was seventeen or eighteen, handsome like the rest of his family and she may have disliked him. He was his mother's favourite and reputed to have been spoilt, but for her to stand up to her parents in the way that she did indicates strong emotions were involved, and at least part of that may have been her intense dislike and fear of Guildford's father, the Duke of Northumberland. Her parents demanded obedience and, when she resisted, they swore at her and beat her until she gave in.

Jane's was not the only marriage which had been arranged. Northumberland had conceived a little web of alliances. Jane's twelve-year-old sister, Katherine, was to marry Lord Herbert, son and heir to the Earl of Pembroke, and Northumberland's daughter, Katherine Dudley, was betrothed to Lord Hastings, the eldest son of the Earl of Huntingdon. Henry Grey had long been a supporter of Northumberland, and the Duke was looking to strengthen their joint ties with key nobility at this critical time.

On 25th May 1553, all three couples were married in a triple wedding at one of Northumberland's London residences, Durham House on the Strand, a grand house with gardens stretching down to the Thames. The King had ordered that the royal wardrobe should be used to provide magnificent clothes for the main participants, including cloth of gold and of silver. The King sent Jane presents of fine jewellery. She and Katherine arrived by barge. Jane was wearing gold and silver brocade decorated with diamonds and pearls, and her hair was flowing loose with pearls plaited into it. After the service there was feasting and entertainment on a grand scale. Some of the effect of this elaborate spectacle was lost when several of the guests, including Guildford himself, were stricken with food poisoning. Many of the Council were there but neither Mary nor Elizabeth had been invited. It had been announced that the King would be present, but his condition was far too serious for him to leave Greenwich.

At the end of May, it was thought that Edward had only weeks to live, and around the 11th June, his doctors believed his death was imminent. Time was of the essence and, at some point, his doctors were dismissed and a woman installed who promised to cure him providing that she had sole charge of him. The medicines she provided did indeed bring a temporary improvement but at a dreadful cost. They probably contained arsenic and soon only added to Edward's sufferings.

Edward's Device for the Succession

For Northumberland, it was essential that Edward lingered a little longer. Edward had drawn up a document, called a Device for the Succession. He excluded both his sisters and initially left the crown to Lady Frances Grey's male heirs, and then to Lady Jane's male heirs. As his condition deteriorated and time became more pressing, he altered the wording, leaving the crown to Lady Jane's male heirs and, finally, he changed it again to Lady Jane and her male heirs. In other words, directly to Jane.

Edward had his reasons to obstruct Mary's claim to the crown, but why did he remove Elizabeth too? He had always had a good relationship with her and she was a firm Protestant. Possibly it proved too difficult to remove Mary without treating Elizabeth in the same way. Certainly, Northumberland would have had his own reasons for excluding Elizabeth. He could not possibly control her in the same way as he expected to control Lady Jane. At nineteen, Elizabeth was much older than her fifteen-year-old cousin and had already proved herself a particularly shrewd and capable young lady, able to withstand pressure from others. Predictably, the official reason the Device gave was that Mary and Elizabeth were illegitimate. They were only of the half blood.

It also added that if either married a foreigner he 'would tend to the utter subversion of the commonwealth of this our realm'.[11]

Edward's Device was written in his own hand and clearly marks the downward trend of his expectations. His first intention was to stick out for a male successor and to give the widest possible chance for that to happen by plumping for a boy which Frances Grey, still in her thirties, might yet have, followed by boys who might be born to Jane, then to Katherine, and then to Mary Grey. As the possibility of his death became more real, then his sights were lowered to those who were actually alive rather than might theoretically be born in the future. That meant there had to be a female succession and he chose Jane in preference to her mother, who would normally have had precedence over her. Henry and Frances Grey would logically have been the first to be told what was afoot and there is no evidence that they had any qualms in depriving Frances's cousin and friend, the Lady Mary, of her crown, or in accepting it for their daughter Jane. They certainly did nothing to prepare her by warning her of what lay ahead.

Time was running out. On June 11th, the day that his doctors reported that the King might die at any moment, the Lord Chief Justice, Edward Montague, the Solicitor General and the Attorney General were summoned to meet with Edward in his bedchamber at the Palace at Greenwich the next day. There, Edward told them about his plans for the succession and they were presented with the Device and told to speedily turn it into a legal document. The lawyers read it with concern and with Edward Montague as their spokesman, explained that turning the Device into a deed of settlement would not make it legal without an Act of Parliament. Edward rallied himself to order them to proceed, for he would not hear of any objections.

The judges examined the Device more fully back in London and agreed that it was illegal. They then appeared before the Privy Council and explained that they could not obey the King's instructions and that to do so would be treason. It would also be treason to implement the Device after the King's death. Northumberland was not present at the time but, shortly afterwards, he burst into the Council Chamber

---

11   Chapman, p. 91.

in a great rage, and threatening physical violence, quite terrifying the lawyers. On the 15th, they faced Edward again and he spoke to them sharply and angrily, asking why his commands had not been carried out, and ordering them to do so, adding that Parliament would be called immediately. Thoroughly frightened, the lawyers gave in.

By the end of June, everybody who mattered had signed Edward's will. There were over a hundred names starting with the Lord Chancellor, Privy Councillors, over twenty peers, Officers of the Household, Secretaries of State, the Lord Mayor of London, judges, bishops and more. No doubt the lawyers were not the only ones with strong reservations and who were intimidated and frightened by Northumberland. Many must have doubted the legality of what was asked of them, but it was hard to stand against the express demand of the sovereign.

Archbishop Cranmer had insisted on a private audience with his godson the King before he would sign, although it was not granted. Edward forcefully insisted he must add his name, and satisfied that it really was what the King wanted and that he would not be able to persuade him out of it, Cranmer reluctantly agreed. No one besides the signatories knew what Edward's will contained and its contents were kept secret as far as was practical. Still, Northumberland was not satisfied. If many of the Council did not trust him, he in his turn did not trust the Council. He presented the Councillors with another document for signature, in which they promised to support Jane as Queen 'to the uttermost of their power, and never at any time to swerve from it'.

Northumberland was still publicly pretending that Edward would recover but that had long ago been seen through. Rumours abounded in London that Edward was dying and even that Northumberland was poisoning him – uncomfortably near to the mark for the Duke. Northumberland was deeply unpopular. Many of those who knew him were frightened of him and of his terrible rages, which he used to impose his will on others.

The ambassadors of France and of the Emperor, Charles V were keenly watching to see how the situation was developing. The Imperial ambassadors had long suspected that there would be a conspiracy against Mary. By the end of May, they were warning Charles that the Duke would prevent Mary from succeeding and was ready to fight against her, bolstered by an agreement that France would offer help. Mary was duly warned to be on her guard and not to trust Northumberland's friendly advances and apparent acceptance of her as the Queen-in-waiting.

Jane's ignorance

The person who was kept in ignorance of developments was Jane. She had returned home to her parents immediately after her wedding and so for a short time she continued in her old way of life, before joining her husband and his family at Durham Place. She had not been there long before she fell ill, very possibly stress-related physical symptoms. In her distress, and unaware of how vital she was to their plans, Jane began to suspect that she was being poisoned by the Dudleys. Accompanied by her mother, she moved out to the Manor at Chelsea, where she had once lived with Katherine Parr, to recover in its peaceful surroundings.

At some stage the Duchess of Northumberland, no doubt impatient and concerned that Jane was unaware of her situation, took matters into her own hands and told Jane that she needed to be prepared for the King's death because he had named her as his successor. Jane found it impossible to cope with such a blunt and unexpected announcement and refused to believe that it could be true: 'Which words being spoken to me thus unexpectedly, put me in great perturbation and greatly disturbed my mind – as yet soon after they oppressed me much more. But I, making little account of these words, delayed to go from my mother.'[12] At long last she had been warned but she could not, or would not, take it in.

Edward's death

Meanwhile Edward's life was drawing to a close, though not quickly enough for those close to him who had to watch his intense suffering. His good friend, Henry Sidney, was in regular attendance on him. Physically, Edward was in a truly pitiable state. His body was covered

---

12   ibid., p. 96.

in many bedsores and ulcers, and his stomach was greatly swollen. He continued to cough constantly and to vomit frequently, and was in much pain. Edward's toes and fingers had become gangrenous, and his hair and nails were falling out.

The afternoon of Thursday 6th July was stormy. Edward woke up about three o'clock and feebly prayed aloud: 'Lord, Thou knowest how happy I shall be may I live with Thee for ever, yet would I might live and be well for Thine elect's sake.'[13] Soon afterwards, he dropped back to sleep and woke again about three hours later. His doctors were there and Henry Sidney. As the thunder and lightning continued to crash and light up the sky, Sidney held Edward in his arms. 'I am faint,' he managed to say and then, 'Lord have mercy upon me. Take my spirit.'[14] Shortly afterwards, he died.

Edward's life had begun with such high hopes. He had been 'England's Treasure' and showed great promise, but he did not have the chance to fulfil it. He had personally championed the cause of religious reform and of the gospel, which meant so much to him, but what would happen now?

JANE THE QUEEN

For Northumberland, the most immediate things which needed to be done were to keep the King's death secret and to capture the Lady Mary. The first was easier to achieve than the second. Timing was everything. Northumberland felt he could not move against Mary too soon, but he had wanted to have her – and Elizabeth – in his grasp before the King died. Around the 4th July, they were both sent an urgent message to go to the King immediately as he was dying. Both were very wary, but whilst Elizabeth took to her bed claiming to be too ill to travel, Mary let concern for her brother overtake her caution. She set off for Greenwich from her home at Hunsdon in Hertfordshire. At Hoddesdon on the evening of the 6th July, she was stopped by a man, probably sent by Sir Nicholas Throckmorton, a courtier and government official,

---

13   A. Weir, *Children of England,* p. 153.

14   N.A. Woychuk, *The British Josiah: Edward VI the Most Godly King of England* (St Louis SMF Press, 2001), p. 107.

who warned her that she was riding into a trap. Mary had to make a momentous decision and she did it quickly. Turning around, she started for her stronghold of Kenninghall in Norfolk, riding into the night with only six gentlemen of her household with her for protection. Mary was a major landowner in the area, in Suffolk and Essex as well as Norfolk. She was very well known throughout the region and would have much support there. As yet, her thoughts were of evading her immediate danger and of her crown, but if she needed to escape the country she was fleeing towards the coast and the safety of the Spanish Netherlands.

Friday 7th July [15]

The following morning, one of Northumberland's sons, Robert Dudley, left to capture Mary at the head of three hundred horsemen, but when he reached Hunsdon he found that she was gone, and he set off in pursuit.

Northumberland began quietly to implement his plans. He had the fortifications at the Tower strengthened and the ports were closed. The Palace Guard were told of Edward's death and will, and they swore allegiance to Queen Jane. Nothumberland's grip on power seemed to be complete. His son Robert was on his way to take Mary prisoner, a woman alone and defenceless. Everything else was under Northumberland's control – the Council and the machinery of government, the Royal Guard, the Navy, and the most powerful of all the fortresses in the land, the Tower, which was also the country's armoury.

That night, Mary stayed at Sawston Hall near Cambridge. Its owner, John Huddlestone, was a Catholic and he arranged for mass to be celebrated in her presence.

Saturday 8th July

The next morning, Huddlestone set off with Mary for the next stage of her journey, but, looking back, they could see smoke rising as the house had been set ablaze. Some Protestants from Cambridge had heard of

---

15   There is some discrepancy about exactly which day things happened during Jane's reign, simply because the original sources differ from each other. To give a clear and coherent description of this time, I have carefully pieced together what I think is the most likely and consistent order of events.

Mary's presence and had torched the house. Mary reassured her host that when she was Queen she would build him a better one.

Back in London, Northumberland was making his next moves. The Lord Mayor, some aldermen and leading merchants were summoned to Greenwich and officially informed of Edward's death and his provision for the succession. They were then sworn to secrecy.

The Achilles heel in Northumberland's arrangements could have been Mary's relationship with the Emperor Charles V – if Charles decided to intervene on Mary's behalf and England found herself invaded by the mighty Hapsburg Empire. To counterbalance this threat, Northumberland had been cultivating his connections with France. If Northumberland could have seen the dispatches leaving the Imperial embassy that day he would have been greatly relieved. A report was sent to Charles V telling him that Mary's situation was hopeless. All the forces of the country were controlled by Northumberland. It would be impossible for Mary to raise sufficient men to oppose him. There was also an urgent message for Mary. All her adult, life Mary had been supported and advised by her cousin Charles and his representatives. Now, those representatives were urging her to give in and submit to Northumberland.

Mary herself was encouraged that day as she received a warm reception at Bury St Edmunds. She spent the night at Euston Hall, near Thetford. A messenger caught up with her there, from Sir Nicholas Throckmorton, informing her of her brother's death. Mary was very surprised and suspicious. Why should he be helping her? She suspected that Northumberland might be trying to entice her to proclaim herself Queen while Edward was still alive and so to commit treason. She would not believe the message until it was corroborated.

Sunday 9th July

There were plenty of rumours swirling about, but up to now Northumberland had mainly managed to keep the King's death a secret. Despite the fact that he had not yet captured Mary, he felt now was the time to present the country with their new Queen. That Sunday the first public intimation of events was given by the Bishop of London, Nicholas Ridley. At the request of the Council he preached at

St Paul's Cross, speaking of both Mary and Elizabeth as bastards, and he especially warned against Mary as she was a Papist. If she became Queen, she would allow foreigners to influence the country and she would oppose true religion. His discourse was badly received, and the crowd were loud in their disapproval.

Mary had received more messages that day, none of them encouraging. She was warned that Robert Dudley was close behind her and also that Norwich had closed its gates against her. Then the courier from the Imperial ambassadors reached her. Their message confirmed that Edward had died, but also warned her that she could not hope to defeat Northumberland and neither could she escape to the Continent, because her route was cut off by several government ships patrolling off the Suffolk coast. They advised her to negotiate with Northumberland while she still had the opportunity.

That day, Jane was still recovering in the peaceful surroundings of Chelsea. In the afternoon she received an unexpected visitor, Mary Sidney, wife of Henry Sidney and one of Northumberland's daughters. Mary told Jane she had come to fetch her as she was expected at Syon, a former convent on the Thames, now converted into a grand house which was owned by Northumberland. Jane said that she was too unwell to go, but Mary emphasised gravely and firmly that it was necessary for her to come and they took to the waiting barge.

When they arrived at Syon, there was no one to greet them and they were shown into a room to wait. They were joined there by Northumberland and some Privy Councillors. The Earls of Huntingdon and Pembroke spoke with Jane at length and she became increasingly uncomfortable, for they were speaking to her with a respect which was far from appropriate for her position. Embarrassed and very confused, the truth did not begin to dawn on her even when they knelt to kiss her hand. They then all proceeded to the Chamber of State where an elaborate set piece was staged. A group were waiting for them each standing in strict order of precedence – her parents, Guildford, the Duchess of Northumberland and Lady Northampton and other nobility. Northumberland led Jane to stand alone under a canopy of estate facing the gathering of distinguished figures. She was becoming ever more disturbed and frightened and was starting to tremble. Northumberland now stepped forward to declare that the King had died and to express his own grief and that of the nation. The room was silent as he went on to explain how Edward had ordered the succession; that he had disinherited both his sisters. It was within his power to do so, and because of their illegitimacy, he had had good reason. 'His Majesty hath named Your Grace as the heir to the crown of England. Your sisters will succeed you in the case of your default of issue.'[16] He assured her that this declaration had been approved by the establishment; the Privy Council, the Judiciary and most of the peers. The crown was unquestionably hers by right. As he finished, all knelt before her.

Jane was struggling to cope both with her grief at the sudden announcement of her cousin's death and to take in Northumberland's shocking declaration. She was overwhelmed and slumped to the ground as she fainted. When she came to no one had moved to help her, and then, in great distress, she began to cry. When at length she had calmed and collected herself, she said clearly, 'The crown is not my right and pleases me not. The Lady Mary is the rightful heir.'[17] It was her listeners' turn to be dismayed and shocked, and they were not slow to respond. First, an angry Northumberland, then her parents demanding her compliance and then her husband cajoling and pleading, all combined to use every means to persuade her to accept the crown, but Jane was immovable. Then, whilst all were impatiently watching, she prayed for guidance. How could she know God's will? It came into her mind that she knew it was right to obey her parents and if so and they were demanding her obedience to them, then she should accept the crown as they were ordering her to do. On her knees she prayed aloud, 'humbly praying and beseeching'. She said, 'If what hath been given to me is lawfully mine, may Thy Divine Majesty grant me such spirit and grace that I may govern to thy glory and service, to the advantage of this realm.'[18]

---

16   Chapman, p. 105.

17   Tallis, p. 152.

18   Chapman, pp. 106-7.

Those watching sighed with relief and came forward each in turn to kiss her hand and swear allegiance even to the death. Inwardly though, Jane felt no relief. Almost as soon as she had made her decision, she felt that it was wrong. She should not have accepted the crown, for it was not hers but Mary's, but she had. The reign of Queen Jane had begun.

When Mary reached her destination, her house next to the old castle at Kenninghall, she received another message about Edward's death and there could be no room for doubt now. Mary did not waste any time. She conferred with her leading officials and then gathered her whole household together, and proclaimed herself Queen, which was met with loud cheering.

Mary was not planning to flee any further or to wait to see if Charles V would send help. She was challenging Northumberland and the Privy Council. She and her staff began to produce the first of a stream of letters. The most important was to the Council itself, writing to them as their Queen and demanding that they proclaimed her as such. She expressed dignified surprise that she had not been officially informed of her brother's death. Her letter was copied and sent throughout the country to men of influence and to towns and to the shires, ordering them to proclaim her Queen. Many other letters were dispatched, appealing for help and urging men to come to swear allegiance to her. Mary had been warned by the Imperial embassy that Edward was dying, and while she waited she had had time to decide what to do when the crisis came. Despite the instructions now coming from the ambassadors, she was fixed in her purpose, and had made careful plans to bring out all the support she could muster and as speedily as possible.

As yet unaware that there were two Queens in the land, Northumberland had arranged for the first public acts of the new reign to take place the next day. The official announcement of Edward's death would be followed by the proclamation of Jane as Queen. She would enter the Tower, the traditional place where the sovereign stayed before their coronation. Jane's was being hastily arranged and in the meantime the royal apartments had been prepared to receive her.

Monday 10th July

At last, Edward's death was officially announced. At seven o'clock in the morning, royal heralds declared the news in the traditional proclamation places in London, and immediately followed it up with the proclamation of Jane as Queen. That was largely met with stunned silence. She was not the Queen people were expecting. To hide the strangely quiet atmosphere, the heralds produced longer fanfares on their trumpets. At midday, Jane was again proclaimed at Westminster, St Paul's and the Tower and at Cheapside at seven in the evening, all with the same lack of response. Criers at street corners gave some explanation, that the Lady Mary and also the Lady Elizabeth were illegitimate and could not succeed to the throne. Additionally, that Lady Mary might marry a foreigner and cause trouble in the kingdom, and she might try to introduce popery.

Early in the afternoon, in bright sunshine, a procession of state barges carrying Jane and her party were rowed to the Tower. The splendid clothes and jewels flashing in the sunlight would have made a grand spectacle for the crowds who had turned out to watch them pass. Jane was wearing the Tudor colours of green and white, though she had to wear chopines, a type of wooden clog, under her shoes in an attempt to give her extra height. Guildford beside her looked suitably regal in white and gold. All was quiet, eerily quiet. No cheers for the new sovereign. None of the normal noisy and exuberant welcome; just a curious and wary watching. Many would have been shocked and dismayed, and probably apprehensive. Everyone knew the Ladies Mary and Elizabeth, and that Mary had been Edward's heir, but Jane was hardly known at all and the fact that she was daughter-in-law to the hated Northumberland was hardly a recommendation.

As they disembarked at the Tower wharf, the silence was broken by a loud welcome, a salvo from the guns. Frances Gray stepped forward to carry her daughter's train, and, to many observers, that too struck a sour note. A mother should not be subservient to her daughter and, in fact, if Jane's mother was living, why was it that the daughter was proclaimed Queen and not her mother?

A Genoese merchant was in the crowd and he watched as Jane walked up to the Tower. He left a description of what he saw: 'Today I saw Lady Jane Grey walking in a grand procession to the Tower. She is now called Queen, but is not popular, for the hearts of the people are with Mary, the Spanish Queen's daughter. This Jane is very short and thin, but prettily shaped and graceful. She has small features and a well-made nose, the mouth flexible and the lips red. The eyebrows are arched and darker than her hair which is nearly red. Her eyes are sparkling and reddish brown in colour. I stood so near her grace that I noticed her colour was good but freckled. When she smiled she showed her teeth, which are white and sharp. In all a gracious and animated figure. She wore a dress of green velvet stamped with gold, with large sleeves. Her headdress was a white coif with many jewels. She walked under a canopy, her mother carrying her long train, and her husband Guildford walking by her, dressed all in white and gold, a very tall strong boy, who paid her much attention. The new Queen was mounted on very high chopines to make her look much taller, which were concealed by her robes, as she is very small and short. Many ladies followed, with noblemen.'[19]

Once inside the Tower, Jane and her family settled into the royal apartments and there she was visited by one of the Council, the Marquess of Winchester, who was the Lord Treasurer. He brought with him a collection of royal jewellery including the crown, which he displayed before her. She had not asked for them and was horrified when he wanted her to take the crown. Although he pressed her and encouraged her to try it on to see if it became her, Jane adamantly refused. The crown was a symbol of kingship, an object of reverence for what it stood for, the authority vested in a monarch by God. It was not to be tried on lightly. Eventually, Winchester persuaded her to let him put it on her to see if it fitted. He added that another crown would be made for Guildford.

It was then, that sickeningly, the reality of Jane's situation hit her. All the deference being shown to her was illusory. If Guildford was to be crowned as King, at the very best he would be sharing equal

_____

19   A. Plowden, *Lady Jane Grey* p. ix.

authority with her, but more likely, real power would rest with him. She had been used to advance him and his father. She was the one who had a claim to be Queen, but he had absolutely none to be King. Jane was having none of it, but she would wait before she responded.

There was business to attend to. Jane signed her accession proclamation, which was immediately printed and posted up all over the capital and all over the country in succeeding days. Jane also signed a letter which would be sent to local officials throughout the country. It informed them that she had rightly taken possession of the kingdom in accordance with Edward's will. She was supported by most of the nobles, all of the Council, and by judges and other important people. They were to defend her just title.

After the momentous events of the day, the main participants were seated at a banquet when a messenger was shown in. He bore a bombshell – Mary's letter from Kenninghall. Not only was Mary still at liberty but, far from being a frightened fugitive, she was defying them and in a letter written with regal authority, was claiming the crown as her own. While the men digested the disturbing news, the two Duchesses, the Duchess of Northumberland, and Jane's mother, the Duchess of Suffolk, both gave way to their emotions and began to cry.

When the meal was over, the Council came together to frame their reply. Mary had carefully provided them with an opportunity to reconsider their position, with a conciliatory note in her letter. 'We take all these your doings in gracious part, being also right ready to remit and fully pardon the same freely, to eschew bloodshed and vengeance.'[20] There was nothing conciliatory in the Council's response. They reminded Mary that she was illegitimate and unable to inherit the crown and threatened punishment if she did not submit to them and their 'sovereign lady Queen Jane'. Thirty-two signatures were added. There was now no going back for either side.

Secretary of State and member of the Council, William Cecil, avoided signing. Despite his strong Protestant allegiance, he was trying to put distance between himself and what was going on around him. He had been involved in Nicholas Throckmorton's attempts to contact

---

20   A. Weir, *Children of England*, p. 161.

Mary and, about this time, he and the Earl of Arundel recognised that they had the same misgivings and began to work together on Mary's behalf.

Jane had been thoroughly dismayed by the incident with the crown, but it was not until after the banquet that she had the opportunity to speak to her husband. She told Guildford bluntly that she would make him a Duke but never King. Even if she had been willing to, it would require an act of Parliament. Furiously, Guildford said he would be King and not a Duke: 'I will be made King by you, and by Act of Parliament.'[21] Jane would not relent and Guildford burst into tears and rushed away to find his mother, who normally smoothed his way for him.

Jane sent for the Earls of Arundel and Pembroke and explained to them, 'If the crown belongs to me, I would be content to make my husband a duke. But I will never consent to make him King.'[22] A very angry Duchess of Northumberland arrived back with Guildford and argued with Jane, but Jane would not back down. Eventually, the Duchess and her son swept out, the Duchess declaring that Guildford should not stay with Jane and they would both return to Syon House that night. Jane immediately ordered Pembroke and Arundel to prevent them from leaving the Tower. She could not make her husband and mother-in-law treat her with the respect which was due to her, but she would not have them openly flouting her authority and doing as they pleased. She would not be treated with contempt. Later, she herself summed up her situation. 'And thus was I deceived by the Duke and the Council, and ill-treated by my husband and his mother.'[23]

On the day that she had been proclaimed in her capital, fifteen-year-old Jane had truly assumed the mantle of Queen as far as she was allowed to. She had defied her husband and mother-in-law and, by implication, the mighty Northumberland. She would not make Guildford King and she had given orders to leading members of the Council which had been instantly obeyed.

---

21   Chapman, p. 117.

22   ibid., p. 117.

23   ibid., p. 118.

Meanwhile, the French and Imperial ambassadors were watching from the sidelines. The French ambassador was confident Northumberland would prevail. He wrote describing Guildford as the 'new King'. His rivals in the Imperial embassy were only officially informed of Edward's death that evening. They were expecting to hear at any time that Mary had been captured and they had not replied to her urgent pleas for help. They had received from Mary a copy of her proclamation speech, and they were appalled at her actions, convinced that she could not succeed and that she had only made her situation much worse.

Tuesday 11th July

For Jane, life in the Tower settled into a pattern over the first few days. The Privy Council met in the White Tower in the mornings. Guildford sat at the head of the table, though as ever Northumberland was the dominant force in their deliberations. Jane was not even present. In the afternoon, Winchester and Jane's father, the Duke of Suffolk, informed Jane of the Council's decisions and presented her with documents which needed her signature. Apart from meal times, when they all ate together, Jane spent much of her time in the royal apartments. She still felt unwell and continued to be convinced Northumberland was trying to poison her, even though his power depended upon her life. Maybe she had heard the rumours that he had poisoned Edward. She was surrounded by people in the royal fortress but she must have felt very alone; not consulted or deferred to, a lonely figurehead, Northumberland's puppet Queen, whom he hoped would provide him with a Dudley dynasty.

Jane was responding to events with dignity and great maturity. She had a real sense of her situation. She did not try to involve herself where she could not influence, but over the coming days where she did have opportunity, she acted effectively and on her own initiative. She gave few orders, but when she did it was with authority and she was obeyed. Guildford, by contrast, was enjoying himself. He liked the attention and the trappings of being King. He was addressed as 'Your Grace' and 'Your Excellency' and began to eat in royal state, all alone.

Meanwhile in Norfolk, support was arriving for Mary. Kenninghall was not large enough to accommodate the arrivals and they set up camp around the house.

Wednesday 12th July

The Council ordered the re-issuing of Jane's proclamation in London and throughout the country. The towns and shires were sent another letter, denouncing Mary for pursuing a false claim and encouraging rebellion. Also, for seeking to bring in foreigners to help her, for subverting God's Word and endangering the realm. Northumberland announced that Guildford and Jane's coronation would take place in two weeks' time at Westminster Abbey.

As messengers rode in to the Tower that day, the news was not good. Mary was still at liberty. Robert Dudley had failed to secure her and various noblemen and gentlemen, accompanied by their retainers had joined her at Kenninghall. She had been proclaimed Queen in Cheshire and Devon. The chance to simply remove Mary from the scene and to present a stunned nation with Queen Jane as Queen without a rival, had gone. Mary now had to be defeated by force and quickly before the situation got out of hand. Orders went out to prepare an expedition to capture her and put down the rebellion.

The Spanish ambassadors had not realised Jane had been declared two days previously and were expecting Guildford and Jane to be proclaimed as King and Queen that day. They were ready to accept their rule and to urge the Council to be lenient with Mary. Two official representatives from the Council visited them to warn the Emperor not to interfere in English affairs, and Northumberland's cousin, Sir Henry Dudley, was dispatched to France. It would be alleged he was ready to offer Boulogne and Calais in return for French aid, but more realistically he was probably seeking firm assurances that the French would help if Charles V invaded on Mary's behalf. In fact, Charles had already decided that he would not get involved and told his ambassadors to maintain good relations with Northumberland and to encourage Mary to do nothing. He had completely abandoned her.

Preparations for the advance into Norfolk were proceeding apace. Ten pence a day, unusually high wages, were offered in order to muster sufficient men. Northumberland faced a critical dilemma. Should he go or should he stay? He really needed to be in two places at once. He was the obvious leader for a military force as the most experienced and able soldier. On the other hand, his strong presence was required in London to direct operations and to ensure the Council stayed together and stayed loyal to him and to Queen Jane. It was agreed that the Duke of Suffolk should take command of the expedition, a risky choice because of his lack of military expertise and application, although he was also a natural candidate because he was the most senior nobleman and the one Northumberland trusted the most.

Some of the Council told Jane of her Father's commission and she became very emotional, bursting into tears and declaring that Northumberland must lead the soldiers and her father must stay with her. Once again she spoke with authority and the Councillors returned to Northumberland to inform him of her decision and also to encourage him to go. He was after all the best soldier in the country, and also, because he had already put down Kett's rebellion in Norfolk just four years previously, they told him that his reputation would deter Mary's sympathisers from resisting. Northumberland very reluctantly gave way and went to tell Jane himself.

Mary's support

Mary's support had significantly grown. From gentry, and even noblemen, with retinues of armed and mounted men to common folk armed with whatever they could find, they had come pouring in and the numbers were becoming impressive. Who were they and why had they come? When Mary had chosen to retreat into East Anglia there had been one significant disadvantage. Her natural support base was in the predominantly Catholic areas of the country, in the north and west. London and the south east were the regions where Protestantism was strongest and so Mary was making her stand in a largely Protestant area. A core of the gentry and common folk who flocked to her were Catholic, for there were still significant numbers in the area. Everyone knew that Mary adhered strongly to the old faith and there were many who either wanted, or were content, to return to the mainly Catholic settlement Henry VIII had left. Mary herself deliberately avoided emphasising religion. Instead, the letters sent out by her household focused on the legitimacy of her claim through the act of Parliament and the will her father had left. This was the reason which drew a very disparate collection of people to Kenninghall. Mary had been Edward's heir and despite what the government had told them since Edward's death, most people believed she was his rightful successor. She was Henry VIII's oldest daughter and the crown belonged to her.

Jane's cause was not helped by Northumberland's unpopularity and nowhere was that stronger than in Norfolk, where his role in savagely putting down Kett's rebellion was still very fresh in people's minds. The peasants of Norfolk and Suffolk hated him because of it and also blamed him for the execution of their hero, the 'Good Duke', Protector Somerset.

Much of Mary's support was Protestant. They rallied to her because they thought she was the legitimate Queen. Nicholas Ridley, Bishop of London, was the only prominent Protestant theologian actively to support Jane. Cranmer had been particularly reluctant and had had to be ordered by King Edward before he would accept the King's Device. Other leading Protestants were outspoken in their support of Mary. John Hooper, Bishop of Worcester and Gloucester, urged those in his diocese to rally to her, and he personally rode about persuading people to go, and also arranged for horses to be supplied to her. John Bale, another bishop, also told his flock to help Mary. Sir Peter Carew supported Mary, and although Jane had already been proclaimed in Devon he managed to have proclamations for Mary made at Dartmouth and Newton Abbot. Such men were under no illusions. They knew the danger Mary represented to their faith and the safety of themselves and of their fellow Protestants, but for them the rule of law and obedience to the monarch had to be placed above concerns for the future, even for the future of the Reformation.

Other Protestants were hopeful that Mary would not threaten their religion. Indeed, John Foxe writing in his *Book of Martyrs* recorded that Mary had promised Protestants in Norfolk that she would not change England's religion. Historians have doubted that staunch Catholic Mary would have done so, but it seems clear that local Protestants were promised some form of religious security. It has been plausibly suggested that some of Mary's household or other officers may have caused people to believe so and nothing was done afterwards to correct that false impression.[24]

The time had come to leave Kenninghall and to march twenty miles or so into Suffolk and towards the coast, to another of Mary's properties, Framlingham Castle. It was an impressive Norman fortress and one whose massive stone walls offered expansive views over the surrounding countryside, an excellent defensive site for Mary to use to make her stand and withstand a siege. She found more supporters waiting for her when she arrived. There was also more good news. Earlier, she had sent a message to Norwich for her to be proclaimed there, but it was met with a refusal as they had not yet had Edward's death confirmed. Within hours they had their confirmation and, not only was Mary proclaimed Queen, but the city immediately sent men and weapons to Framlingham.

Thursday 13th July

In London, rumours and uncertainties abounded and vastly inflated numbers of Mary's supporters were circulated. Throughout the day, all-out preparations continued apace to forge an effective fighting force. Northumberland needed to eliminate Mary's growing army before it became too big, but he was hampered by his own lack of preparedness. He had just not expected to be in this position and, like all Tudor governments, he did not have a standing army at his disposal, so he simply could not muster many men in the short time that he had.

In the morning, Northumberland returned to the Tower to address the Council. With all his sons standing beside him, he began by urging that a second company of soldiers should follow speedily to meet up with him at Newmarket. Then, speaking with his usual forcefulness, he betrayed the concerns which were occupying him. Although he had agreed to go, he was deeply suspicious of those he was leaving behind, that with him gone they would not stay true to Jane. He reminded them that, while he and his companions were going out to fight, they

---

24   J. Ridley, *Bloody Mary's Martyrs: The Story of England's Terror* (London: Constable, 2001), p. 45.

were relying on the Council to protect themselves and their families, and to be faithful to their common cause. He urged them not to betray them and he appealed to them to protect Jane, speaking with a rare honesty, 'Yet shall not God count you innocent of our bloods, neither acquit you of the sacred and holy oath of allegiance, made freely by you, to this virtuous lady the Queen's Highness, who, by your own and our enticement, is rather by force placed thereon than by her own seeking and request'.[25] He reminded them that they were serving God's cause, of their promise of allegiance and that they had all signed Edward's will. Possibly, it was Winchester who replied that he should not distrust them for they were all involved together.

After dinner, Northumberland went with his sons, and other leaders, to take his leave of Jane formally and receive her commission. In two days, he had assembled a fighting force of between three and five thousand horse and foot soldiers, together with an impressive train of artillery. These were not vast numbers, but it was an effective unit, well trained, well led, and well organised. Especially once reinforcements had arrived it should have been enough to crush Mary.

Friday 14th July
Northumberland's troops set out early. They headed east for the Cambridge road and as they passed through the village of Shoreditch plenty of people came out to watch them. Northumberland remarked grimly to Lord Grey of Wilton, who was riding beside him, 'Do you see, my Lord, what a conflux of people here is drawn together, to see us march? And yet of all this multitude, not one wisheth us God-speed.'[26] They spent their first night at Ware, where they tried to recruit more men to augment their numbers.

Northumberland had left Suffolk in charge in his absence but he had none of Northumberland's ability or force of character. Jane herself, though still excluded from Council meetings, began to become more involved. One of the first things she did was to write a letter to the Duke of Norfolk, a prisoner in the Tower ever since the closing weeks of Henry VIII's reign. Although he was a leading Catholic, she

25   Chapman, p. 130.

26   ibid., p. 131.

promised to release and restore him in return for his support. Norfolk made no response.

As news came in, fact was mingled with rumours, but it became clear that more counties had proclaimed Mary, including Buckinghamshire. The Council remained outwardly loyal to Jane, but as they waited for news they weighed their options. The Earl of Arundel sent a message to Mary warning her that Northumberland was on his way. In London the first broadsheets supporting Mary were posted up.

Meanwhile, in Suffolk, the action was hotting up. Sir Henry Jerningham was an important member of Mary's household and he had gone to Ipswich to see about the town's defences. He heard that the government's ships had been forced by the weather to abandon their patrolling and had taken shelter, five in the mouth of the River Orwell and one at Yarmouth. He sensed an opportunity and had himself rowed out to the ships. He found that the sailors were mutinous anyway, for they had not been paid, and they needed little persuasion to turn on their officers, and pressure them to transfer their allegiance to Mary. Later, the soldiers from the warships brought the ships' powerful guns ashore and marched to Framlingham to place themselves at Mary's disposal.

As Jane retired that night, she had no way of knowing that the day had been a turning point, the day when the balance of events had swung away from her and over to Mary. Two critical things had happened a few hours apart. Northumberland's control over the Council and his grip on events had been removed as he marched away from London, and the turning of the fleet for Mary had transformed her chances of success.

Saturday 15th July

Northumberland advanced to Cambridge. He was hampered in his progress by the chronic lack of trust between himself and the Privy Council. They were fearful of Northumberland abandoning them and declaring for Mary if things went against him, and he was determined to maintain joint responsibility for actions by requiring the Council to sign all the decisions taken. The resultant delays led to poor morale in his troops and men began to desert. It also gave Mary more time to prepare her defences.

That night, the Council received a demand from him for reinforcements. They took no action and sent only a brief reply. The Earl of Arundel and William Cecil were putting out feelers within the Council, probing to see if they could find support for Mary.

Sunday 16th July

Northumberland spent the day in Cambridge where he heard wild exaggerations about Mary's army – that it was forty thousand strong. He also heard that his warships had declared for Mary. His troops were continuing to desert and again he wrote sharply to the Council demanding reinforcements.

In the Tower, rumours had reached them that Mary had thirty thousand with her at Framlingham. They also heard that more towns were declaring for Mary, including Oxford, and there was growing support for her in the home counties. The news that the warships had defected was a heavy blow. Also seriously disturbing were reports for some of the noblemen on the Council that some of their own tenants were refusing to fight for them against Mary. That evening, the Earl of Pembroke and the Marquess of Winchester both left the Tower and returned to their own houses. They acted independently and without knowing what the other was doing. When Jane was informed, she sent soldiers to bring them back and gave orders that all the gates to the Tower were to be locked and the keys given to her each night by seven o'clock.

Monday 17th July

Northumberland stayed in Cambridge waiting for reinforcements. His men were still deserting and there was no sign of additional troops arriving.

The Spanish ambassadors continued to send gloomy assessments and to advise Charles V against helping Mary. They were aware that Mary was popular and that Northumberland was universally hated, but they felt, even now, that she had no chance of success.

Tuesday 18ᵗʰ July

Most members of the Council gained permission from Jane and her father to leave the Tower to seek support from the French ambassador, though Suffolk was rightly suspicious of them. It was merely a ruse so that they could escape from the confines of the Tower and they had no intention of returning. They gathered at Baynard's Castle, Pembroke's house, where he and Arundel successfully urged their companions to abandon Northumberland and support Mary. They dispatched a letter to Northumberland demanding his surrender and that he disband the army. They then proceeded to St Paul's to give thanks publicly for England's deliverance from Northumberland's treachery, and after that, to try to appease Mary, they ordered mass to be celebrated.

Northumberland reached Bury St Edmunds, only twenty miles from Mary at Framlingham.

Wednesday 19ᵗʰ July

Jane and her parents had no way of knowing what was happening. The lords of the Council had ominously not returned the previous day, and the only members of the Council still in the Tower apart from Suffolk, were Cranmer and John Cheke.

There had been no reply to the letter the Council had sent to Northumberland, and during the afternoon they took decisive action. They informed Suffolk that Jane was no longer Queen, and told the French and Spanish ambassadors that Mary was. They also ordered the Lord Mayor to proclaim Mary as Queen, and between five and six o'clock at Cheapside he did, amidst scenes of wild jubilation. The pent-up anxieties and emotions of the last few days gave way to noisy celebrations. An observer, Henry Machyn, described what he saw. 'There was such a shout of the people that the style of the proclamation could not be heard. All the citizens made great and many fires through all the streets and banqueting also, with all the bells ringing in every parish church, till ten of the clock at night. The inestimable joys of the people cannot be reported.'[27] London was used to exuberant celebrations at the accession of a new monarch, but this was something

---

27   A. Weir, *Children of England*, p. 179.

else. Many of the eyewitness accounts say that they had never seen such scenes before.

That evening, the Earl of Arundel and Sir William Paget rode hard for Framlingham to bring Mary the Great Seal of England and to tell her she was Queen, and proclaimed as such in London. They were to declare the loyalty and allegiance of the Privy Council.

The faint sounds of Londoners rejoicing could be heard in the Tower precincts. Jane was eating her supper beneath the canopy of estate when her father came to break the news. He tore down the canopy and told her she was no longer Queen. 'You must put off your royal robes and be content with a private life.' Jane told him, 'I much more willingly put them off than I put them on. Out of obedience to you and my mother, I have grievously sinned. Now I willingly relinquish the crown. May I not go home?'[28] Suffolk did not answer her. He could hardly tell his daughter that he was just about to abandon her. He immediately went outside to Tower Hill where he loudly proclaimed Mary as Queen, and then he sought refuge in his house at Sheen, leaving Jane alone to face the consequences.

Jane returned to her private apartments and told her ladies what had happened. They were greatly distressed, but she was composed and told them she was very glad that she was no longer Queen. Later, guards were posted at the doors. The change from Queen to prisoner had been seamless.

At Bury St Edmunds, Northumberland had come as close to Mary as he would get. He did not attempt any engagement and later in the day began to fall back to Cambridge. No blood had been – or would be – shed in his campaign. It is probable that his scouts could now inform him of the facts of Mary's situation, rather than the assumptions he would have been working on until then. Not only was he without his badly needed reinforcements, but he would have been told that Mary's army was around ten thousand strong. They were not an ill-disciplined rabble but organised and stiffened by proper soldiers and leaders of some experience, and, above all, they were supported by a powerful

---

28   Chapman, p. 146.

battery of artillery from the warships. He had no choice but to retire and to seek to build up his own strength.

JANE'S IMPRISONMENT

Thursday 20th July

The Marquess of Winchester visited Jane and removed the royal jewels. He also went through all of Jane's and Guildford's personal possessions and left her without even any money to pay for her necessities. Jane was then moved into the Gentleman-Goalers lodgings which overlooked Tower Green and were adjacent to the Beauchamp Tower, where Guildford was detained. Her retinue had been reduced to four: her nurse Mrs Ellen, Mrs Tilney, Lady Throckmorton, who was wife to Sir Nicholas, and a page. The rest were dismissed. Jane was able to keep some books and writing materials, including a Greek New Testament and her prayer book.

That morning, Northumberland was back in Cambridge and there he received the Council's letter and heard about the developments in London. There was only one thing he could do. He went out into the market place and there proclaimed Mary as Queen, throwing his hat in the air and laughing, whilst his tears of grief ran down his face. Most of his troops faded away, some going straight to Framlingham to transfer their allegiance to Mary, others making their way home.

It was early evening before Mary heard that Northumberland had retreated from Bury St Edmunds and that the immediate danger had passed. Then, Arundel and Paget reached her with news of the amazing turn around in London. Finally, the first soldiers arrived from Cambridge, including some of their leaders such as Lord Grey, anxious to change sides as quickly as possible. For Mary, who had expected to have to fight for her crown, it was a glorious moment. She was Queen without bloodshed and by popular acclamation. She took her household into the chapel to give thanks.

Elsewhere, as the news began to spread, many others would have felt relief. The call for support from both Queens throughout the towns and shires of the kingdom had brought responses from simple proclamations of each as Queen to the raising of armed men to go to fight, but the breathtaking speed with which the cause of Queen Jane had been lost, meant that there was no armed struggle; two queens in one country had not brought civil conflict.

Friday 21st July
Northumberland had his sons and a handful of loyal followers with him. They had been detained the previous day until soldiers arrived from Mary to arrest them. These soldiers were led by the Earl of Arundel, who had been sent on from Framlingham to capture his former leader. A week earlier, as Northumberland had prepared to leave London, Arundel had promised him his support come what may.

A few days later, on Tuesday 25th July, Arundel would bring Northumberland and his group into London at dusk and they were met by ugly scenes. Armed men were positioned along the route through the capital to keep the crowds back, and the mounted escort was increased but there was a terrible noise from the crowd and such was their violent emotion that they were near to breaking through the protection around him and Northumberland was in danger of his life.

By then, most men of any importance had travelled in the opposite direction to reach Mary as soon as possible so that they could pledge their loyalty and plead for forgiveness if they had stood against her. On the whole Mary would prove to be remarkably merciful. She was euphoric at the change in her circumstances and did not want to exact revenge. Of all those who had backed Jane only three would pay with their lives, and of those sent to the Tower most would be released by the end of August.

Appeals to Mary
Among those who went to plead with Mary was Frances, Duchess of Suffolk. Mary was gradually travelling towards her capital and Frances caught up with her at Newhall in Essex and was granted an interview. She lay all the blame on Northumberland, even claiming he had tried to poison her husband. Mary assured Frances that she would be lenient with Henry and was as good as her word for, despite his close involvement with Northumberland, he only suffered a token three days' imprisonment in the Tower. There is no record that on this or any

other occasion Frances pleaded for Jane, or even that her parents ever had any further contact with her.

Although Jane could not have known that her parents were not doing anything for her, she realised she had to present her own case to the Queen, and she wrote her a letter. Her life might depend on its contents and on how the Queen received it. It was long and detailed and covered the events from her marriage until the first days of her reign, explaining her thinking and her actions during that time. She wrote with restraint and with dignity, admitting that she had been very wrong to accept the crown. 'Although my fault be such that, but for the goodness and clemency of the Queen, I can have no hope of finding pardon nor in craving forgiveness, having given ear to those who at that time appeared...to be wise, and now have manifested themselves the contrary...neither did it become me to accept (wherefore rightly and justly am I ashamed to ask pardon for such a crime).'[29] Yet she was not fully to blame: 'For whereas I might take upon me that of which I was not worthy, yet no one can ever say either that I sought it...or that I was pleased with it.'[30]

On 3rd August, Mary made her state entry into London. She was accompanied by the Lady Elizabeth and a great company of nobles, and was received by cheering crowds who gave her a rapturous welcome. She made her way to the Tower, where she would stay in the royal apartments. As she arrived, four prisoners were kneeling before her: Stephen Gardiner, former Bishop of Winchester; the Duke of Norfolk, now over eighty; Mary's friend, the Duchess of Somerset, widow of the Lord Protector, and Edward Courtenay, a young man of royal descent who had been there since childhood. They asked the Queen for pardon and, much moved, she ordered their release.

Mary's advisers

Norfolk and Gardiner found themselves reappointed to the Privy Council. Mary could not realistically remove all those on the Council who so recently had worked against her and called her a bastard. She would chastise, imprison and fine some, but she kept most of them in

29   Tallis, p. 205.

30   Chapman, p. 157.

her government and added some of her own household and some who had served on her father's Council. She would never truly trust her Councillors, but someone she trusted far too much and in preference to them, was Simon Renard. Renard, an able and wily political operator, was one of the Emperor Charles V's ambassadors, whose first loyalty was to his master, but whom Mary trusted and looked to to advise her in secret. Northumberland's warnings of foreign influence in English affairs and of a return to the Catholic faith, were to be proved true from the very start of her reign.

Renard vigorously argued that Mary should not be too merciful, and he especially pressed for Jane and Guildford to be put to death, but Mary refused. She had had time to consider Jane's letter and she believed her cousin had written honestly. She had only known of her elevation to the throne at the last moment and had genuinely not wanted to accept. Others bore responsibility, but not Jane, and Mary could not countenance that she be executed. She did assure Renard, though, that Jane would only be ultimately set free with great care.

In the meantime, Jane's imprisonment was not too unpleasant. She was lodged in the house of Nathaniel Partridge, the gentleman-gaoler. Lady Throckmorton had left her service and was replaced by a Mrs Jacob. After the recent turmoil of events, she probably appreciated the quietness and the opportunity to read her New Testament and study in peace. She could walk in the Queen's garden. Nobody was demanding anything of her and, above all, she seems to have received some assurance that her life was not in danger and even, perhaps, that at some time in the future she might ultimately be freed. That would have been a huge relief and she would have been very conscious of Mary's magnanimity.

The end of Northumberland

Northumberland could not hope for similar mercy. He was tried at Westminster Hall on 18th August. Many of the peers present had supported him merely weeks ago, but now they convicted him of high treason and ordered his execution. He had taken the opportunity to speak for Jane, declaring that she had not sought the crown but had been forced to accept it. His execution was delayed for three days while he was given the time to repudiate his Protestant beliefs and return to the Catholic fold. It may have been simply expediency, hoping that Mary would grant him a reprieve, but if so, he was disappointed. On 21st August, at nine in the morning, Jane watched from her window as Northumberland and four other prisoners were led to the chapel of St Peter ad Vincula across Tower Green. They had come to celebrate mass and Northumberland spoke to the congregation before he received the sacrament: 'My masters, I let you all to understand that I do most faithfully believe this is the very right and true way, out of the which true religion you and I have been seduced this sixteen years past, by the false and erroneous preaching of the new preachers, the which is the only cause of the great plagues and vengeance which hath lit upon the whole realm of England, and now likewise worthily fallen upon me and others, for our unfaithfulness. And I do believe the holy Sacrament here present to be most assuredly our Saviour and Redeemer Jesus Christ.'[31]

It was exactly forty-three years since his father had been beheaded on Tower Hill, and the following day, it was Northumberland's turn. His scaffold speech was similar to his words in the chapel but now repeated before about ten thousand. He added that his conversion was genuine and 'if I had had this belief sooner, I had not come to this pass. Take example of me, and forsake this new doctrine betimes.'[32] It was a propaganda coup for the new regime and they would make the most of it.

Jane's reaction to Catholic converts
About a week later, Jane dined downstairs with her gaoler, Master Partridge, and his wife. He had also invited a friend who lived in the Tower precincts and this friend recorded their conversation in a manuscript he was writing, which has survived and is now known as *The Chronicle of Queen Jane and Queen Mary*. Jane sat in the place of honour and seemed at home amongst the company. She commented that 'the Queen's majesty is a merciful princess. I beseech God she may long continue, and send his bountiful grace upon her.' They then began to speak about religion and Jane asked who had preached at St Paul's

31   A. Plowden, *Lady Jane Grey*, p. 120.
32   Chapman, p. 170.

Cross and was mass celebrated in London? She went on to comment on how strange it was that her father-in-law had converted to Catholicism. Someone ventured that perhaps he had hoped to be pardoned, and this provoked a long indignant speech from Jane. 'Pardon! Woe worth him! He hath brought me and our stock in most miserable calamity and misery by his exceeding ambition.' How could he hope for pardon when he had taken up arms against the Queen and was so generally hated and reviled? 'As his life was wicked and full of dissimulation, so was his end thereafter. I pray God, I, nor no friend of mine, die so. Should I, who am young and in my few years, forsake my faith for the love of life? Nay, God forbid!' Jane was incredulous that someone so much older than her, with a limited number of years of life left, should see that life as so sweet that he clung to it 'he did not care how.' 'But God be merciful to us, for he sayeth, Whoso denieth him before men, he will not know him in his Father's kingdom.'[33]

As the words tumbled out, Jane revealed her resentment and hostility towards Northumberland and was scornful that someone who had urged people to support her as Queen to preserve the Protestant faith, could totally change their religion in order to avoid execution and live a little longer.

Sometime during the autumn she heard that Dr Harding, her first tutor and a former chaplain at Bradgate had also turned his back on his former faith and had embraced Catholicism. The news shocked Jane and she wrote him a letter. She held nothing back as she freely expressed herself in page after page of strong and vivid language. She began, 'So oft as I call to mind (dear friend and chosen Brother) the dreadful and fearful sayings of God, that he which layeth hold upon the plough and looketh back again, is not meet for the kingdom of heaven; and on the other side to remember the comfortable words of our Saviour Christ, to all those that forsaking themselves do follow him, I cannot but marvel at thee and lament thy case; that thou, which sometimes wert the lively member of Christ, but now the deformed imp of the devil... my faithful brother, but now a stranger and apostate; yea sometime my

---

33   A. Plowden, *Lady Jane Grey*, p. 122.

stout christian soldier, but now a cowardly runaway.'[34] Some of Jane's words about Harding seem very distasteful to us, such as 'thou seed of Satan' and 'unshamefast paramour of Antichrist' but they would have sounded quite normal to her contemporaries, even from someone as young and well brought up as Jane. They were used to very robust language and name calling in religious debates.

Jane was particularly horrified that he had turned away from what he had taught others: 'Wherefore hast thou instructed others to be strong in Christ, when thou thyself dost now so horribly abuse the testament and law of the Lord...when thou thyself dost rather choose to live miserably (with shame) in this world, than to die gloriously and reign in honour with Christ, to the end of all eternity...How canst thou, having knowledge, or how darest thou neglect the law of the Lord and follow the vain traditions of men? And whereas thou hast been a public professor of his name, become now a defacer of his glory.'

Scorn and contempt were there and also rebuke and warning, encouragement and reminders of the promises of God and of what Harding was spurning. The whole letter is full of scriptural quotes and biblical truth. It is a passionate letter, written from the heart and the dominant note is concern, concern for him and, above all, for his soul:

'Remember the saying of Christ in his gospel, whosoever seeketh to save his life shall lose it, but whosoever will lose it for my sake shall find it; and in another place, whosoever loveth father or mother above me, is not meet for me, for he that will be my disciple, must forsake father and mother, and himself, and take up his cross and follow me...

Last of all, let the lively remembrance of the last day be always before your eyes, remembering the terror that such shall be in at that time, with the runagates and fugitives from Christ, which setting more by the world than by heaven, more by their life, than by him that gave them their life, more by the vanity of a painful breath, than the perfect assurance of eternal salvation, did shrink; yea, did clean fall away from him that never forsook them. And contrariwise, the inestimable joys prepared for them which feared no peril, nor dreading

---

34   N. H. Nicholas, *The Literary Remains of Lady Jane Grey With a Memoir of Her Life* (Harding, Triphook and Lepard, 1825), p. 22.

death, have manfully fought, and victoriously triumphed over all powers of darkness; over hell, death and damnation, through their most redoubted captain Jesus Christ our Saviour, who even now stretcheth out his arms to receive you.'[35]

In this letter and also in her comments about Northumberland's return to Catholicism, Jane was very vocal in criticising those who succumbed to pressure of whatever kind to reject their professed Protestant faith. She was truly shocked that anyone could do so and was very assured that she would not follow suit. Jane saw the issues in sharp clarity. Christ had died and risen again to give eternal life to those who loved Him and had put their faith and trust in Him. They had been saved by God's grace. How could anyone value more years of life on earth above such glorious and certain hope for eternity? It is possible that she was herself being subject to some kind of persuasion to abandon her own beliefs. Some contemporary writers indicated that she was.[36] She may have been an unexpected choice as Queen, but now everyone knew who she was and that she had been placed on the throne as someone with impeccably Protestant credentials. If she recanted, it would be a huge propaganda gift to those bringing Catholicism back to the country.

Mary's coronation and the question of her marriage

Jane would have been aware that, at the end of September, the royal apartments at the Tower were once more occupied as Mary arrived prior to her coronation. On 1st October, Mary was crowned in a long and splendid ceremony at Westminster Abbey. Stephen Gardiner, now her Lord Chancellor as well as the reinstated Bishop of Winchester, officiated. Both on that day and the previous one, which had seen the usual pre-coronation processions, pageants and celebrations, Mary had been loudly cheered by her loyal subjects, but the enthusiasm of this early period of her reign was not to last much longer. It was quickly to founder mainly because of her marriage.

---

35 Nicholas, pp. 22-34.

36 E. Ives, *Lady Jane Grey : A Tudor Mystery* (Chichester: Wiley-Blackwell, 2011), p. 255.

It was necessary for Mary to marry but the choice of a husband was not straightforward, would become highly contentious, and in the end would have a devastating effect on Jane. As a reigning monarch, Mary was expected to marry. A queen was undesirable, but an unmarried one unthinkable, and also Mary needed to produce an heir, although aged thirty-seven there were obvious risks in having a baby. Should she marry within the kingdom or outside of it? The Privy Council, Parliament and her closest advisers urged her to choose an Englishman, and Edward Courtenay, now Earl of Devon, who had royal Plantagenet blood in his veins as the great grandson of Edward IV, was the preferred candidate of most. Mary would not consider him. Renard had proposed a candidate far more to her liking and in her eyes someone far more appropriate, and though Mary hesitated for some weeks, by the end of October she had made up her mind and given her word to Renard. In early November, her decision was made public. She would wed her cousin, Philip of Spain, the son and heir of the Emperor Charles V. A widower of twenty-six who already had a son, Philip had a strong appeal for Mary as part of her mother's family, who she had turned to for support most of her life, and who, like her, were strong Catholics. What she chose not to consider was how unpopular a foreign marriage would be, even though she had everyone around her urging her against it. Most ordinary Englishmen had a strong prejudice against foreigners, and probably the most disliked of all were Spaniards. Fears that England would be taken over by Spaniards and Spanish interests were widespread and some foresaw that war with France might well result. Mary's choice of a husband could hardly have been more unpopular.

Jane's trial

As the days shortened and autumn set in, Jane reached her sixteenth birthday. She might have been living quietly in her lodgings in the Tower but she was not forgotten and certainly not by Renard. He was sure Mary was being far too merciful for her own good and that there had not been enough executions. He had continued to urge Mary that Jane should die and he was at last gratified when she agreed that Jane and Guildford should be brought to trial.

On 14th November, Jane took a barge from the Tower with Guildford, two of his brothers, Ambrose and Harry, and Thomas Cranmer, all to be tried for treason. They knew that there was no doubt that they would be found guilty but also that there was a hope that, like others before them, including John, the oldest of the Dudley brothers, they would not have their sentences carried out. An attempt had been made to humiliate Jane. The normal place for trials of the nobility was at Westminster Hall, but instead her destination was the Guildhall where, along with the other prisoners she was being tried as a commoner. When they disembarked from their barges they faced a mile's walk through the crowded streets of London, with four hundred halberdiers guarding the route. They walked separately and Jane was followed by her two gentlewomen. She was dressed entirely in black – a black gown, a velvet lined cape, and a black French hood. Her little prayer book was hanging from her girdle, and she held another in her hand, which she read from as she walked. The little procession was led by the Chief Gentleman Warder carrying an axe with its edge facing away from the prisoners indicating they had not been convicted.

All five pleaded guilty and their trial was quickly over. They all faced the death penalty and Jane showed no emotion as her sentence was given. She was to be either burnt or beheaded. The edge of the axe was now turned towards the prisoners for their return journey, to show that they were condemned. When Jane reached the Tower her ladies burst into tears and she tried to comfort them and added, 'Remember I am innocent, and did not deserve this sentence. But I should not have accepted the crown.'[37] Even Simon Renard did not believe the sentence would be carried out.

Early winter 1553

While Jane was in prison, in a rather strange turn of events, the rest of her family were at court. Her sisters had been appointed maids of honour to the Queen and her mother was in Mary's favour, even being given precedence over the Lady Elizabeth. Only her father earned the Queen's displeasure by not conforming to the religious changes, but

---

37   Chapman, p. 181 .

shortly after Jane's trial even he was reinstated into his position at court after he had finally confessed the Catholic faith.

Jane had to continue in her confinement with the threat of her sentence hanging over her. She spent much time studying the Bible, and was still able to walk in the garden, even up to Tower Hill. The Lieutenant of the Tower, Sir John Bridges, visited her from time to time and the two developed a friendship. He encouraged her to hope for a pardon and for release in the future. A little while after her trial, Jane was no longer allowed out for exercise, because of growing unrest in the country, but on December 17th, Bridges was allowed to let her resume her walks. As Christmas approached there was no sign of freedom or of removal to a pleasanter location under house arrest. Jane could only wait unaware that outside the Tower events that she had nothing to do with were beginning to simmer, events which would ultimately drag her into their wake. Only months after Mary's triumphant accession, rebellion was afoot.

Wyatt's rebellion

Antagonism towards the marriage and towards Spain was felt among all classes and throughout the country, and rumour and prejudice were fanning the flames of resentment and opposition. The phrase, 'We will have no foreigner for our king.' was heard on many lips. There were increasing public protests against the marriage and the Council became concerned about the possibility of risings against Mary. They were in a state of alert seeking evidence of revolt.

On 26th November, several men met in London to conspire together. Their leader was Sir Thomas Wyatt, a Catholic who had supported Mary in July, but who hated the Spaniards, and his co-conspirators were both Catholics and Protestants. Their stated aim was to prevent Mary's marriage to Philip. Whether they also intended to dethrone Mary and replace her with Elizabeth is unclear.

There was another meeting a month later on 22nd December. Their plan was for four risings in four different parts of the country, which would happen simultaneously and then converge on London. Sir Thomas Wyatt would lead the revolt in his native Kent, Sir Peter Carew and Edward Courtenay would raise Devon, Sir James Crofts would raise the Welsh borders, and Jane's father, the Duke of Suffolk, would lead Leicestershire against the Queen. His motives for such drastic action are unknown. It was a highly risky venture for, although the hope was that there would be large popular support because of the depth of animosity to Mary's marriage, the outcome was very uncertain. Whatever Suffolk hoped to achieve, he displayed total ingratitude for Mary's great generosity towards him in neither executing him nor properly imprisoning him after he had placed his daughter on the throne, and he was being utterly reckless. It was not only his own life which he was putting at stake, but Jane's as well.

The rebellion was planned for March 1554, but in January Sir Peter Carew fell under suspicion and was summoned to London. A warrant was issued for his arrest. When Courtenay heard this he panicked, and revealed everything to Stephen Gardiner, who had become something of a father figure to him when they were both imprisoned in the Tower. Unaware of how much of the plot was known, his fellow conspirators were forced into premature action.

The date for the uprising was brought forward to 25th January. Sir Peter Carew tried to gather his forces in Devon but people were unwilling to follow him without Courtenay, and he ended up fleeing to France. Sir James Crofts similarly failed to find support in the Welsh Marches. Henry Grey was about to leave his home at Sheen for the Midlands when a messenger arrived summoning him to court. He had been betrayed. He was expecting to meet up with the Earl of Huntingdon, who also held estates in Leicestershire and who had apparently agreed to join the conspiracy, but instead, Huntingdon had immediately informed the Council. While the messenger was given refreshments Henry rode off, hurrying north, and met up with his two brothers before he made for Melton Mowbray and Leicester. There, he issued proclamations against the royal marriage but failed to raise support. He went on to Coventry but found Huntingdon had got there first and the city had barred its gates against him. Grey's men began to desert and with Huntingdon on his heels he gave up and went to ground at his nearby manor of Astley. Here he and his brother, John, spent two miserable days hiding in the park before they were captured and taken to the Tower.

The one part of the rebellion which was effective was in Kent. Wyatt raised his standard at Maidstone and quickly acquired a rebel army several thousand strong. He took over Rochester and some royal ships moored in the Medway went over to him, bringing their guns and ammunition. The Duke of Norfolk led a hastily assembled force against him but it crumbled as most went over to the rebels and others deserted. There was little now to hinder Wyatt and prevent him from entering London, and the city was in confusion and uproar. Mary herself refused to leave for safety elsewhere, and with considerable courage, gave a stirring speech at the Guildhall which steadied her supporters and rallied the capital behind her. When Wyatt arrived in London on 7th February, instead of the widespread support he was expecting, he found it ready to resist him and, although he reached Charing Cross and Ludgate, there were only minor skirmishes before he accepted he could not succeed. He surrendered and his hungry and exhausted troops were rounded up.

Aftermath of the rebellion

This time, there was no question of leniency. Mary and her government had had a fright and would show no mercy to those who had rebelled against them. All the rebel leaders and many of their followers would be executed. Jane of course had played no part but, even if her father had not been involved, the rebellion had shown that Mary's hold on power could not be taken for granted and that if there was trouble Jane, along with Elizabeth, could be figureheads for resistance and opposition. Claims have been made that her father proclaimed her again, though these seem to have been unsubstantiated, but even so it was clear that Jane's continued existence had the potential to threaten Mary. She had been proclaimed Queen once and could be again. Now it was not just Renard, but several members of the Council, men such as Pembroke, Winchester and Arundel, who back in July had helped to put Jane on the throne, who urged Mary to execute her.

Jane would have known about the rebellion. She was not cut off from news of the outside world, and it must have filled her with dread.

All her hopes of pardon were based on the situation in the country staying stable and of Mary feeling secure enough to show clemency. Jane was far too intelligent not to realise that the rebellion changed everything, especially as it became more dangerous. Her death sentence hung over her and it could be enforced at very short notice.

Wyatt's rebellion lasted a mere two weeks and that was all the time Jane, at sixteen, full of life and promise, had to adjust her expectations and deal with the prospect of death. She wrote a prayer, very possibly at this time, and in it she revealed her anguish and struggles, as well as her trust in God and in His control of her circumstances. She began,

'O Lord, thou God and father of my life! Hear me, poor and desolate woman, which flyeth unto thee only, in all troubles and miseries. Thou, O Lord, art the only defender and deliverer of those that put their trust in thee; and therefore, I, being defiled with sin, encumbered with affliction, unquieted with troubles, wrapped in cares, overwhelmed with miseries, vexed with temptations...do come unto thee, O merciful Saviour, craving they mercy and help...O merciful God, consider my misery, best known unto thee; and be thou now unto me a strong tower of defence, I humbly require thee. Suffer me not to be tempted above my power, but either be thou a deliverer unto me out of this great misery, or else give me grace patiently to bear thy heavy hand and sharp correction...

I am thy workmanship, created in Christ Jesus; give me grace therefore to tarry thy leisure, and patiently to bear thy works...for thou knowest better what is good for me than I do...arm me I beseech thee, with thy armour, that I may stand fast...that I may refer myself wholly to thy will, abiding thy pleasure, and comforting myself in those troubles that it shall please thee to send me; seeing such troubles be profitable for me, and seeing I am persuaded that it cannot but be well all thou doest.'[38]

John Feckenham

On the 7th February, the day that Wyatt penetrated so far into London before accepting defeat, the decision was taken to execute Lady Jane and Guildford on Friday 9th, and Mary signed the death warrants.

38   Nicholas, pp. 49-51.

Guildford would be executed on Tower Hill, and Jane would have the privilege of a less public death. Like two of Henry VIII's queens, she would be beheaded within the fortress on Tower Green. On Thursday 8th, as the scaffold was being erected in view of Jane's rooms, she received a visitor. Dr John Feckenham was a Catholic priest in his late thirties. He was Mary's personal chaplain as well as Dean of St Paul's and Abbott of Westminster. A kindly, considerate man, Feckenham was also persuasive and an able theologian, and Mary had sent him to convert Jane to Catholicism.

Feckenham began by sympathising with Jane, and she responded that he was welcome if he had come to give her Christian exhortation. They talked at length and Feckenham then broke off and returned to Mary and asked for a three-day stay of execution so that they could talk further. The Queen not only granted his request but told Feckenham that Jane would be reprieved if she became a Catholic. When Feckenham arrived back at the Tower, Jane was not relieved at what he had thought was good news for her. 'Alas! Sir – it was not my desire to prolong my days. As for death, I utterly despise it, and, Her Majesty's pleasure being such, I willingly undergo it.' Feckenham reiterated that she could be reprieved, but she politely though firmly indicated she would not accept. 'You are much deceived if you think I have any desire of longer life, for I assure you, since the time you went from me the time hath been so odious to me that I long for nothing so much as death. Neither did I wish the Queen to be solicited for such a purpose.'[39]

Feckenham then asked her to take part in a public debate with him. Jane was very reluctant, for her remaining time was precious, but eventually she agreed. They met the next day in one of the Tower's chapels. Jane herself wrote an account of it soon afterwards and one of those present also wrote it down. Feckenham asked Jane a series of questions designed to probe and to unsettle her in her doctrine. They covered the main areas of dispute between Protestants and Catholics and he patiently and persistently tried to put Jane on the back foot. Feckenham began with the nature of faith. He tried to lure Jane into

---

39   Chapman, p. 197.

denying justification by faith alone, by adding the necessity of works to faith. He asked if there was nothing else required of a Christian beyond faith in God. Jane replied that we must love God and our neighbour, but only faith justifies. Feckenham quoted St Paul as saying if I have all faith without love it is nothing. Jane's response was, 'True it is, for how can I love him I trust not, nor how can I trust in him whom I love not; faith and love ever agree together, and yet love is comprehended in faith.'

Feckenham stated that, as love for our neighbour is shown by good works, they are needed for salvation and it is not enough to believe. Jane was quick to refute him: 'I deny that, I affirm that faith only saveth. All Christians should follow Christ in doing good works, but they do not lead to salvation – only faith in Christ's blood and his merits.'[40]

Feckenham moved on to the sacraments and the doctrine of the real presence in the mass. How many sacraments are there? Jane replied that there are two: baptism and the Lord's supper. When Feckenham told her that this was wrong as there are seven, Jane asked him, 'By what Scripture find you that?' Feckenham hedged and said they would return to that later and then came to focus on what Jane had referred to as the Lord's supper. Feckenham asked, 'Why, what do you receive in that bread: do you not receive the very body and blood of Christ?' Jane was very clear in her reply, 'No, surely I do not believe so; I think at that supper I receive neither flesh nor blood, but only bread and wine; the which bread when it is broken, and the wine when it is drunk, putteth me in mind how that for my sins the body of Christ was broken, and his blood shed on the cross.' Feckenham persisted. Christ said, 'Take eat, this is my body: can you require any plainer words: doth he not say, that it is his body?' Jane explained Christ was speaking figuratively, as He did when He called himself the vine and the door. She was appalled at the thought of literally eating Him. She asked and answered a question of her own. Where was Christ when He said, 'Take, eat, this is my body?' He was eating at table with His disciples, very much alive, the day before His death and He was speaking only of bread.

---

40   Nicholas, pp. 35-6.

Feckenham challenged her: 'You ground your faith upon such authors as say and unsay both in a breath; and not upon the church, whom ye ought to credit.' Jane disagreed: 'No, I ground my faith on God's word, and not upon the church. For if the church be a good church, the faith of the church must be tried by God's word; and not God's word by the church.'[41]

Although they debated further this was the main part of their discussions and Feckenham had brought them to the centre of their theology. What was it based on? He stood on the teachings of the Catholic Church. That was where the authority for everything he believed and taught came from. Jane took her faith from the Bible, which she treasured as the Word of God and which had brought her to trust in a person – her Saviour, Jesus Christ. There could be no meeting of minds between them. They were separated by a wide gulf and Feckenham accepted now that he could not hope to bridge it.

There were two unusual aspects about their debate. Firstly, it was conducted in a calm atmosphere. The experienced churchman, over twenty years Jane's senior, would have expected to dominate and to triumph in the discussion, but he allowed Jane to speak freely and without interruption. She was able to present the biblical position clearly and at length. Secondly, respect began to grow between them, for however far apart their beliefs were, they could both see that each spoke sincerely and ably. Such respect between religious opponents was a rare occurrence in Reformation England. When they parted, it was on good terms and they did not expect to meet again.

Jane's final preparations

Jane had stood firm and had refused to compromise her faith in order to accept Mary's firm offer of a reprieve. Now, she had to prepare for her death just days away and to steel herself for the ordeal of beheading. She spent much of her time praying, reading her Bible and meditating, but she also had letters to write and she needed to write her scaffold speech. This would require careful thought. It was a rare opportunity for her to speak for herself and to acknowledge publicly that she had done wrong in accepting the crown, but also to balance that by declaring her

41   Ibid., pp. 35-9.

innocence. She would make a second copy, knowing that it would be published after her death.

Jane wrote letters to her father and her sister, Katherine. Henry Grey was brought to the Tower on Saturday 10th. He was unwell and also belatedly suffering agonies of remorse at the part he had played in bringing his oldest daughter to the scaffold. He, too, was living in the shadow of death and would be executed on Tower Hill on 21st February, just eleven days after Jane, where he would affirm his true Protestant allegiance.

Jane began her letter to him in typical blunt and honest fashion. 'Father, although it hath pleased God to hasten my death by you, by whom my life should rather have been lengthened,' but that was as far as she went, and she showed no signs of bitterness or anger, 'yet I can so patiently take it, that I yield God more hearty thanks for shortening my woeful days, than if all the world had been given into my possession, with life lengthened at my own will.' She had heard he was very upset at her 'woeful' situation and offered him comfort by assuring him that she was ready to die. 'To me there is nothing that can be more welcome than from this vale of misery to aspire to that heavenly throne of all joy and pleasure, with Christ my Saviour...in whose steadfast faith...the Lord that hath hitherto strengthened you, so continue to keep you.'[42]

She wrote him a shorter message in her prayer book, which she would take with her to the scaffold.

'The Lord comfort Your Grace, and that in His word wherein all creatures only are to be comforted, and though it hath pleased God to take away two of your children [herself and Guildford] yet think not, I most humbly beseech Your grace, that you have lost them, but trust that we, by losing this mortal life have won an immortal life, and I, for my part, as I have honoured Your Grace in this life will pray for you in another life, Your Grace's humble daughter, Jane Dudley.'[43]

At some point, Jane was interrupted with the information that Mary had granted a request from Guildford to see her so that they could say goodbye. Jane decided it would be better not to meet as it

42   ibid., p. 47-8.

43   Chapman, p. 200.

might do more harm than good by adding to their distress. 'She let him answer that if their meeting could have been of consolation to their souls, she would have been very glad to see him, but as their meeting would only tend to increase their misery and pain, it was better to put it off for the time being, as they would meet shortly elsewhere and live bound by indissoluble ties.'[44]

Jane's longest letter was for thirteen-year-old Katherine and was written on some blank pages in her Greek New Testament, which she was giving to her. Her affection and concern for her sister show through in what was from start to finish an exhortation to follow Christ and to value the Bible.

'I have here sent you, good sister Katherine, a book, which although it be not outwardly trimmed with gold, yet inwardly it is more worth than precious stones. It is the book, dear sister, of the law of the Lord: it is his testament and last will, which he bequeathed unto us wretches; which shall lead you to the path of eternal joy: and if you with a good mind read it, and with an earnest mind do purpose to follow it, it shall bring you to an immortal and everlasting life. It shall teach you to live and learn you to die.'[45]

She urged Katherine to avoid all distractions of riches and possessions, the world and the flesh. She entreated her to 'live still to die', and to 'delight yourself only in the Lord'. Be ready. 'Rejoice in Christ, as I do. Follow the steps of your master Christ, and take up your cross; lay your sins on his back, and always embrace him. And as touching my death, rejoice as I do, good sister, that I shall be delivered of this corruption. For I am assured that I shall, for losing a mortal life, win an immortal life, the which I pray God grant you, and send you of his grace to live in his fear, and to die in the true Christian faith, from the which, in God's name, I exhort you that you never swerve, nor for hope of life, nor for fear of death...Fare you well, good sister, and put your only trust in God, who only must help you.'[46]

---

44 Tallis, p. 268.

45 *Foxe's Book of Martyrs* Abridged from Milner's edition by Buckley, (London: George Routledge & Sons, 1892), p. 266-7.

46 ibid., p. 267.

Jane's execution

Neither Guildford nor Jane were allowed to have a Protestant clergyman accompany them to their execution. John Feckenham offered to go with Jane and she accepted. Many in the Tower felt sorry for the young couple, and, when Guildford was led from his cell at 10am on the morning of Monday 12th February, a group of gentlemen from among the Tower officials came alongside to support him as Sir John Bridges walked with him to the outer gate. There, the Sherriff of London took over and escorted him the short distance to the scaffold on Tower Hill. Guildford had started out distressed and crying, but he calmed himself and briefly addressed the crowd. Then he knelt and prayed, before he put his head on the block, and was mercifully killed with a single blow.

Jane had stood at her window, watching him go. She was wearing the same black dress and hood she had worn for her trial. She stayed there until the cart carrying his body returned, although her ladies had tried to persuade her to come away. Her composure left her then and she said his name in some distress, but, by the time they came for her, she was ready and calm again. She left Partridge's house on the arm of Sir John Bridges, with Feckenham on the other side of her, and with her two ladies, Mistress Ellen, her nurse, and Mistress Tilney, just behind, both weeping uncontrollably. With her free hand, she was holding her prayer book and she read as she walked for a few moments across Tower Green to her scaffold. When she had mounted it, she turned to Bridges and asked him if she could speak what was in her mind. Then she went to the rail and spoke clearly and steadily to the crowd before her. She began by acknowledging her guilt. She should not have accepted the crown.

'Good people, I am come hither to die, and by a law I am condemned to the same. The fact against the queen's highness was unlawful, and the consenting thereunto by me,' but honesty meant she must also protest her innocence, for she had not wanted it, 'but touching the procurement and desire thereof by me, or on my behalf, I do wash my hands thereof in innocency before God, and the face of you, good Christian people, this day.' She broke off to wring her hands as if washing them, and then continued to confess her faith. 'I pray you all, good Christian people, to bear me witness that I die a true Christian woman, and that I look to be saved by no other means, but only by the mercy of God, in the blood of his only son Jesus Christ; and I confess, that when I did know the word of God, I neglected the same, and loved myself and the world: therefore this punishment is happily and worthily happened unto me for my sins; and yet I thank God, that of his goodness he hath thus given me a time and respite to repent.' She finished by emphasising her Protestant beliefs in that she was only asking for prayer whilst she was alive. 'And now, good people, while I am alive, I pray you assist me with your prayers.'[47]

Jane then knelt down and opened her prayer book at Psalm 51. She turned to Feckenham and asked him if she should say it. Checked by emotion, he could not speak for a moment and then he simply said 'yes'. He knelt beside her and as she recited the nineteen verses of David's psalm of repentance, he followed the words in Latin.

'Have mercy upon me, O God, according to thy loving kindness, according unto the multitude of thy tender mercies, blot out my transgressions. Wash me thoroughly from mine iniquity, and cleanse me from my sin...The sacrifices of God are a broken spirit, a broken and a contrite heart, O God, thou wilt not despise.'

When she had finished they stood together and Jane thanked him. 'God I beseech Him abundantly reward you for your kindness towards me,' and then added with friendly candour that his visit had been more unwelcome to her than her death was terrible. He was silent and then Jane kissed him and they held hands for a moment.

She gave her prayer book to Sir John Bridges, and her handkerchief and gloves to her nurse. She started to untie the top of her gown but when the executioner moved to help her she told him, 'Let me alone' and her two women took her headdress and collar.

The executioner knelt before her and asked for her forgiveness. She gave it 'most willingly' and moved on to the straw and saw the block. 'I pray you dispatch me quickly' she said. When she knelt down she suddenly asked in fear, 'Will you take it off before I lay me down?' He reassured her, 'No, Madam.'

---

47   ibid., p. 267-8.

Jane tied the blindfold over her eyes and reached forward for the block, but she could not touch it. She groped blindly and cried out, 'What shall I do? Where is it?' but those around her froze and none moved to help her. Then someone from below climbed up on to the scaffold and guided her to the block. She laid her head on it and said, 'Lord, into thy hands I commend my spirit.'[48] The axe swung and she had gone.

The executioner held her head aloft and declared, 'So perish all the Queen's enemies! Behold the head of a traitor.' Later that day her body was laid to rest in the chapel of St Peter ad Vincula beside two other beheaded Queens, Anne Boleyn and Katherine Howard.

It had been a difficult day for Sir John Bridges, escorting such young prisoners to their deaths, especially Jane of whom he had grown fond. When he was at leisure to look at her gift to him, her prayer book, he read the message she had inscribed in it for him.

'Forasmuch as you have desired so simple a woman to write in so worthy a book, good Master Lieutenant, therefore I shall as a friend, desire you, and as a Christian require you to call upon God, to incline your heart to His laws, to quicken you in His way, and not to take the word of truth utterly out of your mouth. Live still to die, that by death you may purchase eternal life...The preacher saith, There is a time to be born and a time to die, and the day of our death is better than the day of our birth.'[49]

JANE'S LEGACY

Jane's considerable gifts of speech had been silenced by death, but her words lived on. Her writings – Feckenham's debate, the letters to Katherine and Harding and her scaffold speech – were quickly published in pamphlets and surreptitiously circulated. Jane's courageous death was powerful Protestant propaganda. News of her execution brought sorrow that her life had been so cruelly cut short, but also praise and thankfulness that she had stood with such faithfulness to the end. The signs of coming persecution were growing, and Jane's youth – and the

48   Chapman, p. 206-7.
49   ibid., p. 201.

clarity with which she expressed her faith – only emphasised her example as the first Protestant martyr of the reign. She was an encouragement to those who would follow.

John Banks, a friend of the Grey family, wrote to Jane's former correspondent, Heinrich Bullinger, in Zurich a month after her death, and said she was 'truly admirable not so much by reason of her incredible attainments in literature, by which in the seventeenth year of her age she excelled all other ladies, as by reason of the remarkable firmness with which, though a young girl, she surpassed men in maintaining the cause of Christ'. She had 'persevered in this confession of faith even to the last...All godly and truly Christian persons have not so much reason to mourn over the ruin of a family so illustrious, as to rejoice that the latest action of her life was terminated in bearing testimony to the name of Jesus.'[50]

Peter Martyr wrote to Bullinger on 3rd April. 'I hear nothing else from England, except that everything is getting worse and worse. Jane, who was formerly Queen, conducted herself at her execution with the greatest fortitude and godliness.'[51] Whilst in Geneva, John Calvin commented that Jane was 'A lady whose example is worthy of everlasting remembrance.'[52] John Foxe's monumental *Book of Martyrs* was first published less than ten years after Jane's death and recorded not only the events of her reign, but also her writings and a description of her death. It was a very influential book which would be widely read, especially in the reign of Elizabeth.

At her death Jane stepped into the history books, but only as a very minor character. She is little known or thought of, her reign just the briefest interlude between those of Edward and Mary, although she is one of a very few historical figures to have a tag to her name – The Nine Days Queen. Interest in Jane has ebbed and flowed over the years, but the poignant elements of her life – her youth, her innocence and her violent death – have meant her story has been told and retold again and again right from the 1550s to the present day through

---

50   Tallis, p. 280-1.

51   A. Plowden, *Lady Jane Grey,* p. 152.

52   E. Ives, p. 288.

biographies, poetry, plays, novels, paintings, even operas, and finally films. Most could not resist the lure of romance and so her relationship with Guildford became a love story. As others had used Jane in her life for their own purposes, so, after her death, people projected what they wanted on to her character. Over time, especially in the eighteenth and nineteenth centuries, the robust, honest, independent-minded young girl, with such an ability to express herself, became totally submerged in the idealised picture of a beautiful, meek, gentle, learned and wise paragon of virtue. Since the mid-twentieth century, a more authentic Jane has re-emerged, with an emphasis on her strong character, but in our secular age most recent biographers have struggled to understand her faith and that has tended to distort their view of her. Some have seen her as narrow-minded, and even as a fanatic. Sadly, until Faith Cook's biography, *Lady Jane Grey, the Nine Day Queen of England,* she had rather slipped from view among Christians and in Christian literature.

Jane's faithfulness to her Lord is a challenge to us today as it was in her own time; also her focus and single-mindedness. She seems to have had a remarkable ability, especially for someone so young, to dwell on the important and reject the transient, and was impatient, patronising even, of those who could not see things in the same way. She was not influenced by the adulation she received for her learning, or interested in the trappings of being Queen, but was able to deal with her very sudden elevation to the throne, as well as her equally sudden change to being a prisoner, by focusing on the essentials. That is not to say she found this easy; far from it. Her physical illness from the time she was married and whilst she was Queen, may well have been caused by stress, and her prayer written in the Tower clearly reveals her inner struggles. Jane had a passionate nature despite the self-control she displayed in public, and sometimes it spilled into view, as when she denounced Northumberland at the Partridge's dinner table, and also in the very direct forcefulness of her letter to Dr Harding.

Yet, although Jane felt things deeply, she was remarkably free of self-pity or a sense of grievance at the way she had been treated, except in her comments about Northumberland. As her death drew near, she seemed increasingly aware of her sinfulness, but otherwise her spoken and written words held scant reference to herself. She knew her Bible very well. She had had little time to prepare for her debate with Feckenham but, through her Bible knowledge, was more than ready to withstand him. Her letters and her prayer were full of biblical truth and language. At such a time, her thoughts were not centred on herself and the frightening death awaiting her, but were focused on others and the need to encourage and exhort to stay true to the Bible's teachings and to Christ. She saw God as in control, using the events of her life to teach her and bringing her to the point where she was focused on the reality of heaven and the life to come, which was more important than anything else.

Despite being born to every advantage, Jane's life had not been her own. She had been used by others throughout and their actions brought her to her death, but she did not allow others to define her. Her faith and her strength of character are the two things which shine out from her story. Far from being moulded or swamped by her circumstances, she was her own person, or rather she was God's person, shaped and dominated by her trust in Him. The executioner's axe brutally cut short her life, but nothing could extinguish the light of her faithful testimony to her Lord.

5. CATHERINE WILLOUGHBY 1519 - 1580

A GREAT LADY AND GOD'S USEFUL SERVANT

On 7th September 1533 a wedding took place, probably in London. The forty-nine-year-old bridegroom was one of the most powerful men in the land, Charles Brandon, Duke of Suffolk. He was King Henry VIII's good friend and recently widowed brother-in-law. His bride was his ward, Catherine Willoughby, a young girl of just fourteen. Charles's wife had died only ten weeks earlier, and Catherine would have been stunned when she realised she was to marry the man she had thought of as a second father, especially as she was betrothed to his son.

CHILDHOOD

Catherine had been born in March 1519 at Parham Old Hall in Suffolk. Her father was William, Baron Willoughby of Eresby, a soldier, courtier and substantial landowner. Her mother, who was reputed to be beautiful, was a young Spanish noblewoman, Maria de Salinas, favourite lady-in-waiting and close friend of the Queen, Catherine of Aragon. At their wedding the King made over to the couple a large grant of lands in Lincolnshire and as another sign of his favour, he later called one of his ships after Maria, the *Mary Willoughby*. They had three children, two sons who died in infancy, and their daughter, Catherine, named after the Queen. Both Catherine's parents spent much time at court, where Maria continued as lady-in-waiting, and was a support to her mistress through all the ups and downs of her life. Neither Maria nor the Queen were able to give their husbands a male heir, and no doubt their grief at the deaths of their respective babies and infants would have bound them even closer together. They each had one healthy child who would survive to adulthood: Mary Tudor and Catherine Willoughby. Catherine was the younger by three years, and both girls were raised as devout Catholics, but their spiritual paths would later dramatically diverge.

Just after Catherine's seventh birthday, her father died and she found herself a wealthy heiress, a ward of the crown and with a title in her own right – Baroness Willoughby. Three years later, Charles Brandon, Duke of Suffolk, bought her wardship for a considerable amount of money. Catherine joined him and his wife, Henry VIII's sister, Mary, at their house at Westhorpe in Suffolk, where she was educated and brought up alongside their two daughters, Frances who was a couple of years older, Eleanor, who was about the same age, and their son, Henry, Earl of Lincoln.

The Brandons, as well as Catherine's mother, were becoming caught up in the turmoil taking place within Henry VIII's family. In 1527, Henry began the process which would be known as 'The King's Great Matter' to free himself from a marriage which he no longer believed to be valid, so that he could marry his bewitching new love, Anne Boleyn. When Catherine of Aragon was finally removed from court in 1531, Maria stayed with her until August of the following year when she was ordered to leave Catherine's household and forbidden to communicate with her. The Brandons' sympathies were with their sister-in-law.

In 1533, after their daughter Frances's wedding, Charles Brandon was kept busy in the capital supervising the arrangements for Anne Boleyn's coronation, while his wife's poor health finally gave way. Mary died at the end of June and was buried with great pomp at Bury St Edmunds.

DUCHESS OF SUFFOLK

When Catherine Willougby attended Frances's wedding she might have thought about her own. She was betrothed to Frances's brother, Henry, and at fourteen she would have been considered old enough for marriage, but with Henry being only eleven, there would have to be a delay. In fact unexpectedly, her wedding was at hand, for instead of marrying Henry, her bridegroom was his father, Charles Brandon.

Their contemporaries would not have found this situation either unusual or shocking. Speedy remarriages were not rare and neither were large age gaps between bride and groom. Marriages amongst the nobility were not normally for love but for practical dynastic or financial reasons, and in this case were almost certainly for the latter. Brandon had pressing financial needs and Catherine was a considerable heiress. Henry Brandon was not strong and, in fact, would die just six months later, so it is probable that Charles could see that the only sure way of bringing Catherine's wealth into the family was to marry her himself. As for Catherine, she had to cope with the shock of her sudden marriage, and, in becoming a duchess, of being propelled into the very highest rank of the nobility.

Charles Brandon had not inherited his title. His father was merely a knight, but since his youth Charles had been a close companion of Henry VIII. He was good company, with similar athletic prowess to his King, and his spectacular rise was entirely the result of their strong friendship. Charles was an affable man with abundant personal charm and the valuable gift of being able to deal well with people. He had had his own matrimonial adventures and Catherine was his fourth wife. Catherine would bear Charles two children, providing him with that most valued asset, male heirs. Their first son, Henry, was born in September 1535 followed by a second son, Charles, early in 1537. Despite the large difference in their ages and Catherine's youthfulness at its beginning, it would seem that their marriage was a successful one.

The year 1536 would prove to be significant. It began with the death of Catherine of Aragon. Maria Willoughby had heard that she was failing fast and had urgently petitioned the King for permission to go to her, which was refused. Undeterred and heedless of possible consequences, Maria set out from her London home well before dawn on New Year's Eve to ride through bitter winter weather to Kimbolton, where Catherine was being held under house arrest. When she arrived, Maria bluffed her way in and went straight to her friend refusing to leave, and six days later, Catherine of Aragon died in her arms. Catherine Brandon, accompanied by her mother, was one of the chief mourners at the funeral.

In late spring, Charles sat through Anne Boleyn's trial as one of the commission of peers there to try her, and was present at her execution. That autumn, when insurrection suddenly burst out in Lincolnshire, the beginning of the Pilgrimage of Grace, Brandon was tasked with putting it down. He swiftly gathered troops and arrived at Lincoln to find the rebels dispersing at his approach, although the more dangerous part of the uprising was about to erupt in neighbouring Yorkshire. His prompt actions settled the situation in Lincolnshire. The King then ordered his friend to change his base from Suffolk to Lincolnshire and gave him Tattersall Castle as his main residence. Catherine's mother died in 1539, which brought her daughter possession of Grimsthorpe and other Willoughby estates in Lincolnshire, so that Brandon became the most powerful landowner in the county. He set about rebuilding the medieval fortress of Grimsthorpe, turning it into a comfortable Tudor mansion.

Both of the Brandons were prominent at court and Charles was often busy in the King's service. Catherine was lady-in-waiting to Anne of Cleves, Henry's fourth wife, and Brandon played an important part in persuading Anne to accept the failure of her marriage and the settlement Henry offered her. The Brandons entertained both Henry and his fifth wife, the pretty teenager, Catherine Howard, at Grimsthorpe in August and again in October 1541.

Christian influences

Catherine's position at court brought her into contact with Protestant teaching and, despite her Spanish Catholic background, at some stage her mind and heart began to open to what she was hearing. She has left no record of the process of her path to faith but it appears to have been gradual. Throughout the 1530s, Hugh Latimer and a few other Protestant preachers were invited to preach at court. A very able preacher, down to earth, vivid and clear, Latimer had a particular gift for communicating gospel truth. In 1562, when his servant Augustine Bernher collected his sermons for publication, he dedicated the work to Catherine and might possibly have had her especially in mind when he wrote how God had used Latimer in 'Henry's days to be a singular instrument to set forth his truth, and by his preaching to open the eyes of such as were deluded by the subtle and deceitful crafts of the popish prelates'.[1]

From 1539, Catherine heard evangelical preaching under her own roof when her husband appointed Alexander Seton as their chaplain. Seton was a former friar who had become a Reformer, and he was succeeded as chaplain by another biblical preacher, John Parkhurst, before Parkhurst entered the service of Queen Katherine Parr in 1543.

Catherine Brandon was one of the select few who witnessed the marriage of her good friend Katherine Parr to Henry VIII in July 1543. She was one of Katherine's ladies-in-waiting and became part of the group of Protestant ladies around the Queen who listened to evangelical preachers such as Latimer and Nicholas Ridley, discussed Protestant books, and studied the Bible together. Like Latimer, Katherine Parr undoubtedly had a strong spiritual influence upon Catherine.

In the latter years of Henry's reign, as divisions at court had become increasingly defined along religious grounds, Charles Brandon became prominent on the Protestant side. In 1545, although he was sixty years old, he seemed just as busy as ever about the King's business. Only a year earlier he had been in France with his King, commanding the army which successfully besieged Boulogne, and in the August of 1545, he was active in organising defences in the south east of England against threatened French attack, when he died suddenly at Guildford. Shortly afterwards, the King, who seemed genuinely affected by his old friend's death, paid tribute to him at a meeting of the Privy Council. He said that in all the long years the Duke had served him, he had never tried to hurt an opponent or say anything to injure anyone. 'Is there any of you, my lords, who can say as much?' 'In his will Brandon had requested to be buried at Tattershall, 'without any pomp or outward pride of the world'[2] but Henry insisted that the Duke was buried in St George's Chapel, Windsor. Charles Brandon had not only survived at Henry's

1   D. Baldwin, *Henry VIII's Last Love: The Extraordinary Life of Katherine Willoughby Lady-in-Waiting to the Tudors* (Stroud: Amberley Publishing, 2016), p. 58.

2   E. Read, *Catherine, Duchess of Suffolk: A Portrait* (London: Jonathan Cape, 1962), p. 49.

court, when others of his contemporaries had not, but he had had a closer friendship with Henry than any other man.

Independence

So, after twelve years of marriage, Catherine was left a widow at twenty-six years of age. She had her two young sons to bring up. Henry, who succeeded his father as Duke of Suffolk, was almost ten, and Charles was eight. Catherine assumed control of her own lands, and was able to buy Henry's wardship from the King and see to the administration of his inheritance from his father. She adjusted to independence, as, for the first time, she was no longer under the authority of either a parent or of her husband. One thing she did not relinquish was her title. She would be known for the rest of her life either as the Duchess of Suffolk, or as My Lady of Suffolk.

Catherine had developed into an attractive, charming and lively young lady, with a strong personality. She was energetic – once, when writing a letter, she declared that she was like a sluggard still in her bed at six in the morning – and with a quick, intelligent mind. She was also direct and outspoken, and could be hasty in her speech, certainly not someone known for her tact. Two contemporaries commented that she is 'a lady of sharp wit, and sure hand to drive her wit home, and make it pierce where she pleases' and also 'It is a pity that so goodly a wit waiteth upon so froward a will.'[3] One specific incident during her marriage showed both her wit and her 'frowardness'. The Brandons had gathered guests together for a meal when Charles told the ladies each to invite the gentleman she liked best to accompany her to the dinner table, excluding himself from the proceedings. Catherine immediately approached Stephen Gardiner, Bishop of Winchester, saying, 'Since I may not ask my Lord whom I like best, I ask your Grace whom I like least.'[4]

As gospel truth took root within Catherine, her trust in Christ as her Saviour would come to change and dictate her thoughts and actions. As part of that process, Catherine actively rejected the Catholic faith she

---

3   R. Bainton, *Women of the Reformation in France and England* (Minneapolis: Augsburg Publishing House, 1973), p. 255.

4   E. Read, p. 58.

had devoutly followed in her youth. She could see how it had blinded people to Bible teaching, and that good works, rituals and reverence for the mass were of no benefit to her soul. Being Catherine, she did not hide her loss of respect for the Church and for such an eminent churchman as Stephen Gardiner. Gardiner was her godfather and later he would claim that once they had been close, but that had changed so much that Catherine mocked him by calling her dog Gardiner. On one occasion, she even dressed it in the white vestment of a bishop.

1546

Early in 1546, Katherine Parr's hold on the King's affections seemed to be questioned and there were even rumours at court that she might be removed as Queen. The Imperial ambassador wrote to the Emperor Charles V that 'I hesitate to report there are rumours of a new queen... Madame Suffolk is much talked about, and is in great favour, but the king shows no alteration in his behaviour to the queen.'[5] Catherine Brandon got on well with Henry, but this would appear to be the sole historical reference to her as his possible seventh wife, and would seem to owe more to malicious gossip than reality. If Henry was really tiring of Katherine because of her religious views, it seems unlikely that he would choose to replace her with her great friend, who was far more outspoken and held the same beliefs. Deliberately false rumours would not be surprising, especially if they originated with those who saw the Queen as their enemy and wanted to sow discord in the Protestant camp at court.

Katherine Parr's opponents that year would do their utmost to bring her down, as part of their efforts to gain the ascendancy at court. As they also tried to attack the leading Protestant nobility, such as Edward Seymour and John Dudley, through their wives, all the Protestant ladies around Katherine were at some risk, including Catherine Brandon. In July, Anne Askew was taken to the Tower and tortured in a desperate attempt to get her to implicate some of them. Five specific names were given to her, including Seymour's wife, Anne, and Catherine Brandon, but despite her terrible ordeal Anne did not incriminate anybody. Very soon afterwards, Stephen Gardiner gained Henry's permission to see if

5   ibid., p. 60.

he could find evidence against the Queen. Gardiner intended to arrest a few ladies very close to her, hoping to find 'heretical' books when their rooms were searched, as a preamble to striking against the Queen herself. Katherine was warned and the plot failed, but her ladies, and that probably would have included the Duchess of Suffolk, had to smuggle out to safety any forbidden literature they had at court.

REIGN OF EDWARD VI 1547–1553

Catherine may well have grieved for her husband's old friend, the King, when he died in January 1547, but she would have been thankful for the end of the persecution of Protestants. At Edward VI's coronation in February her eleven-year-old son, Henry, carried the orb, and both he and his brother Charles became Knights of the Bath. The young Duke of Suffolk, just two years older than his new sovereign, was one of the select group of boys who were his companions and were educated alongside him.

As the cause of the Reformation began to slowly advance in the new reign, Catherine took every opportunity to use her position and wealth to promote religious reform and the work of the gospel, especially in her own county of Lincolnshire. The historian John Strype spoke of reform being greatly advanced 'by the helping forwardness of that devout woman of God, the duchess of Suffolk'.[6] Another recorded that: 'She was very active in seconding the efforts of government to abolish superfluous Holy Days, to remove images and relics from churches, to destroy shrines and other monuments of idolatry and superstition, to put an end to pilgrimages, to reform the clergy, to see that every church had provided, in some convenient place, a copy of the large Bible, to stir up the bishops, vicars and curates to diligence in preaching against the usurped authority of the Pope; in inculcating upon all the reading of the Scriptures, and especially the young, the Pater Noster, the Articles of Faith and the Ten Commandments in English.'[7]

Catherine tried to ensure that a Bible was placed in every parish church in Lincolnshire and, where she could, she brought Protestants

6   ibid., p. 66.
7   ibid., pp. 66-7.

into local livings. She was a patron of other evangelical preachers, especially of the influential preacher and her friend and mentor, Hugh Latimer, and she also encouraged the publication of Protestant literature. More than a dozen books were either dedicated to her or bore her coat of arms. She sponsored a mix of publications for a variety of readers – theology, evangelical sermons, and more easily read, basic translations of Protestant works. The translator Nicholas Lesse wrote of her as a patroness 'at whose hands...the common people hath received already many comfortable and spiritual consolations, instructions and teachings'.[8] In November 1547, Katherine Parr's book *Lamentations of a Sinner* was published after encouragement from her great friend Catherine Brandon and also William Cecil. Catherine's involvement was recognised in its title *The Lamentations of a sinner, made by the most virtuous lady Queen Katherine, bewailing the ignorance of her blind life: set forth and put in print at the instant desire of the right gracious lady Catherine duchess of Suffolk...*[9] William Cecil contributed the introduction in which he enthusiastically endorsed the contents.

Protestant refugees

As England was now a safe place to be a Protestant, Continental Reformers who were experiencing persecution in their homeland began to seek a refuge there. Catherine helped some of these Protestant refugees. Around two thousand gravitated to London – from France, Italy, Spain, Germany, the Netherlands and Poland. Catherine used her influence to encourage the authorities to provide a church building and to grant a charter which allowed them to legally worship together in their own way. This was the only congregation in the country which could do so outside of the Church of England. It was called The Strangers' Church and the outstanding Polish Reformer, John à Lasco, was the superintendent over four other pastors, one of whom was a man called Francis Perusell. Catherine was well known to these and to others among the refugees for her practical and financial help.

---

8   J. King, 'Patronage and Piety : The Influence of Catherine Parr' in M. Hannay, (ed) *Silent But For the Word: Tudor Women as Patrons, Translators, and Writers of Religious Works* (Ohio: Kent State University Press, 1985), p. 56.

9   Withrow, p. 84.

Death of Katherine Parr

In September 1548, Catherine lost her close friend Katherine Parr when she died after giving birth to a daughter, Mary. The unfortunate child became an orphan the following spring when her unstable father, Thomas Seymour, was executed for treason, and she came to live with Catherine at Grimsthorpe. When Catherine received Mary she had been assured by the baby's uncle and aunt, Edward and Anne Seymour, that she would receive an allowance for her upkeep and that Mary's other uncle, William Parr, would be willing to also look after the child on occasion. Mary's arrival brought a considerable financial burden, for she came with about a dozen retainers and, as the daughter of a queen, she had to be maintained in an appropriate style. No allowance was forthcoming and in the light of that William Parr was disinclined to get involved. Catherine raised the matter with Anne Seymour, but when she did not get satisfaction, she was determined not to let the matter rest and sought the help of William Cecil, who was Seymour's secretary. Sadly, nothing more was heard of Mary Seymour and it is supposed that she died at a very young age.

William Cecil

Catherine's appeal to William Cecil was only one of many she would send him over the course of her life. Cecil was a year younger than Catherine, and his home at Burghley House, near Stamford was perhaps a dozen miles away from Grimsthorpe. He and his wife Mildred were good friends of hers and, when Catherine needed advice or someone to act on her behalf, she would turn to Cecil. In 1547, he had entered the service of Edward Seymour, the Lord Protector, and then, after he survived Seymour's fall from power, he ended up working for Northumberland, and was given a knighthood. They both recognised Cecil's capacity for hard work and considerable gifts for administration and statecraft, which would reach their heights in the reign of Elizabeth.

Catherine's sons

Catherine's sons were growing up. Henry was fourteen when an approach was made by Edward Seymour to Catherine about his marriage, and he suggested to her a very suitable match with his own daughter, Anne. There was a lot to commend the idea. A duke would be marrying the daughter of a duke and two families committed to the Reformation would be uniting. Catherine gave her reaction in a letter to Cecil written in May 1550 and it showed that on the subject of marriage she had very unusual and 'advanced' views for her time. She did not want the two young people to be committed to a formal betrothal but to be given time to see if that was what they themselves wanted. While it was the norm for all her contemporaries to decide themselves who their children would marry, she wanted the pair to be given the opportunity to marry for love.

'They, marrying by our orders and without their consents, as they be yet without judgement to give such consent as ought to be given in matrimony, I cannot tell what more unkindness one of us might show another, or wherein we might work more wickedly than to bring our children into so miserable a state not to choose by their own liking... This I promise you I have said for my Lord's daughter as well as for my son, and this more I say for myself and say it not but truly: I know none this day living that I rather wish my son than she, but I am not, because I like her best, therefore desirous that she should be constrained by her friends to have him whom she might peradventure not like so well as I like her; neither can I yet assure myself of my son's liking...But to have this matter come best to pass were that we parents keep still our friendship, and suffer our children to follow our examples and to begin their loves of themselves without our forcing.'[10]

Catherine may well have been influenced by her own experience of a sudden marriage in which she had no choice, even though, in the event, she and her husband had made it a successful union, but the letter also indicates the independence of her thinking. She was not one to be influenced by what others thought or did. As it turned out, the Duke of Somerset was not willing to wait to dispose of his daughter in marriage, and instead she became the bride of John Dudley, eldest son of John Dudley, the future Duke of Northumberland.

---

10   Read, p 76-7.

Cambridge

Catherine's priority at this stage for her sons was to ensure that they had the best education. In the autumn of 1549, aged fourteen and twelve, they both began to study at Cambridge University, at St John's College. William Cecil was a former student as was the gifted group of Reformers including John Cheke and Roger Ascham who, as tutors, so influenced their royal pupils, King Edward and the Lady Elizabeth. Catherine's boys received a rigorous education, studying long hours in spartan conditions. Even allowing for the exaggerated compliments commonplace in Tudor times, there appears to have been something special about them. They were very intelligent, attractive lads, who showed great promise. They lived in college but Catherine rented a house a few miles away in the village of Kingston, to be near them.

Shortly after they had started at St John's, Cranmer was able to use his influence to secure the appointment of Martin Bucer as Regius Professor of Divinity at Cambridge. Bucer, a well-known and distinguished German Reformer, had arrived in the country as a refugee. The brothers studied under him, and their mother too was able to attend some of his lectures. Catherine became a good friend to Bucer and his family, providing them with some practical support and helping his wife to nurse him in the weeks before his death in February 1551. Then, in July of the same year, tragedy struck. The dreadful illness known as the sweating sickness broke out in the town and university at Cambridge. It would strike without warning, carrying off its victims with terrifying speed. The sufferer passed from the 'cold phase' to one of fever and delirium accompanied by drenching sweat, and very few survived. Catherine's boys were immediately removed to Buckden, but not in time. Henry sickened soon after arrival and died within hours. Catherine herself was not well at Kingston but roused herself and rushed to Buckden. She was too late to see Henry, but did get to Charles before he too succumbed, both sons taken from her on the same day. Catherine was devastated and retired to Grimsthorpe to mourn her great loss.

Response to tragedy

Early in September she felt able to write to Cecil, but was still not ready to see him. Her letter reveals how she saw God's hand of goodness even in this time of deep trial, and also knew His help. She believed in God's sovereignty, His control over her circumstances. 'I give God thanks, good Master Cecil, which it has pleased Him to heap upon me; and truly I take this last (and to the first sight, most sharp and bitter) punishment not for the least of His benefits; inasmuch as I have never been so well taught by any other before to know His power, His love and mercy, my own weakness and that wretched state that without Him I should endure here.' She freely admitted she could not trust herself to contain her grief if she saw Cecil. 'And to ascertain you that I have received great comfort in Him, I would gladly do it by talk and sight of you. But as I confess myself no better than flesh, so I am not well able with quiet to behold my very friends without some parts of these vile dregs of Adam to seem sorry for that which I know I ought rather to rejoice.'[11]

The loss of her dear sons led to some practical changes. Properties which Henry VIII had granted to Charles Brandon and his male heirs reverted to the crown. With the death of her younger son, the title of the Duke of Suffolk died out, but in October Henry Grey, her stepdaughter Frances' husband, was newly created Duke of Suffolk, in the right of his wife. The Grey family were now her nearest relatives and she spent Christmas that year with them and their daughters, Jane, Katherine and Mary.

Second marriage

Catherine was helped in her grief by Hugh Latimer. He had retired from preaching at court, and he stayed with her at Grimsthorpe as her chaplain from November 1551 to the spring of 1552, preaching a series of sermons to her household on the Lord's Prayer. During 1552, someone else gave Catherine comfort and support, and that was her gentleman usher, Richard Bertie. He had joined her household in the late 1540s and his role as usher was to walk before her in processions and to escort her to court functions, but he also managed Catherine's

11   Baldwin, p. 105.

business affairs for her. A couple of years older than Catherine, he was a gentleman and a graduate of Oxford University, a capable and intelligent man. Importantly, he also shared Catherine's evangelical faith. They were falling in love and were married, probably early in 1553, by Hugh Latimer. Catherine had chosen well; they were well-matched and he would make her a good husband, but not everyone saw it that way, and she had to face censure, even ridicule, for marrying so far beneath her. As a great lady, Catherine was expected to marry someone of similar rank, certainly not anyone who was far from having noble blood, but she was not likely to have been bothered by such criticism. Her joy would have been capped in the summer of that year when she realised that she was expecting a baby.

Catherine played no part in the national crisis which played out that summer, when, after Edward VI's death, Northumberland put Lady Jane Grey on the throne, although Catherine's family were very much involved and she knew the key players well. When she heard that Mary was to be Queen, Catherine, like others of her faith, must have wondered what lay in store for them, and she would not have to wait long to find out.

BACKGROUND. THE REIGN OF MARY 1553 –1558 (PART 1)

In the extraordinary events of July 1553 which brought Mary to the throne, she owed much to Protestant support, but she was to show no gratitude. Her devotion to Catholicism meant that she would have wanted to return her kingdom to the Catholic fold on her accession whatever the circumstances, but Mary was deeply grateful for what she saw as God's intervention on her behalf, and this meant that she was even more determined to put the clock back to pre-Reformation days. She thought that much of her support came from those wanting the same, instead of understanding that many people had flocked to her not because of her faith, but because they thought she was the rightful queen. They saw her as Henry VIII's oldest child, who was being cut out of her inheritance by the hated Duke of Northumberland. Mary had spent most of Edward's reign living quietly on her estates surrounded by loyal Catholics and she had no idea of the spread and depth of Protestantism within her realm. She believed that it had been foisted on to the populace by a self-serving and cunning government and by eloquent fanatical Protestant preachers. Once they were removed, her people would gladly return to their Catholic past.

The first arrests were not slow to come. On Sunday 13th August, just ten days after Mary's triumphant arrival in London, a riot was near to breaking out when Dr Bourn, a Catholic priest, was preaching at St Paul's Cross in front of London dignitaries. He was violently heckled by Protestants in the crowd and the intervention of two prominent Protestant clerics, the Bible translator, John Rogers, and the leading preacher, John Bradford, was needed to ensure Bourn's safety, only for Rogers and Bradford to be accused of being behind the incident themselves and be arrested. It was the beginning of a roundup of prominent Protestant churchmen, first in London and then across the land, including leading bishops Hooper, Ridley, Latimer and Cranmer. At the same time, only men licensed by the authorities, and therefore Catholics, were allowed to preach or read the Bible in church. Parliament met in October and legislation restored the Church to its position at the death of Henry VIII, but without the heresy laws. The mass and the doctrine of the real presence were back, as were services in Latin, the old rituals and ceremonies, and the burning of Protestant books.

In March 1554, clerical celibacy was reimposed and this led to the ejection of married clergy from their positions, unless they were willing to put away their wives and children. Large numbers were deprived of their livings. All the foreign Protestant refugees who had settled during Edward's reign were ordered to depart. They were not the only ones making the journey to the Continent. There were many who felt the best course was to leave England and seek safety abroad. Some Protestant leaders, such as Bishop Hooper, urged others to take the opportunity to go, although he himself remained at his post until arrested. Over time, at least eight hundred Protestants would flee and those who went in the early part of the reign did so with little difficulty. Most settled in either Germany or Switzerland at such places as Strasbourg, Frankfurt,

Zurich and Geneva, and they included many clergy and Oxford and Cambridge students, as well as gentry and merchants. The two chaplains from Bradgate Park, James Haddon and John Aylmer, both reached the Continent, settling in Germany. John Foxe eventually made for the printing centre of Basel, where he continued to work on his book and where he would receive details of the persecution in England. Others of the refugees were also active. Printers and pamphleteers produced material which was smuggled back to England, and over a hundred young men were trained for the ministry.

THE BERTIES' REACTION TO MARY'S REIGN

Interview with Gardiner

Catherine would have watched events unfolding with deep concern. She did what she could, and sent financial support to Nicholas Ridley and Hugh Latimer, incarcerated in the Tower. Her baby, a girl they named Susan, was born within a short time of the execution of her step-granddaughter, Lady Jane Grey, in February 1554. The Berties were based at Grimsthorpe and must have wondered if they would be left alone by staying quietly in the country. Did Catherine hope that the special friendship between their mothers would lead Mary to regard them more favourably? If so, they were disappointed. During Lent, Richard Bertie was summoned to appear before Stephen Gardiner in London. Gardiner had spent much of Edward VI's reign imprisoned in the Tower for his opposition to religious reform, but Mary had not only released him and restored him as Bishop of Winchester, but had also appointed him her Lord Chancellor, in effect, her chief minister. Gardiner began in an aggressive way by rebuking Bertie for ignoring two previous subpoenas and threatening to make an example of him in Lincolnshire, although Bertie quickly declared that he had not received them. Gardiner told Bertie that Charles Brandon still owed four thousand pounds to the crown at the time of his death and Catherine, as his widow and executor, was responsible for the debt. Mary required that the sum should be immediately repaid. Bertie was able to assure him that since Henry VIII's reign the debt was being paid back in instalments and this was ongoing. Somewhat mollified, Gardiner switched tack and came to what was probably the main reason for the interview – religion.

'If it be true that you say, I will you favour. But of another thing, Master Bertie, I will admonish you as meaning you well. I hear evil of your religion, yet I hardly can think evil of you' for he knew his mother to be a godly Catholic and that he had benefited from other Catholic influences. Gardiner said he spoke as Richard's friend, 'Wherefore, I will not doubt of you; but I pray you if I may ask the question of my lady your wife, is she now as ready to set up the mass as she was lately to pull it down?' It was Gardiner's opportunity to pay back Catherine for her pointed playfulness at his expense, and he came out with a list of complaints against her: about her dog, her insult to him when she had declared she liked him least, and also a more recent comment made when he was in the Tower. One day, when Gardiner was at the window of his cell, he had seen Catherine outside and had doffed his bonnet to her. Catherine had called up to him that it was merry with the lambs now that the wolf was shut up. Bertie replied as best he could to defend his wife and respectfully reminded Gardiner that her views on the mass had been taught by learned churchmen and were universally accepted for the last six years. 'If she should outwardly allow [the mass] she should both to Christ show herself a false Christian and unto her prince [Mary] a masking [deceiving] subject. You know, my Lord, one by judgement reformed is more worth than a thousand temporizers. To force a confession of religion by mouth contrary to that in the heart worketh damnation where salvation is pretended.' Gardiner enquired whether she might be persuaded to change and remarked, 'It will be a marvellous grief to the prince of Spain and to all the nobility that shall come with him, when they shall find but two noble personages within this land of the Spanish race, the Queen and my Lady your wife, and one of them gone from the faith.'[12]

Catherine and her husband were disturbed by this interview. They could not feel secure. Gardiner might choose to interview either of them again and they could be exposed to far more serious and searching questioning. The time had come for big decisions and they concluded

12   Read, pp. 99-101.

they must follow others of their persuasion and go abroad. Richard would go first to make preparations and then Catherine could follow. He would need authorisation and so Bertie presented himself before Gardiner again, claiming he needed to travel to seek repayment of money owed to Charles Brandon's estate by some on the Continent including the Emperor Charles V. Gardiner told him to wait until after Mary's wedding to Charles's son, Philip of Spain, but Bertie plausibly argued he was more likely to be successful before the wedding rather than afterwards, which Gardiner accepted, and he allowed Bertie to obtain his passport. There is a sense that Gardiner was enjoying a game of cat and mouse with the Berties and he was no doubt glad to have the opportunity to pressurise Catherine who had bested him too many times in the past. He may well have felt that the Berties abroad would be far less troublesome than at home, and that an enjoyable show of menace, moderated by overtures of friendship, would be effective in persuading them to go.

Bertie left from Dover in June and Catherine waited for his summons to follow him in London, at her house in the Barbican. It was a long and no doubt anxious wait, , for once, Catherine must have carefully guarded her tongue. In the meantime, significant events were taking place elsewhere.

Queen Mary's marriage to Philip of Spain was celebrated at Winchester Cathedral in July of that same year, 1554. Philip had accepted strict limits on his role as King and, aware of his unpopularity, he made efforts not to antagonise his new subjects, apparently even trying to rein in some of Mary's enthusiasm for restoring Catholicism and persecuting Protestants, although it may have been a different story in private. In November, Reginald Pole, Cardinal and Papal Legate arrived in England. It was what Mary had been longing for. He formally pronounced the realm absolved of schism and fully rejoined to the Catholic Church. After Parliament had ensured there would be no removal of the old monastic lands from their new owners, they reinstated all the previous heresy laws, and the horrors of burning were once again ready to be unleashed.

Escape

It must have been with a great sense of relief that, soon afterwards, Catherine finally received instructions to depart. Up to now she had always travelled in the state expected of her rank, surrounded by abundant servants and luggage. Now, she had to embark on her long journey with very few necessities and a minimum of servants. She was dressed as a merchant's wife and carried her baby daughter, who was not quite a year old, in her arms, when on 1st January 1555, between four and five in the morning, Catherine cautiously emerged from her house accompanied by six servants. There was an immediate alarm when the watchman heard something and came out to investigate. They had to leave behind a bag containing the baby's clothes and also a pot of milk, but the watchman was distracted and inspected them, which gave Catherine the chance to send the men on ahead, while she and the two female servants slipped into the shadows beyond the gate of the nearby Charterhouse. When the watchman emerged on to the street, it was deserted and he turned back inside.

When it was safe, Catherine and her two women set off for their destination, the Lion Quay. They were unsure of the route, but, on the way to Moorgate, they were joined by the men and went on together. A barge was awaiting them at the quay, but its rowers were reluctant to push off in the thick mist and had to be persuaded to proceed. The Council were soon informed that Catherine had fled and they took steps to find her, setting a watch at the ports.

Bertie had sent a friend, an elderly gentleman called Robert Cranwell, to help Catherine and he was there to meet her when her barge arrived at the Essex port of Leigh. Cranwell had a friend who lived at Leigh, a merchant called William Gosling, who had a married daughter who lived elsewhere and was not known in the town. Catherine was given shelter in Gosling's house and he gave out that she was his daughter. The others stayed elsewhere and, at some point, Catherine had the joy of being reunited with her husband. At last they were able to set out from Gravesend for Flanders. Tantalisingly, they had almost reached their destination when the wind changed and drove their ship back across the sea towards England, when the wind veered, and again the coast of the Low Countries came into view. Then it disappeared for the second time as they were blown right back almost to where they had started from. The captain could not set off again without taking on more supplies and he sent a seaman ashore to fetch them. Suspicions had been aroused and the man was questioned about the ship's passengers, but his reply – that there was only a mean merchant's wife, was apparently taken at face value. The ship set sail again and this time successfully made the crossing and the Berties disembarked in Brabant. They had made their escape to the European mainland, and now an uncertain future lay ahead of them.

EXILE 1555-1559

Cleves

The next stage was a journey of about a hundred miles and, with the women now wearing local dress, they set out without delay. Their destination was the town of Wesel in the Duchy of Cleves. This was then in the Holy Roman Empire, but is now part of modern Germany. A number of Walloons, French speaking Protestant refugees, had settled there and formed a church, and their pastor was Francis Perusell, although at the time he was using the name Francis de Rivers. This was the same man who, not long before, had been pastor of the French congregation in the Strangers' Church in London during Edward's reign, and he not only knew Catherine, but he was one of the refugees she had personally helped. The Berties headed inland and stopped a few miles short of Wesel in the town of Xanten, or as Foxe called it, Santon. Richard contacted Perusell asking him to apply to the town authorities for a permit for them to stay in Wesel and they waited in Xanten while he did so. They were living very quietly and may have felt secure, but if so, that was not to last. Late in February, Bertie was warned that some of the townsfolk were suspicious that their little group was not as unimportant as they appeared to be, but that they thought they were people of consequence. These rumours had reached the Bishop of Arras and he planned to question them without warning about their status and religion. The prospect was alarming and Richard decided they must move on at once, but carefully, so as not to draw attention.

About three that afternoon Catherine and Richard, carrying baby Susan, left their house as if going out for a stroll, and their two female servants followed at a distance behind. They dared not carry their goods with them or use horses or a waggon, but once out of the town they hurried forward through the fading light of the cold winter's day. It began to rain which not only soaked them, but turned the icy ground under their feet into slush, which was difficult to walk through. The servants tried to hire some kind of conveyance from the villages they passed but without success, and so they pressed on reaching Wesel a little before seven. They were not expected and, not knowing where to go, they sought accommodation in the town's inns, only to find that they were refused entry to them all, for it was assumed that they were a lance-knight (a common foot soldier who had a very poor reputation) and his woman. At last, Bertie found a resting place in a church porch, and, in a pitiable state, wet through, cold and hungry, they thankfully took shelter. Then Richard went out again to try to find Perusell's house, but though he was fluent in French, Latin and Italian, he could not make himself understood to anyone he met. Eventually, to his relief, he heard two boys talking in Latin and he offered them money if they would take him and his family to the house of a Walloon. This they did and, when the householder came to the door, Richard explained that they were English and were seeking the house of Master Perusell. They had been brought to the very house where Perusell was dining with a friend. A few moments later, Perusell himself appeared in the doorway and when he saw who it was and the bedraggled, exhausted state they were in, he was momentarily speechless. Then he drew them in for an emotional welcome and they were provided with dry clothes and warm food and the glad news that he had just obtained permission for them to stay in Wesel.

Within a few days, Perusell found a house for them and so they began to settle into life in Wesel, none the worse for their adventures. They must have been especially thankful for this as Catherine, who was thirty-six and in her time would have been considered old for such things, was in the early stages of pregnancy. They lived quietly in Wesel, able to worship freely and to have fellowship with others who held similar beliefs. Other English refugees settled there too and, for a while, the Bible translator and former Bishop of Exeter, Miles Coverdale, was their pastor. In October, Catherine gave birth to a son, who was called Peregrine because he had been born during their wanderings or peregrinations.

Unfortunately for the Berties, those wanderings were soon to start again. Sometime during the winter of 1555 to 1556 Sir John Mason, the English ambassador in the Netherlands, acting against his own government, sent them a warning that they were in danger of arrest. A leading member of Mary's Council, Lord Paget, who was in the Netherlands, had made up a reason for visiting the baths which were near Wesel. He had arranged for the Duke of Brunswick, who was passing by Wesel, to take the Berties into custody. They could not delay but must move on as soon as they could.

Weinheim

They decided to seek safety in the Palatinate in the town of Weinheim. The Prince-Elector who ruled the Palatinate, Otto Heinrich, was a strong Protestant. He had succeeded his brother and both of them had been friends of Martin Bucer, the theologian Catherine had befriended in Cambridge. The Berties faced a daunting journey some two hundred miles up the Rhine in winter with two very young children, one of them only a few months old. When they arrived in April 1556, they must have hoped that travelling away from England and further into Germany would take them well away from danger. Miles Coverdale had already moved from Wesel into the Palatinate and he sought help from the Prince-Elector on their behalf, who responded by putting a castle at their disposal, which was perched on the top of a hill near the town.

Once again they began to settle into their new home, but only three months later, they were made aware that Philip and Mary had certainly not forgotten about them. Catherine bore the highest rank and the highest profile of all those who had fled England, and especially with her Spanish Catholic background it irked that she should flout the religious laws of her homeland. Stephen Gardiner's antagonism was no longer an issue as he was now dead, but Catherine was too important for Mary to be content to leave her in peace. Philip and Mary dispatched an agent called John Brett to deliver letters to several refugees, including the Berties. He arrived outside the walls of the castle one day in July and when he explained to the gatekeeper that he had letters for the Duchess from some friends, he was told to wait where he was while she was informed. Not long afterwards a stone was dropped from the turret over the gate, which narrowly missed his head, and then some servants rushed out and pursued him down the hill to the town. There, local officials became involved, and William Barlow, whom Mary had removed as Bishop of Bath and Wells, and was now Catherine's chaplain, appeared to say that the Berties did not approve of their servants' actions, and to find out what Brett's letters were about. Were they simply messages or were they subpoenas? They would not accept the latter for in the Palatinate they were under the jurisdiction of the Prince and not an outside authority. Brett refused to answer and he was confined for a while before the authorities decided that he was not allowed to deliver his documents and he had to depart. What the letters actually were was never ascertained, but they may well have been warrants ordering the Berties to return to England.[13]

They were safe again for the time being, but it was not long before another problem began to rear its head, for they were running out of money. Over time, the little group who had fled England together had grown in number, and besides William Barlow, Catherine now had a small entourage around her, probably other refugees who had moved on with her from Wesel. They may all have been in some degree dependent on her financially. At the same time, the Berties' own resources were diminishing. They would have brought as much money as they could with them but that was now running low. It could have been even worse, for in December 1555, members of Parliament had dug in their heels and successfully blocked a government bill which would have forced Protestant exiles to forfeit their property unless they returned to England. Even so, Mary's government had hardened their attitude towards those who had gone abroad and were actively trying to prevent money being sent to them. Although the Berties had made careful

---

13   Baldwin, p. 156.

plans for the administration of their estates, the amount of income they were able to receive from them was limited.

Poland

The solution to this pressing problem came unexpectedly and, once again, was linked to the Continental Reformers Catherine had helped in England. One of them was John à Lasco, a prominent preacher and teacher, who had been the superintendent of the Strangers' Church in London. He had left England early in Mary's reign in a ship full of members from the Church and he was now back in his native Poland, at the invitation of the King, to take a prominent role in advancing the Reformation there. He knew what the Berties had been going through and informed his King of their need, and also the Count Palatine of Vilna, a part of modern-day Lithuania, who was a Calvinist. About a decade earlier the Polish King, Sigismund, had considered marrying Henry VIII's daughter Mary, but the negotiations had failed and afterwards it was rumoured that he was then interested in marrying Catherine, the widowed Duchess of Suffolk, but nothing came of it. Now, both he and the Count sent letters to the Berties offering to provide for them in Poland.

The proposal was very welcome, but such a long journey was not to be undertaken lightly, and so their chaplain, William Barlow, was dispatched to go to Poland and have the arrangements confirmed before the family uprooted themselves and followed on. Barlow travelled across Germany and into Poland, where he was given an audience with the King. He conveyed the Berties' gratitude, and presented Sigismund with a present of the few jewels they had left from those they had brought with them from England. In return, Sigismund gave Barlow a document with a formal offer for Richard and Catherine and sealed with his great seal.

Now there was nothing to detain them and, in April 1557, a year after they had arrived, the Berties left the castle at Weinheim at the start of their long journey. They had not gone far before they ran into trouble. They were travelling in a little group. Catherine with her children and some female servants were seated in a wagon, while her husband and four other men rode their horses alongside. The Duchess's pet spaniel was with them and for some reason this dog was made the excuse for a group of horsemen to attack them. They were led by the captain of a Landgrave (nobleman), and they outnumbered their victims, fighting with Bertie and his men and even thrusting their boar spears into the waggon though fortunately missing its occupants. The captain's horse was killed under him and Catherine signalled to her husband to get away to bring help. Bertie abruptly made off and rode hard for the nearest town. One of their attackers had got there before him and was spreading the tale that the captain had been killed by some Walloons. When Bertie arrived, it was assumed that he was the man who had killed the captain and the town's men, led by the captain's brother, fell upon him. He would probably have been murdered but he noticed a ladder leaning against a house, and somehow managed to get to it and dart up it and into a first floor window. Once inside, he went up further to the top of the house to the garret and there he was able to fend off his assailants for a while, with his dagger in one hand and his rapier in the other. Then the burgomaster and a magistrate appeared and, speaking in Latin, urged him to give himself up, which Bertie did once he was satisfied that they would protect him from the crowd. He was taken into detention, and while there wrote letters to the Landgrave and another local nobleman, the Earl of Erbach, seeking their help. The next day, Catherine's wagon arrived in the town and the Earl of Erbach also appeared. When he saw the Duchess he greeted her with deference and courtesy, which dismayed the townsfolk, especially as they now knew that the captain was still alive, and, becoming frightened of what they had done and fearing repercussions, they began to slink away. The Berties were free to continue their journey and they went on as far as Frankfurt.

Weinheim to Frankfurt was only a small stage of the long journey of over a thousand miles which lay before them, but it was where many English Protestants had congregated and they had established their own church. Even though the Church had been marred by deep divisions, for Catherine and Richard it must have been a welcome interlude to meet up with their fellow countrymen and fellow believers, to worship together and catch up with news. From Frankfurt, their route took them through difficult mountainous terrain before they reached the great plains of north Germany and then they travelled on across the border into Poland. King Sigismund graciously welcomed them, and offered them a home and a position in an area called Crozan in Samogitia, near the Baltic Sea, which today is part of Lithuania. Bertie was to administer the region on behalf of the King. It was a mainly Protestant area and Sigismund had been looking for a suitable Protestant to appoint as governor. For the Berties, it meant that at last they were safe and could look forward to a secure future in Poland, doing what they could to encourage the spread of Bible teaching, for as long as they needed to be there. Just how long that might be they, like all the exiles, simply did not know, and they had to be prepared to stay there long term. There was no prospect of a return home while Mary reigned and, in the late summer of 1557, which was when they probably arrived at Samogithia, Mary would have been forty-one, with possibly many years of life ahead of her.

Catherine's correspondence with William Cecil was necessarily halted while she was abroad, but news of what was happening in England must have filtered through to her, even when they were in Samogitia. It was distressing, and the Duchess and her husband would have been grieved by what they heard, including about Hugh Latimer, who meant so much to Catherine as a friend and spiritual teacher, and whose old age was no protection against the heresy laws. These had been passed by Parliament in November 1554, Catherine had left her home at the beginning of January 1555 and the first execution took place early in February. The Berties had escaped with very little time to spare.

BACKGROUND. MARY'S REIGN (PART 2)

The aims of Queen Mary's religious policy were simple: to remove Protestantism from her realm, to destroy it through fire. The theory was that if the leading stubborn core died a horrible death, the rest would be frightened into submission, and she did not expect the resistance she was to encounter.[14] Such men as Edmund Bonner, now reinstated as Bishop of London, and her Lord Chancellor, Stephen Gardiner, once again Bishop of Winchester, until his death in November 1555, energetically pursued the 'heretics'. But the drive behind the policy came personally and directly from Mary herself, encouraged by Reginald Pole, who had succeeded Cranmer as Archbishop of Canterbury.

The martyrs

On 4th February 1555 John Rogers, a well-known preacher and the compiler of the Matthews Bible, was led to his execution at Smithfield. He recited Psalm 51 as he walked and died calmly and bravely, the first martyr to be burnt and a strong example to those who would follow after. Very soon afterwards, a group of leading clerics including John Hooper, Bishop of Gloucester, and Robert Ferrar, Bishop of St David's, were sent back to die where they had officiated, and within a year most of the leading theologians and Protestant bishops who had not fled abroad, had been burnt. Among them were the outstanding preacher, Hugh Latimer, and the former Bishop of London, Nicholas Ridley. In Oxford in October 1555, the night before his death, Ridley spoke cheerfully of his wedding in the morning. Many other martyrs viewed their deaths as bringing them to their spiritual wedding or to a feast in heaven with Christ their Saviour. Latimer and Ridley were burnt together and, as normally was the case at Protestant executions, they were not allowed to address the onlookers, but Latimer exhorted his friend with words which have resounded through the years: 'Be of good comfort, Master Ridley, and play the man. We shall this day light such a candle, by God's grace, in England, as I trust shall never be put out.'[15]

Ridley's had been a particularly horrible and protracted death and Thomas Cranmer had been forced to watch. His timid, scholarly mind was not suited to withstand the intense pressure he was being put under to recant, as was his strong belief in the importance of obedience to the monarch. He was being subjected to special treatment to undermine his resistance. It was partly because of the key role he had played in

14 E. Ives, *The Reformation Experience : Living Through the Turbulent Sixteenth Century* (Oxford: Lion Hudson, 2012), pp. 221, 223.

15 *Foxe's Book of Martyrs*, p. 422.

the English Reformation, but Mary also saw him as her personal enemy, the man who had brought about her parent's divorce. Early in 1556, Cranmer was broken down by his treatment and recanted, which normally would have saved his life, but Mary insisted he should still be burnt. On 21st March just before his execution, Cranmer gave a speech which was supposed to be his final and public recantation. Instead, before his astonished audience could stop him, he repudiated all his previous recantations, and declared they were contrary to his true faith and came from his fear of burning, and then denounced the Pope as anti-Christ. He died bravely, holding the hand with which he had signed his recantations into the flames, and though the authorities tried to suppress what had happened, their great coup from his series of recantations was completely turned into a propaganda disaster when the truth was spread abroad.

Although they came from every social class including the gentry and clerics, the majority of the martyrs were humbler folk such as craftsmen, shopkeepers and labourers. Once again, the doctrine of transubstantiation, of the real presence of Christ's body in the mass, was the usual test of their 'heresy'. Over two hundred and eighty died in the fires and many more, perhaps even another hundred, died while held in prison awaiting trial or execution, in poor conditions and often suffering maltreatment. A large number of the martyrs were young, in their late teens or twenties. Around one in five who died were women.

There was only one burning in the whole of the north of England. The vast majority were in the south east, where the greatest number of Protestants were, and also where they were sought out more vigorously, especially in London and the counties to the east: Sussex, Essex, Suffolk and Norfolk. Sympathy for the victims grew and, in time, there was so much obvious support for them that demonstrations of sympathy at burnings were forbidden and those who disobeyed were threatened with death. Yet, they still continued. Some were brought to faith themselves by the courage and faith that they observed.

Far from all Protestants stood firm. Many who were arrested recanted, though of those some took advantage of their freedom to flee abroad, and others later returned to their faith, some being rearrested and burnt. A particularly sad case was that of Sir John Cheke, King Edward's tutor, who had safely fled abroad, but was kidnapped in Flanders and returned to England, where, despite his initial resistance, John Feckenham was instrumental in persuading him to recant.

Worse things were happening on the Continent. In Spain and the Spanish Netherlands as well as in France, Protestants were dying in larger numbers and even more cruelly, but the years of Mary's persecution in England left an unanticipated legacy. The burnings were on a scale undreamed of before. There were ten in the twenty-four years when Henry VII was King, and eighty-one in Henry VIII's thirty-eight-year reign, compared to nearly three hundred in the three and a half years of Mary's persecution. That period became known as England's Terror and Mary as Bloody Mary. The revulsion and horror did not simply evaporate afterwards but left an indelible memory. John Foxe returned from exile after Mary's death to interview eyewitnesses of what had happened not long before, to authenticate the material for his *Book of Martyrs*. The enduring popularity of his book meant that the nation remembered for far longer than the first generation or two. Catholicism would come to be seen as a foreign religion, intolerant and cruel, and this affected the nation's attitude to the Catholic Church and to the Pope for hundreds of years.

Elizabeth

Some Protestants formed secret congregations, although they were likely to be burnt if caught. Far more compromised. To avoid drawing attention to themselves and risk arrest, they attended their parish church as they were required to do and participated in the mass. The most high-profile person to compromise was the Lady Elizabeth. At first, Mary had tried to persuade Elizabeth to attend mass at court, but Elizabeth had resisted as long as she dared. When she gave way and participated in both the mass and confession, Mary was highly suspicious of her motives. After Wyatt's rebellion, Elizabeth had endured a period of imprisonment in the Tower, while strenuous but abortive efforts were made to find links between her and the rebels. Imperial ambassador Simon Renard was not the only one pressing for her death, or at least her removal from the succession, but Mary eventually released her.

Mary disliked Elizabeth, not least because she was daughter of the hated Anne Boleyn, whom Mary saw as the author of her own, and her mother's, misfortunes. The fact that Mary did not trust her and thought her apparent conversion to Catholicism was probably only play acting, made it unbearable that Elizabeth was her heir. She feared that, unless something changed, the unthinkable would happen at her death, and Elizabeth would take the realm back to Protestantism again. The only certain way to prevent this was for Mary to have a baby and, late in 1554, as her stomach swelled, to Mary's great joy she thought she was pregnant. The following April, she retired to her private apartments at Hampton Court to await the birth. Humiliatingly, weeks – and then months – passed, but no baby appeared. She had experienced a phantom pregnancy and something similar would happen again three years later. How different things would have been if either of these had been a real pregnancy and Mary had succeeded in giving birth to a Catholic heir.

The summer of 1558 was a grim time all round. Mary's people were enduring particular economic hardships and the effects of a series of poor harvests. A further round of prosecutions and burnings was underway. The national mood was depressed by the loss of Calais the previous winter. Philip of Spain had succeeded in drawing England into a war with France for his own advantage and the upshot was that Calais, the one part of France that England still held, had been won back by the French. As the year advanced, Mary's health deteriorated. She wrote to Elizabeth pleading with her to keep the country Catholic on her accession. Mary had stomach cancer and, on 17th November, it claimed her life. Elizabeth was on her estate at Hatfield when two Council members arrived with the news of Mary's death. They found her in the park reading her Greek New Testament and, at first, she was too overcome to speak. Then she sank to her knees and quoted from Psalm 118 in Latin.

'This is the Lord's doing; it is marvellous in our eyes.'[16] That same day, she ordered the persecution to stop.

REIGN OF ELIZABETH 1558-1580

Letters from Poland

Mary had ended up being a most unpopular Queen and London was overjoyed at the accession of her twenty-five-year-old half-sister. The news would have taken a while to reach the Berties in Samogitia, but there, and among all the exiles, it would have been received with much relief and rejoicing. On 28th January 1559, Catherine wrote to her new Queen a letter exuding thankfulness to God for placing her on the throne and so delivering her subjects, and anticipating that God would use Elizabeth to establish a clearly Protestant church.

'The almighty and ever-living God so endue your Majesty with his Spirit, that it may be said of you as of his servant David, "He hath found one even after his own heart"...Wherefore now is our season, if ever anywhere, of rejoicing, and to say after Zachary [Zachariah], "Blessed be the Lord God of Israel," which hath visited and delivered your Majesty, and by you us, His and your miserable and afflicted subjects. For if the Israelites might joy in their Deborah, how much we English in our Elizabeth that deliverance of our thralled conscience. Then first your Majesty hath great cause to praise God that it pleased Him to appoint you the mean whereby He showeth out this his great mercy over that land; and we generally ought to praise, thank, and honour Him in you, and you in Him, with an unfeigned love and obedience all the days of our lives.' Catherine prayed that God would give her 'a prosperous journey once again presently to see your Majesty, to rejoice together with my countryfolks, and to sing a song to the Lord in my native land. God for his mercy grant it, and to your Majesty long life, with safe government, to his glory, your honour, and [your] subjects comfort.'[17]

At last, Catherine could have contact again with the Cecils. William's fortunes had come full circle. He had not served Mary, although he had

---

16   A. Weir, *Children of England,* p. 363.

17   Reprinted in M. Haykin, pp.110-11.

had to compromise and attend mass and Catholic services in order to keep his freedom and indeed his life, but for some time he had been administering Elizabeth's estates and she well knew his worth. One of Elizabeth's very first actions as Queen was to appoint Cecil as her Principal Secretary, and for the next forty years he would serve with distinction as her chief minister; together, they forged an extremely effective partnership.

As for Catherine, a measure of sadness and disillusionment must have come to her not long after she wrote to the new Queen. She received a letter from the Cecils and on 4th March she responded to it in a very different tone to her letter to Elizabeth. She had learned that things were not moving in the way she had expected and she urged Cecil onward to restore the Church and reproached him for the reports she had heard that he was hanging back.

'I would to God all our whole nation were likewise one in Jesus Christ...for the love I bear you I cannot forbear to write...and if it shall please you to heed a simple woman's mind.' She spoke of Edward Seymour 'that good duke, your old master...when God had placed him to set forth His glory (which yet of himself he was always ready to do)' he was held back by worldly friends and 'gave over his hot zeal to set forth God's true religion as he had most nobly begun, and turning him to follow such worldly devices, you can as well as I tell what came of it: the duke lost all that he sought to keep, with his head to boot... Wherefore I am forced to say with the prophet Elie[Elijah], How long halt ye between two opinions?' How could the Queen and any councillor still attend mass? Catherine emphasised the importance of acting quickly: 'To build surely is first to lay the sure cornerstone, today and not tomorrow...There is no fear of innovation in restoring old good laws and repealing new evil...Christ...hath left His Gospel behind Him a rule sufficient and only to be followed. Thus I write after my old manner, which if I persuade you, take it as thankfully and friendly as I mean it...With my hearty prayer that He will so assist you with His grace that you may the first and only seek Him as His eldest and chosen vessel.'[18]

---

18   Read, pp. 133-5.

For Catherine, it was very straightforward. Christ's gospel, the Bible, should be the sole authority for everything. She herself might have come to faith gradually over a period of time, but her love for God and her trust in Christ her Saviour, had then turned her life upside down. In Edward's reign, she had used what she had, her money, her position, her influence, to promote her faith, and, in Mary's reign, she had given up what she had, her home, lands, position, comfort and country to flee abroad to save her life, for she would not compromise. Now that Protestant Elizabeth had replaced Mary, what was to stop the Church being immediately restored to how it had been before Mary's changes? Other developments could follow on afterwards.

For Elizabeth, it was anything but straightforward, and she and Cecil were indeed moving very cautiously, even though a new religious settlement was imperative. She faced a daunting situation. Internally, the economy was at a very low ebb. War with France was further depleting her limited resources. Externally, it was a dangerous moment for the nations around her were watching. Would she repudiate her sister's Catholicism? Her powerful Catholic neighbours were presently at war with each other, and England needed to maintain good relations with Philip II's Spain to offset the perils posed by her old enemies France and the dominant pro-French influence in Scotland, positioned in between them as she was. Elizabeth still carried the label of illegitimacy and the Pope might choose to call the Catholic nations to unite to remove her if Protestantism was restored. In that case, there was a Catholic replacement candidate to hand in her nearest rival for the throne, her cousin, the teenage Mary Queen of Scots, who was married to the heir to the French throne. With typical canniness, Elizabeth began by keeping everyone guessing as to her intentions, but that was only sustainable in the short term. She was also ruling a country where probably the majority wanted an end to the twists and turns and changes in religious policy. There was a yearning for stability and for the continuance of the familiar, without the extremes of either zealous Catholicism or zealous Protestantism. Elizabeth was in tune with the mood of many of her subjects.

BACKGROUND. ELIZABETH'S RELIGIOUS SETTLEMENT

The first Parliament of the reign assembled on 25th January 1559. Inside the House of Commons there was an influential, well organised and skilful group of committed Protestant members, especially some who had already got home from their exile abroad, and they were advised and supported by some leading churchmen who had also scrambled to return from the Continent. This group of men were determined to seize their opportunity and to make the most of this moment. The result was that they may have succeeded in moving the government further and faster than they had intended going at this time.

When Elizabeth dissolved Parliament in early May, an Act of Uniformity and an Act of Supremacy had been passed, and a Protestant framework for the Elizabethan Church was set in law. Once again there was a prayer book, which was largely based on Edward VI's Second Prayer Book of 1552, with some minor alterations. Probably the most contentious of these would prove to be about clerical robes or vestments which were retained, despite being a hangover from the medieval Church, and the returning exiles' desire for plain black Geneva style preaching gowns. Unlike her father who had been the Supreme Head of the Church of England, Elizabeth was now styled Supreme Governor, in essence a very similar position, although in practice she had slightly less authority than him. The Pope, once again, had none. It was a compromise, but not with Mary's Catholic Church, for this was clearly a Protestant Church, but between the different strands of Protestantism itself, in a similar way to how Cranmer had melded them in the Edwardian Church.

By January 1560, all but one of Mary's bishops had refused to take the oath of supremacy and were removed from office. Elizabeth had to appoint twenty-five new bishops and did so by reinstating some her sister had removed and by choosing most others from the returned exiles. Her new Church had a gifted and committed leadership. Clergy were also able to have wives again. Attendance at church was compulsory and absentees were fined, but this was a moderate settlement which could be accepted by most and was deliberately not too zealously enforced. Elizabeth was supposed to have once said that she did not want to make windows into men's souls. She was not too concerned with what people believed in their own hearts, as long as they outwardly obeyed her laws. The repeated use of the Prayer Book services Sunday by Sunday, all in English with readings from the English Bible, meant that they became increasingly familiar and helped the new order to be accepted gradually.

Over the next four years, Elizabeth's Church was further established, especially with the issuing of the Thirty-Nine Articles in 1563, basically a mild revision of Edward's Forty-Two Articles. The same year, Foxe's *Book of Martyrs* was first published in English, and this would go on to be hugely influential as it was read across the land whether in churches or in the homes of those who could afford it, where it was normal to see it alongside the Bible and the Prayer Book. Once the Pope excommunicated Elizabeth in 1570, denying her right to the throne and calling on English Catholics to refuse to obey her, Catholics became suspected enemies of the state. There were several Catholic plots to assassinate or remove the Queen and replace her with Mary, Queen of Scots, but all of these were thwarted. Mary was executed in 1587 and her death was followed by attempted invasion when the Spanish Armada of 1588 aimed to dethrone Elizabeth and reimpose Catholicism. All of this meant that Protestantism now became linked with loyalty and patriotism.

The expectation was that this Church settlement was just the beginning, and that over time, it would be modified and built upon, certainly taken further, but Elizabeth had no such intention. As far as she was concerned this was it, and she would be deaf to the pressure which would grow for further reform, especially from within the Church itself. As the reign proceeded both Catholics and Protestants would fall foul of her. Some Catholics faced not merely fines, but execution for treason, and some Protestants, with advanced views for a church outside of the Church of England model, were prosecuted for sedition if these ideas were promoted to others.

Homecoming

Catherine and Richard Bertie returned home as soon as they could, probably in the late spring or the summer of 1559, over four years after their exile had begun. Their lands and goods, some of which had been seized by Mary, were restored to them, and they were released from any debts owed to the crown. Almost immediately, Catherine was active to help others and to work for the gospel. Miles Coverdale and his family returned to England in the autumn of that year and were in financial need. Catherine appointed him as her chaplain and tutor to her children, and he stayed with her for nearly five years until he accepted a living in a London church. He was not reappointed to his former bishopric at Exeter, possibly because he felt he was too old.

The Bertie family settled back to living at Grimsthorpe and to picking up the threads of their former life. Catherine was now forty and the children six and three. The family owned several properties, but their main homes continued to be at Grimsthorpe and the Barbican in London, where they would stay for part of each winter or when they needed to be in the capital. They regularly visited their friends, and from time to time they also stayed at court.

While Catherine was still a duchess and a great lady, in Elizabeth's reign she would not have the same importance or prominence at court that she had had under Henry and Edward, when she had been at the centre of court life, a lady-in-waiting and a good friend of both Edward Seymour, Duke of Somerset and John Dudley, Duke of Northumberland. Now, despite her friendship with Cecil, there would be a gradual disintegration in her relationship with Elizabeth. They stood for such different things and they had such different personalities. Elizabeth was carrying the weight of government and responsibility for the peace and stability of her kingdom, which involved, in her eyes, a relatively static national Church. Her own preferences were for a conservative Protestantism, and she could not stand those who were too enthusiastic about their religion, and those who pushed their own viewpoint too hard. Her early life had been so difficult, and at times precarious, that she had learned the hard way to be devious, calculating and opaque; like her father, she was a powerful figure who no one could take lightly or for granted. She frequently prevaricated and changed her mind, and at times Cecil must have had his patience tried to its limits. Catherine was very direct in her thinking and speech and saw things with her own particular brand of clarity. Nothing must stand in the way of the progress of God's work and that was what mattered. She stood in the Puritan camp, wanting the Church purified from all lingering Catholic practice. From the very beginning of the reign, she opposed vestments and anything which would smack of the old Church and obscure the message of the new and of the Bible itself, and she pressed for further change at every opportunity. At times, Cecil must have wearied of her letters and Elizabeth quickly tired of her. Elizabeth would not be pushed by anyone and, with her imperious nature, she resented those who tried. It is likely that she utterly disliked Catherine of Suffolk.

Towards the end of 1561, Catherine was staying at the court at Greenwich but in November had to move to the Barbican when she went down with smallpox. This was a dangerous disease, often leading to permanent disfigurement and not infrequently death, but Catherine seems to have escaped relatively lightly and, by February 1562, she was much improved. A year later, Richard became an MP. For four years from 1563, he sat in the House of Commons representing Lincolnshire, along with William Cecil. He was a member of a parliamentary committee established to look into the succession, which would not have endeared him to Elizabeth, for whom it was a very touchy subject; indeed, she resisted all attempts to make her name an heir.

Mary Grey

Over the years Catherine's wider family gave her some cause for concern. When she returned to England in 1559, her stepdaughter Frances Grey was ill and she died that November. Frances's two daughters, Katherine and Mary, both ladies-in-waiting, were now orphaned, although they did have a stepfather, Adrian Stokes, through her second marriage. Their lives were tainted by their proximity to the throne. If Henry VIII's will was still followed then they were Elizabeth's immediate heirs. Only if it was ignored would the normal rules of inheritance apply and Mary Queen of Scots, the granddaughter of Henry's older sister would succeed, instead of the Greys, who were granddaughters of his younger sister. With Elizabeth still unmarried, the line of succession was very much a pertinent and live issue.

In July 1565, Mary Grey married secretly. She and her husband, Thomas Keyes, were an unlikely match. At nineteen or twenty, Mary was diminutive and with royal blood in her veins. Keyes was an exceptionally large man, the largest at court, much older than Mary, a widower with a family from his first marriage. He was also merely the sergeant porter, and Mary was marrying far beneath her. Her sister Katherine had married in 1560, secretly and without the Queen's permission, and had been separated from her husband and imprisoned or under house arrest ever since Elizabeth had found out. Mary too had not sought the Queen's permission first, as any lady-in-waiting should have done, yet alone one so near to the throne. In August, Mary's secret came out and the furious Queen had Keyes immediately imprisoned. Mary herself was placed under house arrest at Chequers in Buckinghamshire. Two years later, in August 1567, she was transferred to Catherine's charge, delivered to her at another London house, the Minories, just as the Duchess was about to set off for Grimsthorpe.

A couple of days later, Catherine voiced her concerns in a letter to Cecil. She complained that Mary had arrived with virtually no possessions and declared that she herself was unable to supply her needs. She asked Cecil if he thought it was appropriate to ask the Queen to provide suitable furniture and household goods to equip one room for Mary and her maid. Could Catherine really not provide for her step granddaughter herself, or was she annoyed at the way Mary had been dumped on her, and wanting to make a point, and also make sure that the Queen knew just what a poor standard of living her cousin had been reduced to by Elizabeth's harsh treatment of her? Catherine sounded really shocked at Mary's pitiful lack of the most basic of personal possessions, and even more shocked at her physical and mental state. 'I hope she will do well hereafter, for notwithstanding that I am sure she is now glad to be with me, yet I assure you she is otherwise, not only in conscience but in very deed, so sad and ashamed of her fault...so that I am not yet sure she [Mary's maid] can get her to eat, in all that she hath eaten these two days not so much as a chicken's leg. She makes me even afraid of [for] her, and therefore I will be the gladder for them [furnishings and basic necessities]. I think a little comfort would do well.'[19]

Mary stayed in Catherine's custody for two years. They would have mourned together when the news reached them that Mary's sister, Katherine, had died in January 1568, but living with the Berties was probably the happiest time of Mary's confinement. She was staying with family and she got on well with Susan and Peregrine. Then, in 1569, she was moved on to the charge of Sir Thomas Gresham and stayed with him until she was released in 1572 after the death of her husband. She died in 1578, possibly of the plague, still only in her mid-thirties.

Reginald Grey

The last years of Catherine's life were marked by other stressful and sad events and by various frustrations. On top of all these difficulties, Catherine also had to cope with growing ill health.

In 1570, her sixteen-year-old daughter, Susan, was betrothed to a young man called Reginald Grey and she married him within the year. Reginald's father should have been the Earl of Kent, but he had had insufficient money to claim the title. Catherine decided to step in, and enlisting Cecil's help, she also approached Elizabeth herself to try to have the title bestowed on Reginald. At the same time, Catherine wished to see her husband with a title, and pressed for him to become Lord Willoughby during his lifetime, and after his death for the title to revert to Peregrine. Even though she was unwell, Catherine pursued both her objectives with tenacity. She found Elizabeth's sudden changes of mood difficult to handle, but kept a spiritual perspective on the situation, writing to Cecil, 'Surely I must confess her Majesty's strange countenance...was no little grief to me, and more than I was able in the sudden to digest, but when with better leisure I remembered that though men might fail me yet God would be merciful to me, it made me of better comfort.'[20]

---

19   ibid., p. 145.

20   ibid., pp. 174-5.

At one time, she told Cecil she had wondered if her son-in-law's case was hindered by Elizabeth's negative attitude to herself and her family. Reginald Grey did become Earl of Kent, and he obviously shared Catherine's faith, for Catherine's former chaplain, John Parkhurst, now Bishop of Norwich, wrote to her wishing that Reginald lived in Norfolk, 'that having such a one as he is, in commission, we might together travel to reform that is out of frame, to the advancement of God in his glory and the suppression of Popery in these parts, wherein for want of help I cannot do that I desire'.[21] Sadly, Reginald and Susan had only a short time together as he died in 1573.

Peregrine

Although the case for Bertie went to both the Attorney General and the Solicitor General and then waited for a decision from Elizabeth, that never came and he would not acquire a title. It was disappointing for Catherine, but far more serious issues were raised by Peregrine's marriage. Peregrine was very different to Catherine's other sons. As a youth, he had spent time in William Cecil's household, but he was not the outstanding scholar his half-brothers had been and his lively, wayward nature caused Catherine anxiety both at Cecil's and afterwards. Then, in 1577, he became deeply attached to a most unsuitable young lady. In July, Catherine told Cecil in a letter that 'I had rather he had matched in any other place'.[22] At the age of twenty-two, Peregrine had fallen in love with Lady Mary de Vere, maid of honour to Elizabeth and sister to the Earl of Oxford. Her brother was a very unpleasant man, who had made the lives of his wife, Ann, and her parents, William and Mildred Cecil, miserable. Mary, too, appeared to have a difficult personality and Catherine was deeply concerned about the relationship and clearly feared Mary might turn out like her brother. In fact, Catherine felt helpless. Peregrine had made up his mind and had committed himself to Mary, so his mother could only make the best of a bad job. In July 1577, just a fortnight after her previous letter, Catherine was unburdening herself again to Cecil. 'I cannot express how much it grieveth me that my son in this weightiest matter hath so

21   ibid., p. 176.
22   ibid., p. 181.

far forgotten himself to the trouble and disquiet of his friends. He is like enough to be his own undoing and the young lady's too.' She also spoke of Peregrine's 'wilfulness and uncourteous dealings'.[23]

Despite her deep misgivings Catherine had come to see that she had to promote the match. Not only was Peregrine determined to marry Mary, but he might be rash enough to do it without the Queen's approval. As a maid of honour, Mary needed Elizabeth's permission to marry and the pair's future would be blighted without it. Catherine had too much personal experience of the implacable, harsh treatment Elizabeth could mete out to those who crossed her, in the lives of Katherine and Mary Grey, to be casual about the necessity for royal sanction of the match. She would normally have gone through Cecil, but his own feelings were so involved because of Mary's brother, that she could not openly ask for his help, only confide the situation to him.

Catherine tried to befriend Mary and form a relationship with her herself. By December they were on better terms. The Queen gave her consent for the marriage and the wedding took place early in 1578. Catherine and Richard vacated Grimsthorpe so that the young couple could live there, and moved to Hampstead. Their house at the Barbican, now called Willoughby House, was perhaps in too central and busy a location for a long stay, and Hampstead was quiet and countrified. The newlyweds did not stop causing problems and anxiety even now. They were quarrelling, drinking too much and failing to look after the property.

In September 1578, Cecil's eldest son, Thomas, visited Grimsthorpe and reported to his father that Catherine had already gone to see them to try and help their marriage relationship. Catherine must have been sorely tried, particularly as she was not well. For some years, she had suffered from periodic illnesses and her poor health could only have made it harder to cope with the ongoing stress and upset over Peregrine and Mary. A year later, Catherine was ill and in pain, and distressed when she found out that her footman had implied to Cecil that she was 'senseless'. She wrote to him to put the record straight. She was indeed

---

23   ibid., p. 182.

ill, but was in her right mind. 'But whatever I am in weakness of body, [I am]Your Lordship's very assuredly till it will please God to call me.'[24]

The situation was to get worse. Mary was not only behaving badly to Peregrine but to Catherine too and, in the spring of 1580, Catherine thought the danger went beyond threatening her peace of mind but instead was to her life itself. With some agitation, she wrote not to Cecil, but to the one person who might have an even better chance of influencing the Queen in her favour, Elizabeth's long-time favourite, Robert Dudley, Earl of Leicester. Catherine had known Robert since he was a child for his father, John Dudley, was a protégé of her first husband and the two families were friendly.

Catherine did not go into specifics but, in her letter, she told Dudley that her daughter-in-law was spreading rumours that Catherine was trying to harm her and was also passing around a letter written by Catherine which could be interpreted in a bad light, such a bad light that Catherine came to fear that she would be executed. Catherine could be intemperate and express herself forcibly, and she herself described the letter as 'sharp', but she believed it was being used maliciously against her and given a meaning she had never intended, and she was clearly frightened about what the Queen's reaction might be.

Nothing is known about what happened next, but in April, Catherine had mentioned the situation to Cecil and was also asking once more for his help with Peregrine. Although the last thing she wanted in her old age was for him to go abroad, Peregrine was keen to see military service and Catherine could not bear to see his 'doleful pining and vexed mind at home,' and so petitioned Cecil to obtain Elizabeth's permission for him to go. Her distress is obvious and so is her faith. 'Oh my good Lord, you have children and therefore you know how dear they be to their parents...in place of comfort I myself must be the suitor for his absence, to my great grief and sorrow. But God's will be fulfilled, who worketh all for the best to them that love and fear Him; wherefore were not that hope of Him thoroughly settled in me, I think my very heart would burst for sorrow.'[25]

---

24   ibid., p. 188.
25   ibid., p. 190.

In time, in fact two more years, these family upsets would die down. Peregrine did not go overseas until 1582, and by then he and Mary had put the very rocky start to their marriage behind them and had settled down together. They would go on to have seven children, calling their only daughter after Catherine, and Peregrine would have a successful career as a soldier and military commander, and would be well thought of by his Queen. Susan married again, also in 1582, to a friend of Peregrine's, Sir John Wingfield, and so she too was settled and would have children.

Gospel work

In March 1579, Catherine had reached her sixtieth birthday, which meant that in those days she would have been regarded as an old lady. To add to her family anxieties and her own ill health, she had the frustration of seeing her hopes for the country's religious settlement unfulfilled. She must have seen the twenty years of Elizabeth's reign as a wasted opportunity. In 1559, Catherine had viewed the situation at the end of Edward's reign as a mere starting point, but the differences between Edward's and Elizabeth's religious settlements were all in the wrong direction, which meant that Elizabeth's had not even gone quite as far as Edward's. Nothing Catherine had impatiently pushed for in the following years had been achieved; indeed, her interventions may well have been counterproductive. Yet Catherine herself had used her time well to faithfully and consistently encourage the spread of the Bible's message, especially where she had influence in her own county of Lincolnshire.

On her return from exile, Catherine resumed the spiritual activities she had pursued under Edward. She sponsored and encouraged the publication of Calvinistic theology and religious works in English.

Once again, she paid for the printing of Hugh Latimer's sermons. Latimer's former servant, Augustine Bernher, prepared them for publication and their collaboration ensured they could be read not only at the time, but that they would survive for posterity. She continued to use her influence and patronage to promote able gospel preachers and to bring Bible truth to the many, including those who were ignorant and untaught. Increasingly, Catherine's support for clerics was for those who were of a Puritan persuasion and some of them were openly critical of the official Church. Twice, she used her influence to help her chaplain, John Browne, when he had to appear before the Star Chamber for criticising the Anglican Church. She had connections with the parish of the Holy Trinity Minories in London, which was a centre where Puritan preachers were nurtured.

Catherine's death

Catherine, sadly, would not live to see her daughter marry again or Peregrine and Mary resolve their differences. The distresses of 1580 came while she was ill and only months before her death in September of that year. She was buried at Spilsby, near her estate at Eresby. Richard died eighteen months later and was laid to rest beside her, and a fine monument to them stands in the church. Surely Catherine's death must have felt like the end of an era. She was sixty-one when she died and had held the title of Duchess of Suffolk for forty-seven years, since she had become a bride at fourteen in the far-off days of Henry VIII. She had lived through the reigns of two of his children and well into the reign of his third. She had been born into a staunchly Catholic family in pre- Reformation days and had lived through all the changes which the Reformation had brought. She herself had come to believe the key doctrines, not with a mere mental assent, but with a wholehearted giving of her heart and life to God. She believed in justification by faith and also that He had directed her life for good, and still believed that in the traumas of her last months. God 'worketh all for the best to them that love and fear Him'. She may have been a great lady, but she had also lived usefully, fruitfully and faithfully as God's servant.

CATHERINE'S LEGACY

In 1562, Augustine Bernher dedicated his book of Latimer's sermons to Catherine, Duchess of Suffolk. He wrote of 'the excellent gifts of God bestowed upon your Grace, in giving unto you such a princely spirit, by whose power and virtue you were able to overcome the world, to forsake your possessions, lands and goods, your worldly friends and native country, your high estate and estimation with the which you were adorned and to become an exile for Christ and His Gospel's sake'.[26] Shortly afterwards, Catherine received more praise, and her story a far wider audience, when she was included in Foxe's *Book of Martyrs*, with an especially detailed account of her adventures on the Continent. She had not been a martyr but she had made substantial sacrifices and Foxe felt she had earned a place in his book. Perhaps not surprisingly, she acquired the reputation of a Protestant heroine. Unusually, in the years following her death, she had both a song and a play written about her. In about 1588, a ballad appeared called, 'The Most Rare and Excellent History of the Duchess of Suffolk and Her Husband Richard Bertie's Calamity'. In 1623, 'The Life of the Duchess of Suffolk' took to the stage at a theatre in Cripplegate.

Catherine was known for her faith by friend and foe alike. In Elizabeth's reign, a Spanish Catholic called her, 'One of the worst heretics in England' and described her as someone 'who had studied at Geneva'.[27] Catherine lived a life of faithfulness and consistent Christian witness at the top of society and in the public eye, and used the opportunities her position gave her. Her aim was to do what she could to help to spread biblical truth. She saw the importance of good preaching and teaching, and of making the Bible and good Christian literature available, and in English. She helped many Reformers, giving money for their support, displaying a caring nature, and showing willingness to roll up her own sleeves when needed, as when she nursed Martin Bucer.

Catherine knew much loss in her life. Within six years, she suffered the deaths of her first husband, one of her closest friends in Katherine Parr, and then the rest of her first family, with the deaths of her two sons. Four years later, she chose to lose her status and everything she had in England, for the danger and uncertainty of exile and a completely unknown future. She met these situations without self-pity and with trust in God, whom she strongly believed was in control and working everything for her good, and teaching her through her trials and circumstances. At the end of her life, she had lost her health and

---

26   Baldwin, p. 167.

27   M. Haykin, p. 104.

feared she would lose her only son to live abroad. She was near to heartbreak, but again, was helped through her trust in God and His good purposes. She was a good example of a godly woman showing endurance, looking for God's will to be done and strengthened by her belief in His sovereignty.

Catherine was also very human and openly displayed her faults. She was tenacious, but probably unwise in the way and frequency with which she pressed for further religious reform. Although there may have been an attractive side to her honesty and directness, she undoubtedly went too far at times, sometimes expressing herself too forcibly, and she was well known for her temper.

Catherine was a strong and lively character and modern historians have found her interesting and something of a personality. Most have had little understanding of her faith, but on the whole she has been treated with respect, and regarded as having lived a significant life, and as being an outstanding woman of the Tudor age. The Christian historian Michael Haykin has dubbed her 'The Puritan Duchess'. Her contemporary, Augustine Bernher, called her a 'valiant spirit'. It seems right to leave the last word to him for he knew her personally and was well placed to assess her influence. He wrote that for thirty-five years she had been a mainstay to preachers, a comfort to martyrs and God's instrument for the spread of the gospel.[28]

---

28 *Oxford Dictionary of National Biography* Vol , p. 487.

A SELECTION OF SIGNIFICANT PEOPLE

John Aylmer 1520/21–1594

He studied at Cambridge and was then tutor to Lady Jane Grey. As a married priest, he was deprived of his church living in March 1554 and spent the rest of Mary's reign in exile on the Continent. He became Bishop of London in 1577.

John Bale 1495–1563

He was Cambridge educated and a friar until he became a Reformer in the early 1530s. He was a prolific writer and playwright. He went into exile from 1539 at Wesel in the Duchy of Cleves and was a very outspoken Protestant propagandist. He returned to England after Edward VI's accession and became Bishop of Ossory in Ireland. Despite his faith, he encouraged support for Mary against Lady Jane Grey, but fled to Europe again after Mary succeeded to the throne and finally returned to England after Elizabeth became Queen. He provided important encouragement, practical help and information to John Foxe when he was compiling his martyrology.

Edmund Bonner c. 1500–1569

After his student days at Oxford University he was ordained about 1529 and went on to become a leading Catholic churchman. He was appointed Bishop of Hereford in 1538 and Bishop of London from 1539–1549 and 1553–1559 and, in that office, actively persecuted Protestants. He was removed from office and imprisoned during Edward VI's reign for opposing religious changes, restored by Mary and deprived again by Elizabeth. He has a bad reputation for the enthusiasm with which he persecuted Protestants and the way in which he interrogated them, though he claimed some of his harshness was to frighten his victims into recanting, and so save their lives.

Charles Brandon c. 1484–1545

A soldier, courtier, and nobleman who was active and loyal in the service of Henry VIII. He owed his rapid rise to their friendship. Viscount Lisle 1513. Duke of Suffolk 1514. He married Mary Tudor, King Henry VIII's younger sister in 1515, so giving their descendants a place in the line of succession to the throne. After Mary's death, he married the young heiress, Catherine Willoughby, in 1533. A powerful East Anglian magnate and leading figure in the Protestant group at court in the 1540s.

William Cecil 1520/1–1598

He was an able administrator. In the reign of King Edward VI he was secretary to Edward Seymour, Duke of Somerset and then to John Dudley, Duke of Northumberland. In 1550, he became a member of the Privy Council and Third Secretary of State. He was knighted in 1551. He was not involved with Mary's government because of his Protestant convictions. In 1558, he became Secretary of State and Elizabeth's outstanding chief minister, remaining in post for the rest of his life. In 1571, he was made Lord Burghley.

Charles V, Holy Roman Emperor 1500–1558

Duke of Burgundy 1506–1555, King of Spain 1516–1556, Archduke of Austria and Holy Roman Emperor 1519–1556. This meant that he ruled Spain, the Netherlands, Austria, parts of Italy, and much of Germany and was the most powerful ruler in Europe. He sought to defend Catholicism in Europe against the advancing Protestant Reformation. He abdicated as Duke of Burgundy in 1555 and from his other roles in 1556, passing control of Spain and the Netherlands to his son Philip and of the Empire to his brother Ferdinand, and then entered a monastery.

Miles Coverdale 1488–1569

He studied at Cambridge University and was an Augustinian friar until he came to believe Reformation doctrines in the late 1520s. His first exile was from 1528–1535. He worked with Tyndale and translated the first complete English Bible, which was published in 1535 and translated from Latin and German. His revision of the Matthews Bible was published as the Great Bible in 1539. His second exile was from 1540–1547. In Edward VI's reign, he served as almoner to Katherine Parr, as a royal chaplain and Bishop of Exeter. He was imprisoned after Mary's accession but his life was spared and he was sent into his third period of European exile, only because of the personal intervention of the King of Denmark. In Elizabeth's reign, he was appointed chaplain to Catherine, Duchess of Suffolk and tutor to her children.

Thomas Cranmer 1489–1556

He studied and lectured at Cambridge University. From 1529, he was asked to work on Henry VIII's divorce. Archbishop of Canterbury 1533–1555. He worked steadily and cautiously to change the Church over this period. His own theology gradually continued to change throughout this time. Cranmer was a moderate and scholarly man with a very strong conviction of the need to obey the monarch. He was responsible for the Prayer Books of 1549 and 1552 and their memorable liturgy. Although he had interceded on Mary's behalf with King Henry VIII, she was implacably opposed to him, and he was imprisoned in 1553 and executed in 1556.

John Dudley 1504–1553

A protégé of Charles Brandon, Duke of Suffolk, and an able soldier, courtier and administrator who gradually rose in Henry VIII's service and was a leading Protestant at court. 1542 Viscount Lisle. 1547 Earl of Warwick. In 1549, he ousted Edward Seymour and replaced him as effective regent, styling himself Lord President of the Privy Council. 1551 Duke of Northumberland. He proved to be an unusually dominant character who developed a good relationship with Edward VI. At Edward's death, he tried to put his son Guildford and daughter-in-law, Lady Jane Grey, on the throne. A last-minute reversion to Catholicism failed to save his life and he was executed in 1553.

Duke of Norfolk
See Thomas Howard

Duke of Somerset
See Edward Seymour

Duke of Suffolk
See Charles Brandon
Also Henry Brandon (eldest son of Charles and Catherine Brandon), Henry Grey (husband of Frances nee Brandon and formerly Marquess of Dorset).

John Foxe 1516/17–1587
He studied and lectured at Oxford University. From 1547, he was tutor to the Earl of Surrey's children. He left for Europe early in 1554, settling in Frankfurt and then Basel. He worked on his book of martyrs with significant help from John Bale. He returned to England after Elizabeth's succession and, in 1559, a short version was published in Latin. The first edition of the much larger English edition, *Acts and Monuments of these Later and Perilous Days Touching Matters of the Church,* was published in 1563 and changed and expanded in 1570, with further editions in 1576 and 1583. It was quickly universally known as Foxe's *Book of Martyrs.* Although others were involved, it was a massive undertaking and affected his health.

Stephen Gardiner c. 1495/1503–1555
He was educated at Cambridge University. From 1524–1529, he served Cardinal Wolsey and, in 1529, entered the service of the King, Henry VIII. He was Bishop of Winchester from 1531–1551 and 1553–1555 and leader of the Catholic group within the Church and at court. An important, wily and able politician, but divisive and not trusted by King Henry. From 1548–1553, he was imprisoned in the Tower for opposition to Edward VI's religious reforms. In 1553 Mary appointed him her chief minister as Lord Chancellor.

John Hooper 1495/1500–1555
He was a student at Oxford University and was a Cistercian monk before he became an evangelical. He was strongly influenced by the Swiss Reformer, Ulrich Zwingli. He left England for the Continent in 1540 and again in 1544 and returned in 1549. He had a good relationship with both Somerset and Northumberland and was one of the most influential churchmen during Edward VI's reign. He became Bishop of Gloucester in 1551 and Bishop of the new diocese of Gloucester and Worcester in 1552. At Mary's accession, he sent his wife and children to safety in Frankfurt but did not attempt to escape himself before he was imprisoned. He was executed in Gloucester in 1555.

Thomas Howard 1473–1554
He was prominent in royal service and as a soldier for much of his life. Earl of Surrey 1514. Duke of Norfolk 1524. He was a significant rival to Thomas Cromwell. A staunch Catholic, he was one of their most influential leaders at court. He was imprisoned in the Tower for not denouncing his treasonous son to King Henry VIII, but survived into the next reign although he spent all of it still incarcerated in the Tower. Released by Mary, he was then tasked by her with defeating Wyatt's rebellion, even though he was in his eighties.

Hugh Latimer c. 1485–1555
One of several leading Reformers who were brought to evangelical faith and rejected their earlier Catholicism while at Cambridge University. An oustanding preacher, he was a court preacher under Henry VIII from 1534 and under Edward VI. From 1535–1539, he was Bishop of Worcester, but resigned over the Act of Six Articles and was briefly imprisoned and again in 1546. A friend and spiritual help to Catherine, Duchess of Suffolk. He was imprisoned after Mary's accession in 1553 and executed with Nicholas Ridley in 1555.

William Parr 1513–1571
Katherine Parr's brother. His career was advanced by his sister's marriage to Henry VIII. A courtier, prominent nobleman and soldier. Baron Parr 1539. Earl of Essex 1543. A member of the Privy Council

from 1545–1548, and from 1558–1571. Marquess of Northampton 1547–1553 and 1559–1571. A Protestant who supported the Duke of Northumberland and was one of the most important men at Edward VI's court. He was imprisoned in the Tower in 1553, convicted of treason and fortunate not to be executed for his support for Lady Jane Grey. Mary removed his land and titles. He was reinstated as Marquess of Northampton and to the Council under Elizabeth, and had a good relationship with her.

King Philip II of Spain 1527–1598

The son and heir of the Emperor Charles V. Duke of Milan from 1540. King of Naples and Sicily from 1554. King of England as husband of Queen Mary from 1554–1558. From 1555, ruler of the Netherlands. King of Spain from 1556–1598. King of Portugal from 1580–1598. He persecuted Protestants in his territories and, like his father, tried to protect the Catholic Church in Europe against the inroads of the Reformation. Following the death of the Catholic claimant to the English throne, Mary Queen of Scots, who was executed in 1587, Philip launched the Spanish Armada in 1588 to overthrow Elizabeth and re-establish Catholicism.

Nicholas Ridley c.1502–1555

He had a long association with Pembroke College, Cambridge, from his entry as a student in 1518 to being Master from 1540. Bishop of Rochester 1547. Bishop of London 1550. A leading Reformer within the Church and the most prominent churchman to support Lady Jane Grey as Queen. He was imprisoned by Queen Mary in 1553 and executed in October 1555 with Hugh Latimer.

John Rogers 1500–1555

He was a student at Pembroke College, Cambridge. He left in 1526 and entered the Church. In 1534, he became a chaplain in Antwerp and got to know William Tyndale who was probably instrumental in his conversion. Unlike Coverdale, he was proficient in both Greek and Hebrew. After Tyndale's arrest, he amended and combined Coverdale's translation of the Old Testament with Tyndale's New and partial

Old Testament translation, which was published in 1537 under the pseudonym 'Thomas Matthews'. From 1540–1548 he was a pastor in Germany. On his return to England, he ministered as a clergyman and prominent preacher in London. He was arrested in 1553 and executed in 1555, the first martyr to be burnt in Mary's reign and his calm steadfastness was an encouraging example to those who would follow.

Edward Seymour c.1500–1552

He became increasingly prominent after his sister Jane married Henry VIII, as a soldier and in national affairs. He was a member of the Council from 1537 and Earl of Hertford. Duke of Somerset from 1547 and Lord Protector from 1547–1549, in effect regent for his underage nephew, Edward VI. An unusually humane man, which stemmed from his sincere Protestant faith but, facing significant difficulties, including his own brother's treachery, he did not prove a very effective ruler. He was popular with the common people who called him the 'Good Duke.' He became a victim of his failure to maintain his support on the Council and of the machinations of John Dudley. He was imprisoned in the Tower from October 1549 to February 1550 and then rearrested in October 1551 and executed in January 1552.

Nicholas Shaxton c.1485–1556

A protégé of Anne Boleyn. He was an evangelical court preacher from 1534 and Bishop of Salisbury from 1535–1539. He resigned his bishopric over the passing of the Act of Six Articles. He was arrested in 1546 and sentenced to death for heresy, but was persuaded to recant. He did not return to his Protestant beliefs after the accession of Edward VI, but remained a Catholic until his death.

William Tyndale c.1494–1536

He was a student at Oxford University. Afterwards, he worked as a tutor in Gloucestershire and preached in the area. About 1523, he sought support from the Bishop of London to translate the New Testament into English, but did not obtain it and about 1524 he left England and went to Germany. His English New Testament was printed in 1526 and, among other works, the *Obedience of a Christian Man* in 1528.

His revised New Testament was published in 1534. He was captured and imprisoned in Vilvorde Castle in 1535, and executed in 1536. He left an incomplete Old Testament translation, but his work formed the basis of other sixteenth-century Bibles and a very significant part of the Authorised Version of 1611, including probably at least 80 percent of the New Testament. An unexpected legacy was his great influence on the development of the English language.

JULY 1553 ROUTES OF MARY & THE DUKE OF NORTHUMBERLAND

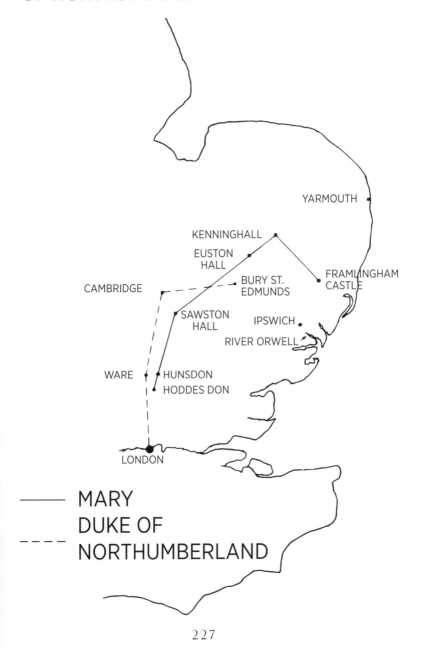

YARMOUTH

KENNINGHALL

EUSTON HALL

BURY ST. EDMUNDS

FRAMLINGHAM CASTLE

CAMBRIDGE

SAWSTON HALL

IPSWICH

RIVER ORWELL

WARE

HUNSDON

HODDES DON

LONDON

—— MARY

- - - - DUKE OF NORTHUMBERLAND

CATHERINE AND RICHARD BERTIE ON THE CONTINENT

Samogitia

Poland

Denmark

HOLY ROMAN EMPIRE

WESEL

FRANKFURT

R. Rhine

WEINHEIM

France

LONDON

HOUSE OF TUDOR

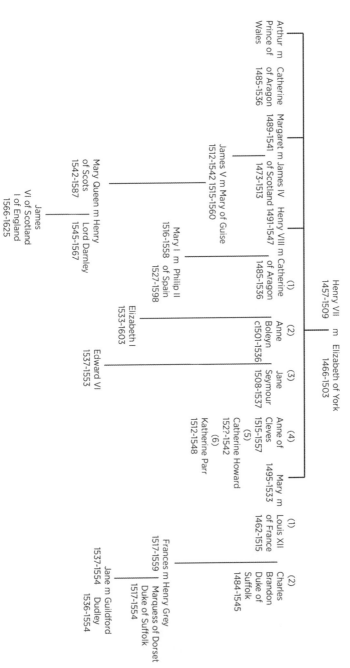

Henry VII m Elizabeth of York
1457-1509   1466-1503

Arthur m Catherine
Prince of of Aragon
Wales   1489-1541

Margaret m James IV
of Scotland 1491-1547
1473-1513

Henry VIII m Catherine   Mary m Louis XII
1485-1536   (1) of Aragon   1495-1533 of France
                1485-1536   1462-1515

James V m Mary of Guise
1512-1542 1515-1560

              Mary I m Philip II   (1)
              1516-1558 of Spain   Charles
              1527-1598   Brandon
                                   Duke of
              Elizabeth I   Suffolk
              1533-1603   1484-1545

Mary Queen m Henry
of Scots   Lord Darnley   (2) Anne   (3) Jane
1542-1587   1545-1567   Boleyn   Seymour
                            c1501-1536   1508-1537

James
VI of Scotland
I of England
1566-1625

Edward VI
1537-1553

(4) Anne of
Cleves
1515-1557

(5) Catherine Howard
1521?-1542

(6) Katherine Parr
1512-1548

Frances m Henry Grey
1517-1559 Marquess of Dorset
           Duke of Suffolk
           1517-1554

Jane m Guildford
1537-1554 Dudley
           1536-1554

229

HOUSE OF SUFFOLK

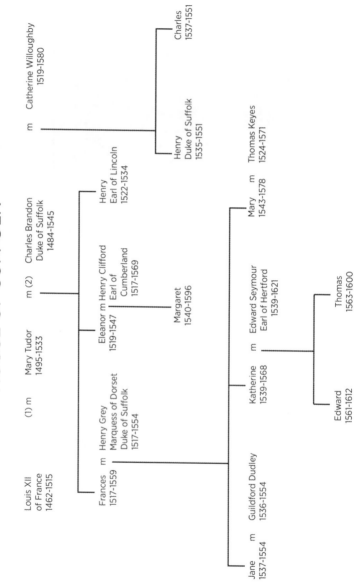

Louis XII
of France
1462-1515

(1) m

Mary Tudor
1495-1533

m (2)

Charles Brandon
Duke of Suffolk
1484-1545

m

Catherine Willoughby
1519-1580

Frances
1517-1559

m

Henry Grey
Marquess of Dorset
Duke of Suffolk
1517-1554

Eleanor
1519-1547

m

Henry Clifford
Earl of
Cumberland
1517-1569

Henry
Earl of Lincoln
1522-1534

Henry
Duke of Suffolk
1535-1551

Charles
1537-1551

Margaret
1540-1596

Jane
1537-1554

m

Guildford Dudley
1536-1554

Katherine
1539-1568

m

Edward Seymour
Earl of Hertford
1539-1621

Mary
1543-1578

m

Thomas Keyes
1524-1571

Edward
1561-1612

Thomas
1563-1600

Some Discussion Starters

1. Bible knowledge

Both Lady Jane Grey and Anne Askew knew the Bible well and were able to use it from memory at the right time and under the pressure of intense questioning.

How well do we know the Bible?

What priority do we give to studying, meditating on, and memorising Scripture?

What actions can we take to know the Bible better?

What helps are available?

How much does the Bible mould our minds?

2 Timothy 3:16-7, Deuteronomy 11:18-20, Psalm 119:11,97,105, Luke 12:11-2.

2. Education

Many Reformers linked education with biblical faith. Katherine Parr believed in the value of education and Edward, Elizabeth and Lady Jane were strongly influenced by theirs.

Has that link been mainly lost today?

What does the Bible say about educating and training up a child?

What place is there for Christian schools and Christian home education? Should Christians do more to support Christian schools?

Has the state taken away too much of the role of a parent?

What can parents do when their children are taught anti-Christian values?

Proverbs 22:6, Ephesians 6:4, 2 Timothy 3:15-17, Deuteronomy 11:18-20.

3. Speech

Some in the sixteenth century seemed to think it was perfectly acceptable to contend with and condemn religious opponents using robust and disrespectful language. In many ways it was quite normal. Anne Askew and Jane Grey did so and Catherine Willoughby acted disrespectfully to Stephen Gardiner.

Are there things in our own day which Christians commonly accept but which do not meet biblical standards?

What does the Bible teach about speech?

How should the gospel be presented?

How should open air preachers respond to those who heckle and try to disrupt them?

Does anything justify speaking harshly or disrespectfully?

Colossians 4:6, Galatians 5:22-3, Psalm 19:14, James 3:1-8, Ephesians 4:29-30.

4. Obedience to the authorities

In the early Reformation years,there was a strong emphasis placed on obeying the government. Tyndale's book on *The Obedience of the Christian Man* was particularly influential. So much so that some Protestants found it hard to disobey Mary when she became Queen, even though she was ordering them to worship against their conscience. By contrast, also during Mary's reign, some Protestants in exile on the Continent, most prominently John Knox, promoted the theory that Christians could and should remove an ungodly ruler.

What does the Bible teach about obedience to the government and others in authority over us?

Does the Bible place any limits on respect for those in authority and our need to obey?

How does the authority of the state relate to the authority of the Church to govern its own affairs?

Should Christians be better or worse, or just different citizens than others?

Does the fact that many governments have abandoned any Christian ethos limit our need to respect and obey them?

How do we value and use our vote and our voice in our democracy?
How much do we pray for our country, our leaders and our elections?
Romans 13:1-7, Titus 3:1, 1 Peter 2:13-17, Matthew 22:15-21.

5. **How should we respond if we are badly treated by others?**
Lady Jane Grey was used by others. Her parents and others disregarded her welfare and used her for their own ends, and her death sentence came about through the actions of others.
How do we react to the frustrations, limitations and disappointments we might meet with in life?
How does the Bible tell us to react when others treat us badly? What can help us to obey this teaching?
How do we deal with hurt and bitterness?
Romans 12:17-21, Luke 6:27, 35-6, Colossians 3:12-13, Matthew 5:44, Matthew 6:12.

6. **Trials and difficulties**
Anne Askew, Catherine Willoughby and Jane Grey responded to them with Christian maturity.
What can we learn from them?
How can we deal with trials and problems in a positive way?
When we face difficult circumstances do we ask 'Why me?'
Have we had times when we could see that our troubles were part of God's plan for us, and that, despite the pain, they were for our good?
Romans 8:28, Genesis 50:20, Psalm 18:30, 2 Corinthians 1:3-4, James 1:3.

7. **Inconsistent living damages Christian witness**
Edward Seymour displayed his faith in some of his policies, by being unusually humane and enlightened, with genuine concern for the poor, but his testimony was marred by his pride and grand lifestyle.
How can we deal with the danger of drift and creeping worldliness?
Are we aware of inconsistencies in our own life?
Is a desire for material comfort a snare for us?
How can we avoid the danger of complacency?

James 4:4, I John 2:15, Matthew 10:28, Colossians 3:1-4, 1 Timothy 6:6, Hebrews 13:5, Romans 8:5-6.

8. Persecution

Mary's reign saw the worst period of persecution in British history. There is much persecution elsewhere in the world today, and even in our own country, things are becoming increasingly uncomfortable for Christians.

What does the Bible teach about persecution?

How can we pray for and support those experiencing persecution?

Do we expect persecution?

Matthew 5:11-12, John 15:18-21, 2 Timothy 3:12, 1 Peter 4:12-16, Joshua 1:9, 2 Corinthians 12:9-10.

9. Loss

Loss is a recurring theme in these ladies' lives, not surprisingly when people died so much younger and life was more precarious. That loss included loss of liberty.

Do we fear loss?

What brings comfort and encouragement in the face of loss?

How can we support those who are bereaved or are coping with other significant loss?

If we should live well into old age, loss is almost inevitable – of health, friends or spouse. Can we prepare for that in advance?

Philippians 3:7-8, Luke 12:15-21, James 4:13-15, Romans 8:28, 2 Corinthians 1:3-4.

10. Pressure

All four women faced pressure of one kind or another. Pressure to conform is as strong today as it was then. As in the sixteenth century, some in society want people all to think the same on certain issues, rather than valuing the freedom to differ. Free speech is under attack and Christians have lost their jobs for stating the biblical position on social and moral issues.

If we feel pressurised where does it come from? Ourselves or others?

What will help us deal with pressure?

How can we advise children/teenagers to cope with peer pressure?
Is it difficult for Christians to now work in certain jobs or careers
which would have been fully open to them in the past?
How can we cope with the pressure to conform?
Romans 12:1-2, Philippians 3:20, Colossians 3:23, John 16:33,
James 4:4.

SELECT BIBLIOGRAPHY

Atherstone, Andrew, *Travel with the Martyrs of Mary Tudor* (Leominster: Day One, 2005)

Bainton, Roland, *Women of the Reformation in France and England* (Minneapolis: Augsburg Publishing House, 1973)

Baldwin, David, *Henry VIII's Last Love: The Extraordinary Life of Katherine Willoughby Lady-in-Waiting to the Tudors* (Stroud: Amberley Publishing, 2016)

Beilin, Elaine ed, *The Examinations of Anne Askew* (New York: Oxford University Press, 1996)

Chapman, Hester, *Lady Jane Grey* (Jonathan Cape: London, 1962)

Cook, Faith, *Lady Jane Grey Nine Days Queen of England* (Evangelical Press: Darlington, 2004)

D'Aubigne, J.H. Merle, *The Reformation in England 2 volumes 1866 –1878.* (Reprinted Edinburgh: Banner of Truth Trust, 1985)

De Lisle, Leanda, *The Sisters Who Would Be Queen : The Tragedy of Mary, Katherine and Lady Jane Grey* (London: Harper Press, 2008)

Dickens, A.G., *The English Reformation,* (London: Collins, 1967)

Edwards, Brian, *Travel With William Tyndale : England's Greatest Bible Translator* (Leominster: Day One, 2009)

Elton, G.R., *England Under the Tudors* (London: Methuen, 1962)

Foxe, John, *Acts and Monuments Online.* www.dhi.ac.uk> foxe

Foxe, John, *Foxe's Book of Martyrs* (Abridged from Milner's edition by Theodore Buckley. London: George Routledge & Sons, 1892)

Fraser, Antonia, *The Six Wives of Henry VIII* (London: Arrow Books, 1998)

Hannay, M., ed, *Silent But For the Word : Tudor Women as Patrons, Translators, and Writers of Religious Works* (Ohio: Kent State University Press, 1985)

Haykin, Michael, *'Katherine Suffolk, the Puritan Duchess'* (Haddington House Journal, 2018)

Ives, Eric, *Lady Jane Grey : A Tudor Mystery* (Chichester: Wiley-Blackwell, 2011)

Ives, Eric, *The Reformation Experience : Living Through the Turbulent Sixteenth Century* (Oxford: Lion Hudson, 2012)

James, Susan, *Kateryn Parr: The Making of a Queen* (Aldershot: Ashgate, 1999)

MacCulloch, Diarmaid, *The Boy King: Edward VI and the Protestant Reformation.* (Los Angeles: University of California Press, 2002)

Needham, N.R., *2000 Years of Christ's Power: Part 3: Renaissance and Reformation* (London: Grace Publications, 2004)

Nicholas, N.H., *The Literary Remains of Lady Jane Grey With a Memoir of Her Life* (Harding, Triphook and Lepard, 1825)

Oxford Dictionary of National Biography (Oxford, 2004)

Porter, Linda, *Katherine the Queen: The Remarkable Life of Katherine Parr* (Pan, 2010)

Plowden, Alison, *The House of Tudor* (Stroud: The History Press, 2010)

Plowden, Alison, *Lady Jane Grey and the House of Suffolk* (London: Sidgewick & Jackson, 1985)

Plowden, Alison, *Lady Jane Grey: Nine Days Queen* (Stroud: Sutton Publishing, 2003)

Read, Evelyn, *Catherine Duchess of Suffolk: A Portrait* (London: Jonathan Cape, 1962)

Reeves, Michael, *The Unquenchable Flame : Discovering the Heart of the Reformation,* (London: IVP, 2016)

Ridley, Jasper, *Bloody Mary's Martyrs : The Story of England's Terror* (London: Constable, 2001)

Ridley, Jasper, *The Life and Times of Mary Tudor* (London: Weidenfeld & Nicolson, 1973)

Starkey, David, *Six Wives : The Queens of Henry VIII* (London: Chatto & Windus, 2003)

Stevenson, Joan & Squires, *Anthony, Bradgate Park : Childhood Home of Lady Jane Grey* (Newtown Linford: Kairos Press, 1999)

Tallis, Nicola, *Crown of Blood: The Deadly Inheritance of Lady Jane Grey* (London: Michael O'Mara Books Limited, 2017)

Weir, Alison, *Children of England: The Heirs of Henry VIII* (London: Pimlico, 1997)

Weir, Alison, *The Six Wives of Henry VIII* (London: Pimlico, 1997)

Wilson, Derek, *The Queen and the Heretic : How Two Women changed the Religion of England* (Oxford: Lion Hudson, 2018)

Withrow, Brandon, Katherine Parr. *A Guided Tour of the Life and Thought of a Reformation Queen* (Phillipsburg, P&R Publishing, 2009)

Woychuk, N.A., *The British Josiah: Edward VI the Most Godly King of England* (St Louis: SMF Press, 2001)

Zahl, Paul F.M., *Five Women of the English Reformation* (Grand Rapids: Eerdmans, 2001)

Christian Focus Publications

Our mission statement –

STAYING FAITHFUL

In dependence upon God we seek to impact the world through literature faithful to His infallible Word, the Bible. Our aim is to ensure that the Lord Jesus Christ is presented as the only hope to obtain forgiveness of sin, live a useful life and look forward to heaven with Him.

Our Books are published in four imprints:

CHRISTIAN FOCUS

popular works including biographies, commentaries, basic doctrine and Christian living.

CHRISTIAN HERITAGE

books representing some of the best material from the rich heritage of the church.

MENTOR

books written at a level suitable for Bible College and seminary students, pastors, and other serious readers. The imprint includes commentaries, doctrinal studies, examination of current issues and church history.

CF4•K

children's books for quality Bible teaching and for all age groups: Sunday school curriculum, puzzle and activity books; personal and family devotional titles, biographies and inspirational stories – Because you are never too young to know Jesus!

Christian Focus Publications Ltd,
Geanies House, Fearn, Ross-shire,
IV20 1TW, Scotland, United Kingdom.
www.christianfocus.com